MOTHER TERESA and the MYSTICS

MOTHER TERESA and the MYSTICS

TOWARD A RENEWAL OF SPIRITUAL THEOLOGY

Edited by Michael Dauphinais, Brian Kolodiejchuk, MC, and Roger W. Nutt

Foreword by H. James Towey

SAPIENTIA PRESS OF AVE MARIA UNIVERSITY

Sapientia Press
of Ave Maria University
5050 Ave Maria Blvd.
Ave Maria, FL 34142
800-537-5487

Distributed by:
The Catholic University of America Press
c/o HFS
P.O. Box 50370
Baltimore, MD 21211
800-537-5487

Cover Image: Mother Theresa, © photograph by Raghu Rai/Magnum Photos

Printed in the United States of America.

Library of Congress Control Number: 2017964739

ISBN: 978-1-932589-81-8

CONTENTS

~

FOREWORD

~

I remember exactly where I was when I first learned that for most of her life Mother Teresa of Calcutta had lived in spiritual darkness. I was in a hotel room in Newark, New Jersey, when a clerk delivered galley proofs of a forthcoming book by Fr. Brian Kolodiejchuk, *Come Be My Light*. I had the privilege of serving as legal counsel to Mother Teresa from 1985 until her death, and it was not uncommon for the Sisters or priests of the Missionaries of Charity, the religious congregation she founded, to ask me to review materials of consequence. I was grateful for the chance to get a first look at this highly anticipated work.

I was astonished by what I read. Mother Teresa's correspondence contained previously unknown accounts of her extraordinary visions in 1947 when Jesus directly conversed with her. And, in heartbreaking detail, she recounted the prolonged "dark night" she endured from the time of these visions until her death nearly fifty years later.

These letters that described her vulnerability and struggles collided with my own observations of who Mother Teresa was. To me, she was always the strong one, the person who encouraged others and led by example and never gave the slightest hint of interior strife. She was forever praying, rosary in hand, exhorting those around her to "be all for Jesus, through Mary," and she spoke as if they both were walking next to her. When she talked of Jesus in public, she did so with tender love and conviction. This closeness with God explained the unmistakable holiness that seemed to reside in and radiate from her. She was no ordinary soul.

That is why the effect of her letters left me grateful but confused. The accounts of her conversations with Jesus deepened my faith because there was no way on earth that Mother Teresa would fabricate such stories. Indeed, she only revealed these supernatural occurrences to the Archbishop of Calcutta because she was ordered to. She was not one to talk about herself and her experiences. She seldom spoke of her past and even less frequently of her own spiritual journey. So if Mother said that she saw Jesus and spoke with him, she did. Period. Lying or exaggerating was not in her nature.

On the other hand, the revelation of the agonizing darkness she lived, and the pervasive doubts about the presence of God in her life, perplexed me because I felt she was as close to God as a human could be. The intimacy with God I perceived explained why she was so cheerful, full of energy, and upbeat. I concluded early on that God equipped her with a unique strength because her heroic work with the lepers and dying required it. The rapid expansion of her religious order throughout the world—when she died she had seven hundred missions in over one hundred countries—provided objective proof that God was granting her graces that mere mortals did not receive.

And if anyone needed such fortification, it was she. Mother Teresa was one mortified soul. She drove herself hard and never rested. I was in my thirties when she was in her eighties, and she seemed to never tire. I recall one day in Mexico in 1989 when I drove her from appointment to appointment and was her companion throughout the day, and by nightfall I was thoroughly exhausted. When we returned to the convent late that evening and I walked her to the door, I could see a line of her beloved Sisters waiting to get one-on-one attention from her—a request she never refused. Such demands on her life were standard. She rose each morning at 4:40 a.m. and was full speed ahead.

She also was no stranger to physical suffering. During the twelve years I knew her, she had numerous injuries and illnesses, from recurring bouts of malaria to broken bones. When she traveled to America, which she frequently did, I would see her arrive missing a tooth or sporting an eye patch. She had such crippling back pain toward the end of her life that on one occasion she had to be carried by stretcher onto a private plane just to be transported from Washington to New York. She had so many close brushes with death due to her failing heart that each time I said goodbye to her made me think it was the last.

But she always seemed to will herself to recovery so that she could continue to "love and give until it hurt," as she often said. I remember once in Memphis she had been sick all night and was to attend a mass that morning where nearly ten thousand of the faithful were to gather. She was in no condition to go, but there was no way she wouldn't. At the end of mass, as she passed out Miraculous Medals to hundreds of attendees who formed a spontaneous receiving line when word circulated that she was still in the coliseum, I held her hand and felt it burning with fever. Mother and comfort rarely met.

This was her life. As I said, I was certain celestial compensation provided a superabundance of graces that gave her special strength and assured her of Jesus's intimate presence.

So it was utterly remarkable to read her letters in Fr. Brian's book and discover that the exact opposite was true—that in fact she felt abandoned, forsaken, forgotten by God. I immediately wondered how it could be possible for her to endure this profound darkness for decades and never let on. I took the first chance I could to ask her successor as general superior of the Missionaries of Charity, Sister Nirmala, a person within Mother's inner circle who could legitimately claim to "know" her, whether she had known that Mother was enduring such a prolonged dark night. She responded no; all others close to Mother followed suit. Sister Gertrude, who at age nineteen was the second woman to join the Missionaries of Charity and was holding Mother when she breathed her last, told me the same thing. Mother had fooled everyone. As Mother herself explained in her letters, her smile was a "cover" that concealed her true spiritual condition. Today we know that smile did not make her a hypocrite. It made her a saint.

It has now been twenty years since Mother went home to God, and I have thought a great deal about how difficult it must have been for her to carry to her grave a secret of this magnitude, a secret she expected to last forever, as she had explicitly asked all those to whom she had revealed it to destroy her letters (thank God they didn't!). I can only conclude that the strength to hide her interior destitution began with the signal graces she received on a train ride to Darjeeling on September 10, 1946, when she received a supernatural communication of Jesus's thirst for love and souls. This mystical experience led her to transition from a teacher of geography and history in a Calcutta boarding school to a servant of the poorest of the poor in the adjacent slums. The significance of this event on the train would be displayed throughout the world in every single chapel opened by the Missionaries of Charity, as the words from John 19:28, "I Thirst," are displayed alongside the crucifix. Every year on September 10, her Sisters, Brothers, and priests celebrate "Inspiration Day" to commemorate what God communicated to their foundress.

As was the case with her conversations with Jesus, Mother was reluctant to ever speak of her experience on the train, or how it came about. Only toward the end of her life, and at the insistence of one of her Missionaries of Charity Fathers, Joseph Langford, did she expound on the "I Thirst" spirituality that was mysteriously infused into her very being and the charism of the Missionaries of Charity. The letter she wrote on her encounter with God's infinite yearning, or thirst, for love, was the only first-person account we have from Mother on the one mystical experience the world knew she had.

To learn after her death that this experience on the train was followed by a series of three visions and face-to-face encounters with Jesus and his holy mother is to begin a study of precisely what God communicated to her—and entrusted to us—about this mysterious "thirst." As with SS. Francis of Assisi, Margaret Mary, and Faustina, for example, the revelation of intimate dialogue between them and God invites such thoughtful reflection. Surely the Lord intends his words to Mother Teresa, and the message of his thirst, to nourish the generations who follow her.

Questions abound: What are we to make of the spiritual darkness that enshrouded Mother Teresa so tightly? Could the words and experiences of this little Albanian woman from Skopje (present-day Macedonia) with no advanced formal education have anything to say to the challenges that the twenty-first-century presents?

Ave Maria University convened a gathering of esteemed theologians to begin the process of answering these questions and more. The lectures from this symposium, titled "Mother Teresa and the Mystics," as well as a previous lecture on campus by Fr. Brian Kolodiejchuk, constitute the contents of this book. To my knowledge, this assembly of scholars was the first such academic conference ever held on Mother Teresa.

Academics looking to "unpack" Mother Teresa's words and life face significant obstacles in their research and contemplation. She penned nothing beyond her correspondence, except for a couple of major speeches (her Nobel Peace Prize acceptance speech in 1979 in Oslo and her address at the National Prayer Breakfast in 1994 in

Washington, DC, are the only two that come to mind). It may be hard to believe, but the talks that Mother Teresa gave at venues as diverse as Vatican assemblies or university commencements were given extemporaneously. She would get to the podium, make a sign of the cross on her lips, and trust that she would receive from the Holy Spirit the words she was intended to say. This same confidence explains why, whether meeting with popes or prelates, presidents or royalty, she went into their company without notes (but not without specific appeals; she never wasted a solitary opportunity to ask those in authority for something for her poor).

Although she was not prone to write down her own thoughts, the record of what she left behind is more than ample. It will both command the attention of the academy and enrich the Catholic intellectual tradition for centuries to come. My sense is that the more one studies what Mother Teresa said and did, the more significant her contributions to the treasury of the faith will be. This very phenomenon happened after the death of her patron saint, St. Thérèse of Lisieux, who also had little formal education, not even holding a high school diploma. Today she is a Doctor of the Church. Her "Story of a Soul" and her many letters, as well as the testimony of those who knew her, led to a growing realization that beyond the simplicity of her words was a compelling erudition. Scholars plumbed the depths of her writings and discovered a bounty of riches.

A similar epiphany is likely to develop the more we study Mother Teresa. She had insights and a wisdom that only Divine Providence could convey. I was struck by the story I heard from one of the Missionaries of Charity about the last meeting Mother Teresa had with the great St. John Paul II about two months before she died. The meeting took place in his private study, and Mother was brought in her wheelchair into this magnificent chamber. The two of them faced each other in silence, and then the Holy Father, after slowly nodding his head for some time, said knowingly, "I thirst." It was as if those simple words of John's Gospel said everything that needed to be said about the mystery of Mother's life.

The Church now ponders together the life of this newly canonized Saint in the context of this cry of Jesus from the cross, as well as his promise that "whatever you did to the least of my brethren, you did it to me." Many scholars have begun to study her teaching that the poor were "Jesus in His distressing disguise" and what it means in a world where the sanctity and dignity of life are threatened. They realize her maternal love and care for the unwanted and unloved were a continuation of that offered by the preeminent virgin and mother, Mary of Nazareth, to whom she was so devoted. Studies of Mother Teresa's radical embrace of evangelical poverty and "choosing not to have" so that she could be free to "cleave" to Jesus (her description) further illuminate the contribution of a vow that has been the lifeblood of consecrated life, and contribute to the understanding of the heights of spousal love attainable by consecrated religious. Indeed, there are countless avenues of examination.

It should come as no surprise that a little, relatively unknown university like Ave Maria University would be at the forefront of this scholastic endeavor. Ave Maria is honored to be "Mother Teresa's University," as his Eminence Sean Cardinal O'Malley of the Archdiocese of Boston famously and fairly declared. Church history reveals that it is precisely from such unexpected places—like Skopje and Wadowice—that the Lord sows seeds along the path of faith. The little, hidden, and humble are fertile soil for the Good News.

Has any age ever needed the joy of the Gospel more? Our youth crave the truth and long to give their lives to high purpose, but instead find themselves failed by a generation of adults who put their interests ahead of those they were to shepherd. Our elderly often face what Mother Teresa described as the worst of all diseases known to mankind: loneliness. In between these poles rests a great spiritual and material poverty that pervades modern existence. It is not unique to this age, but our response must be.

The more we fathom the mysticism of Mother Teresa, the better formed we will be to follow his holiness Pope Francis's exhortation at her canonization to be carriers of God's merciful love to a world thirsting for it. Let the inquiry begin.

H. James Towey

MOTHER TERESA and the MYSTICS

INTRODUCTION

~

Roger W. Nutt

Why hold a conference and publish a corresponding book dedicated to St. Teresa of Calcutta and her relation to the Christian mystical tradition? There are several reasons. First, Mother Teresa occupies a special place in the communal life of Ave Maria University (AMU). As concrete manifestations of the inner meaning of its Catholic, liberal arts mission, SS. John Paul II and Mother Teresa are special inspirations for AMU's academic community. In addition to presenting the lives and teachings of these great contemporary saints in the classroom, AMU students enjoy many service and mission opportunities under the auspices of the unique Mother Teresa Project. AMU's campus is also home to a one-of-a-kind museum honoring Mother Teresa that is open to students, local residents, and pilgrims, and includes a collection of many original documents and artifacts associated with the Saint of Calcutta. Mother Teresa is, in short, a resource and inspiration for the academic, spiritual, and communal life at AMU.

Since the early 2000s, the Aquinas Center for Theological Renewal and the Patrick F. Taylor Graduate Programs in Theology at AMU have held annual theological conferences on various topics. Several of these conferences have been devoted to aspects of the thought of St. John Paul II, but until 2017, we had not dedicated a complete conference to Mother Teresa. A conference exploring the theological richness of Mother Teresa's life and thought was long overdue. Most of the papers included in this volume are the fruit of this conference, which took place February 10–11, 2017.

Why not, one may ask, devote such a conference to missionary activity or love for the poor? Such topics—and many others—could easily be considered in relation to Mother Teresa's life and work and are worthy candidates of theological exploration. Why focus on mysticism and renewing spiritual theology?

Mother Teresa's spiritual life, especially as revealed in the volume of her posthumously published private writings referenced here as *Come Be My Light*, seemed to us to be a topic of both deep theological intrigue and timely importance. All saints, because of their graced intimacy with God, teach us important truths about the meaning of the Gospel. Mother Teresa enjoys a unique relevance for Christians today. She teaches us in so many ways the paradox of Christ's ever-present, but always hidden, engagement with the world. To the eyes of the world, Mother's own life and the charism of the religious order that she founded, the Missionaries of Charity, seem futile and pointless. After all, what can a few—or even a few thousand—Catholic women religious, brothers, and priests who constitute the Missionaries of Charity—devoted to the vow of "whole-hearted and free service to the poorest of the poor" and consecrated to Christ by the vows of poverty, chastity, and obedience—do to fix the world's problems of poverty and injustice? For Mother Teresa, this way of thinking misses the mark. She never grew tired of pointing out that she was not a social worker or political reformer. For her, the most important thing, what really mattered, was deep, spiritual intimacy with Christ. Her solidarity with the poor in Calcutta and around the world was not a social work program or the product of a partisan political agenda. Her work was a way of living in union with Christ. Christ's words on the Cross—"I thirst"—reflect the inner meaning of Mother's life and work. She sought to satiate Christ's thirst by loving him above everything—material possessions, money, honor—and everyone. Her work with the poor was service to the thirsting Christ. Her hours of quiet prayer and her devotion to Christ in the Eucharist were not fragmented escapes from her missionary activity—they were its very source. She shared God's love for the world with the poor by first living for God in deep but simple intimacy with Christ. Service to the poor, in Mother's teaching, is the fruit of a prior interior union with Christ. One does not start with action—social work—Mother teaches; one starts with a life of interior silence and prayer, which then bears fruit in authentically charitable action. This is aptly summarized by the aphorism that she often shared with people, paradoxically on what she called her "business card":

> The fruit of Silence is Prayer
> The fruit of Prayer is Faith
> The fruit of Faith is Love
> The fruit of Love is Service

Mother Teresa's core doctrine is quite manifest in these simple words. For her, true service animated by Christian charity is the fruit of an anterior spiritual life.

On these points alone Mother Teresa offers much food for thought for spiritual theology and the realization of Vatican II's "universal call to holiness." But there is more. Despite the deep impact that Mother Teresa had on the Church and the world, despite the power of her words and the courage of her public witness, she lived for decades in intense spiritual aridity—darkness. Even those who knew Mother well and personally, as H. James Towey relates in the foreword to this volume, were surprised by what they read in *Come Be My Light*. Most of us, for obvious reasons, expected Mother's interior life to be filled with tangible consolations from God—special favors. *Come Be My Light* reveals the opposite. For decades, even while she exuded joy to those around her and the Missionaries of Charity grew exponentially, Mother scarcely ever felt the presence of God in her life of prayer. Prayer was arduous for her—there were no tangible consolations of God's presence—and her spiritual life was lived in a painful darkness in which God's presence was hidden from her.

After coming to know Mother Teresa through her public life and the work of the Missionaries of Charity, the details of the spiritual ordeal revealed in her letters were difficult for readers—Christian and non-Christian alike—to come to terms with. These details seem to call into doubt everything that we hold true about the spiritual lives of saintly people. For some Catholic and Christian devotees of Mother Teresa, the revelations of *Come Be My Light* were a source of scandal or embarrassment. For others, some of whom are taken up in the essays in this volume—such as her critics and the popularizing "new atheists"—the struggles unveiled in Mother's private spiritual writings exposed her as a fraud, hypocrite, or even a closet atheist.

This brings us to the unifying theme of this volume: the Christian mystical tradition and the renewal of spiritual theology. Mother Teresa's toil in spiritual darkness, while arresting and contrary to our expectations, confronts us with a basic truth of the Christian mystical tradition. It is a simple truth, mostly forgotten today, but manifest in the Bible and through all of the great Christian mystics. Namely, true intimacy with God—mystical union—in this life is normally shrouded in darkness and accompanied by suffering. And why should this not be the case? Christ's own life was imbued with renunciation and suffering. Christ's arresting words on the Cross—"My God, my God, why have you forsaken me?"—should remind us of this. Does anything that Mother says disturb more than Christ's words from Psalm 22? The Fathers of the Church portrayed Moses as the paradigmatic mystic. Curiously, in Exodus, when God tells Moses that he will meet him on Mt. Sinai (true mysticism always entails a divine motion of creaturely ascent away from our own safe ground toward God), he indicates that the encounter will take place in a shrouded fashion: "Lo, I am coming to you in a thick cloud" (19:9). Pondering Moses's ascent to meet God in the dark cloud, the author of one of the first great works in mystical theology, the sixth-century Syrian monk Dionysius the Areopagite, taught that "Moses breaks free … away from what sees and is seen, and he plunges into the truly mysterious darkness of unknowing. Here, renouncing all that the mind may conceive, wrapped entirely in the intangible and the invisible, he belongs completely to him who is everything."[1]

Heaven—Christian beatitude—is knowing by means of seeing, but in this life the infused theological virtues of faith, hope, and love unite the soul to God and draw it toward eternity in a hidden way. The theological virtue of faith, the Letter to the Hebrews teaches, bestows a knowledge of things that are "unseen" (11:1). This Christian truth is often forgotten, and it creates a tension between our popular expectations for tangible manifestations and spiritual consolations and real life in a fallen world. God does not exult the human creature by indulging the ego; he has redeemed us from eternal loss by means of his Son's suffering and death. The way to eternal life for each and every Christian is to follow this path. We don't follow Christ so as to avoid suffering and ultimately dying; we follow Christ so as to be able to die—to accept ultimate weakness and vulnerability—in union with God. Mother Teresa's spiritual darkness accentuated this point for her. In his essay, Fr. Brian Kolodiejchuk quotes her words to the

---

1. Dionysius, *The Mystical Theology*, in *Pseudo-Dionysius: The Complete Works*, trans. Colm Luibheid (Mahwah, NJ: Paulist Press, 1987), 137 [1001 A].

Sisters: "My dear children—without our suffering, our work would just be social work, very good and helpful, but it would not be the work of Jesus Christ, not part of the redemption.—Jesus wanted to help us by sharing our life, our loneliness, our agony and death. All that He has taken upon Himself, and has carried it in the darkest night." Jesus did not preach—or live—a gospel of monetary prosperity or this-worldly honor. He taught us that sin and its consequences are real, but that if we live for him and not the things of this world, our own sufferings, and ultimately our death, have been redeemed.

Monastic spiritual writer Fr. Thomas Merton penetrates this truth when he writes:

> The way to contemplation is an obscurity so obscure that it is no longer even dramatic. There is nothing in it that can be grasped and cherished as heroic or even unusual. And so, for a contemplative, there is supreme value in the ordinary everyday routine of work, poverty, hardship and monotony that characterize the lives of all the poor, uninteresting and forgotten people in the world.[2]

Jesus died a death of intense physical pain and suffering, as well as the psychological suffering of extreme injustice, humiliation, and betrayal. He did all of this without fanfare while being mocked and tortured by the very people for whom he was suffering. All the disorders of sin in the world surrounded Christ during his passion. Likewise, it is no accident that Mother Teresa of Calcutta, who devoted her life to serving Christ in the poorest of the poor, experienced intense spiritual poverty and suffering—the dark absence of God's presence. Her life with Christ was not mediated by pampering and consolations. Her union with Christ was hidden in the dark, unseen realities of Christian faith.

2. Thomas Merton, *New Seeds of Contemplation* (New York: New Directions, 1961), 250.

This leads us to one final theme taken up frequently in this volume: dark nights. "Dark nights" like Mother's spiritual suffering are often spoken of without proper theological nuance, thus giving well-intentioned souls false expectations about their own progress and the true itinerary of the Christian spiritual life. The great mystics of Church tradition understood spiritual progress on a continuum of growth in union with God. Teresa of Avila's mansions start in the outer, external parts of the castle and move gradually away from externalities to the deeper, more hidden but more profound chambers of intimacy between God and the soul. Mother Teresa, like Christ on the cross, was no doubter, nor was she a spiritual novice. She was advanced in religious life, she had received locutions from Christ, and she gave no evidence of struggling with sinful attachments or of needing beginning purgations during the decades of her spiritual darkness. To make the point directly: Mother's darkness was not that of the "dark night of the sense"; her darkness was not the cauterizing flame of the first stages of the interior life. Mother's darkness was of a higher and profounder order, which helps to explain the intensity of her suffering. In 1947, for example, she mentions to her bishop that she is aware of already having undergone the initial purgations associated with the mystical doctrine of St. John of the Cross: "In the work there will be complete surrender of all that I have and all I am—I have given Him everything—I have not been seeking self for sometime now … *God has done everything. He simply took everything.—Now I am His.*"[3] During the decades of spiritual darkness, she was well advanced on the path of mystical ascent.

Like the dark cloud of the divine presence that encircled Moses at Mt. Sinai, Mother lived the darkness of God's hiddenness precisely because the highest union with God in the highest parts of the soul

---

3. Brian Kolodiejchuk, MC, ed., *Mother Teresa: Come Be My Light* (New York: Doubleday, 2007), 57. Emphasis added.

is not something that is mediated or experienced by the lower faculties—it lacks the visible drama of the beginning stages of spiritual growth. The further one is moved away by grace from created, sinful attachments, and even created goods, and the closer that God draws a soul to himself, the further one is from the tangible, fallen world. Many of the essays in this volume take up the question of Mother's darkness in relation to the categories of traditional mysticism for the sake of properly appreciating and understanding the nature of her sufferings, which were not that of the beginner. On this score in particular, Mother Teresa cracks open for us today the great truths of the Christian mystical tradition. The true spiritual master, Dionysius taught some 1,400 years ago, is one who knows the faith not only through teaching but also by "suffering divine things."[4] If there is anyone who can refamiliarize us with this elusive truth of "suffering divine things," it is surely Mother Teresa of Calcutta.

We thank especially Fr. Brian Kolodiejchuk, MC, for visiting AMU's campus to deliver a paper on Mother Teresa several years ago, for sharing his knowledge of Mother's writings with us, for his submission to this volume, and for his editorial support and guidance during the production of this volume. Mrs. Grace (Farley) De Salvo helped with the organization of the conference. Without her faithful service and logistical efficiency, the idea of the conference would have remained a mere abstraction. Mrs. Ashleigh McKown polished all the essays and guided the entire production process—she could, in justice, be credited with coauthoring the entire volume! We thank H. James Towey for bringing his personal, firsthand knowledge and love for Mother Teresa to AMU and for his ongoing support of the Aquinas Center for Theological Renewal and the Patrick F. Taylor Graduate Programs in Theology. Finally, we are grateful to all who

4. Dionysius, *The Divine Names*, in *Pseudo-Dionysius*, 65 [648 B].

attended the conference; their presence at AMU was a joy for us and enriching to our topic.

~

Mother Teresa's spiritual darkness, like Christ's cry to the Father on the cross, is a gift to the Church in which God seeks to lead us to union with himself through the hidden secrets and treasures of the interior life. It is our hope that the essays in this volume open new avenues of theological exploration—through the lens of Mother Teresa's spiritual suffering—by which this gift can be more widely received and understood. We certainly could have hosted a conference on missionary activity or some other topic related to Mother's life. But we hope that the contemplation of Mother's spiritual darkness will invigorate spiritual theology such that our service to others is truly the fruit of our love, and that our love is the fruit of our faith, which is fruit of our prayer, which can only issue from the mystical fruitfulness of silence.

1

MOTHER TERESA

Rich Resource for Contemporary Theology

~

Brian Kolodiejchuk, MC

St. Pope John Paul II, in his Apostolic Letter of January 6, 2001, *Novo Millennio Ineunte*, reminded us of an important principle for the Church:

> Many things are necessary for the Church's journey through history, not least in this new century; but without charity (*agape*), all will be in vain. It is again the Apostle Paul who in the *hymn to love* reminds us: even if we speak the tongues of men and of angels, and if we have faith "to move mountains," but are without love, all will come to "nothing" (cf. 1 Cor 13:2). Love is truly the "heart" of the Church.[1]

This paper was originally delivered as a lecture at Ave Maria University in February 2013.

1. St. Pope John Paul II, Apostolic Letter *Novo Millennio Ineunte*, January 6, 2001, http://w2.vatican.va/content/john-paul-ii/en/apost_letters/2001/documents/hf_jp-ii_apl_20010106_novo-millennio-ineunte.html, no. 42.

The pope then goes on to say that St. Thérèse of Lisieux understood this well and that he proclaimed her a Doctor of the Church precisely because she is an "expert in the *scientia amoris*."[2] This "science of love"—what St. John Paul referred to in *Novo Millennio Ineunte* as "the lived theology of the saints"[3]—is inseparable from and complementary to the *scientia fidei*, the "science of faith" or of "thought" or speculative theology.[4]

Emeritus Pope Benedict XVI also spoke of the knowledge of the saints as a resource or reference point for academic theology at the General Audience of October 21, 2009, dedicated to St. Bernard:

> St. Bernard, … solidly founded on the Bible and on the Fathers of the Church, reminds us that without a profound faith in God, nourished by prayer and contemplation, by an intimate relationship with the Lord, our reflections on the divine mysteries risk becoming an empty intellectual exercise and losing their credibility. Theology refers us back to the "knowledge of the Saints," to their intuition of the mysteries of the living God and to their wisdom, a gift of the Holy Spirit, which become a reference point for theological thought. Together with Bernard of Clairvaux, we too must recognize that man seeks God better and finds him more easily "in prayer than in discussion." In the end, the truest figure of a theologian and of every evangelizer remains the Apostle John who laid his head on the Teacher's breast.[5]

The saints, and especially the mystics, serve as an important resource for theology; indeed, they can be considered as theologians

---

2. Apostolic Letter *Novo Millennio Ineunte*, no. 42.

3. Apostolic Letter *Novo Millennio Ineunte*, no. 27.

4. See François-Marie Léthel, OCD, "La teologia dei santi: I santi come Teologi," *Alpha Omega* 8, no. 1 (2005): 81–108, for this discussion. Italics added to the quote from *Novo Millennio Ineunte*.

5. Pope Benedict XVI, General Audience, St. Peter's Square, October 21, 2009, https://w2.vatican.va/content/benedict-xvi/en/audiences/2009/documents/hf_ben-xvi_aud_20091021.html.

themselves. For example, Father Harvey Egan, SJ, makes this general observation concerning mystics in the preface to his book on Christian mystics.[6] St. Teresa of Calcutta was already considered one of the great saints of the last century. Now, however, as we can discover from her writings collected in *Come Be My Light*,[7] she can be regarded as one of the Church's great mystics as well.

By turning to St. Teresa's experience and words—her "lived theology"—we may discover a rich resource for "thought" theology, perhaps more than might be expected. This is primarily because of what Fr. Egan refers to as Mother Teresa's "unique holiness and mystical depths."[8]

Perhaps a fruitful entryway into demonstrating how St. Teresa can be a rich resource for theologians is a statement by the theologian Rosemary Haughton in her book *The Passionate God*. There she states, "The poetry of passionate love is the accurate language of theology."[9] Although Mother Teresa exhibited poetic talent,[10] she *lived* the poetry of passionate love rather than express it in verse.

If there is one short phrase that describes Mother Teresa, it is that she was a woman passionately in love with Jesus. From childhood, she fell in love with Jesus, her first and only love. Later she resolved to love Jesus "as He had never been loved before,"[11] a daring resolution to take seriously, which she did throughout her long life. If her private writings in *Come Be My Light* reveals her passionate love for Jesus, they also reveal her intense interior suffering over the course of decades.

---

6. Harvey D. Egan, *Soundings in the Christian Mystical Tradition* (Collegeville, MN: Liturgical Press, 2010), xi.

7. Brian Kolodiejchuk, MC, ed., *Mother Teresa: Come Be My Light* (New York: Doubleday, 2007).

8. Egan, *Soundings*, 368.

9. Rosemary Haughton, *The Passionate God*, quoted in Susan Pitchford, *God in the Dark: Suffering and Desire in the Spiritual Life* (Collegeville, MN: Liturgical Press, 2011), 1.

10. See her poem in Kolodiejchuk, *Come Be My Light*, 15.

11. Kolodiejchuk, *Come Be My Light*, 47.

In her book *God in the Dark: Suffering and Desire in the Spiritual Life*, Susan Pritchford observes:

> "Passion" is one of those strange words—like "sanction"—that has two distinct and seemingly opposite meanings. It has both positive and negative connotations: strong desire, on the one hand, and suffering, on the other. The mystics and troubadours of medieval Europe understood this well, and they could not conceive of a love that didn't include both faces of passion.[12]

Here I explore how St. Teresa, mystic and theologian, lived these two meanings of the word "passion"—her passionate love for Jesus and her intense interior suffering that she referred to as the "darkness"—and thus show one of the ways that she can contribute to the theological apostolate in the Church today.

THE PASSIONATE SAINT

Mother Teresa's letters in *Come Be My Light* make evident the previously hidden roots of her call to be a Missionary of Charity (MC). An essential key to grasp the meaning of Mother Teresa's "darkness," therefore, is to understand it in light of her vocation to be a Missionary of Charity.

In his Apostolic Exhortation *Redemptionis Donum* of March 25, 1984, John Paul II stated to religious that the call to consecrated life "springs from the interior encounter with the love of Christ," which is a "redeeming love" that "directed to a particular person" takes on "a spousal character"; it becomes "a love of choice."[13]

As a consecrated religious, Mother Teresa understood herself to

12. Pitchford, *God in the Dark*, 2.

13. John Paul II, Apostolic Exhortation *Redemptionis Donum*, March 25, 1984, http://w2.vatican.va/content/john-paul-ii/en/apost_exhortations/documents/hf_jp-ii_exh_25031984_redemptionis-donum.html, no. 3.

be the spouse of Jesus Crucified, who chose her with a personal and tender love; in that choice, she became his spouse. Jesus's choice of Mother Teresa and her response to his call are already manifest in three special graces granted to her while still at home. First, as she testified years later, "from childhood the Heart of Jesus has been my first love."[14] Second, she received an extraordinary grace at First Holy Communion: "From the age of 5½ years, when first I received Him the love for souls has been within. It grew with the years until I came to India with the hope of saving many souls."[15] Third, both she and her confessor in Skopje, Jesuit Father Jambreković, shared a desire for martyrdom.[16]

These special graces were nurtured by the good Christian formation received in her family (and particularly through her mother, since her father had died when she was eight or nine years old), the fervent Jesuit parish of the Sacred Heart in her home town of Skopje, and in her teen years, Mother Teresa's contact with St. Thérèse (beatified in 1923, canonized in 1925, and declared co-patroness of the missions in 1927). All this served as the fertile soil in which Mother Teresa's religious vocation could grow until her departure for Dublin to join the Loreto Sisters in September 1928 and her arrival to India on January 6, 1929.

During her years as a Loreto nun, Mother Teresa kept growing in her union with God, passing through the active and passive nights of sense and spirit described by St. John of the Cross.[17] A letter to Fr. Jambreković in 1937, the year she professed her final vows, gives an indication of her experience during her Loreto years:

14. John Paul II, Apostolic Exhortation *Redemptionis Donum*, no. 14.

15. John Paul II, Apostolic Exhortation *Redemptionis Donum*, no. 15.

16. Mother Teresa to Fr. Stjepan Krizin Sakač, SJ, June 17, 1958. See also Kolodiejchuk, *Come Be My Light*, 92.

17. See Ralph Martin, STD, "John of the Cross and Mother Teresa: The Truth about Dark Nights," chap. 2 in this volume, where he discusses in depth these nights.

Do not think that my spiritual life is strewn with roses—that is the flower which I hardly ever find on my way. Quite the contrary, I have more often as my companion "darkness." And when the night becomes very thick—and it seems to me as if I will end up in hell— then I simply offer myself to Jesus. If He wants me to go there— I am ready—but only under the condition that it really makes Him happy. I need much grace, much of Christ's strength to persevere in trust, in that blind love which leads only to Jesus Crucified. But I am happy—yes happier than ever. And I would not wish at any price to give up my sufferings. But do not, however, think that I am only suffering. Ah no—I am laughing more than I am suffering—so that some have concluded that I am Jesus' spoiled bride, who lives with Jesus in Nazareth—far away from Calvary....Pray, pray much for me—I really need His love.[18]

Johannes Tauler vividly describes the suffering of the person going through such a trial:

Then we are abandoned in such a way that we no longer have any awareness of God, and we fall into such anguish that we no longer know if we were ever on the right path, nor know if God even exists, or if we ourselves are alive or dead. And so an anguish besets us that is so strange, it seems as if everything in the entire world were joining together to afflict us. We no longer have any experience or awareness of God, but everything else seems repugnant to us as well, and it seems we are trapped between two walls.[19]

Mother Teresa reached a key point in her spiritual development in 1942: she was so advanced on the path of holiness that she made a private vow with the permission of her confessor: "I wanted to give

---

18. Mother Teresa to Fr. Stjepan Krizin Sakač, SJ, June 17, 1958.

19. Johannes Tauler, quoted in R. Cantalamessa, "Mother Teresa, 'The Night' Accepted as a Gift," originally published in Italian in Avvenire, August 26, 2007. English translation by Matthew Sherry, accessed September 25, 2012, http://chiesa.espresso.repubblica.it/articolo/164985%26eng%3Dy.html.

God something very beautiful" and "without reserve," she wrote. "I made a vow to God, binding under [pain of] mortal sin, to give to God anything that He may ask, 'Not to refuse Him anything.'"[20]

Four years later, Jesus tested that vow. Beginning in September 1946, after revealing to her that he wanted her to establish a new religious community—the Missionaries of Charity—dedicated to the service of the poorest of the poor, Jesus referred to her private vow: "In all my prayers and Holy Communions He is continually asking 'Wilt thou refuse?'"[21]

At this time, she received a series of locutions and visions, and (most probably) experienced moments of ecstasy as well. Her confessor Jesuit Father Celeste Van Exem wrote of her "continual, deep and violent union with God." Years later, she remembered that while in Asansol (where she was residing during the first half of 1947), "there as if Our Lord just gave Himself to me—to the full. The sweetness and consolation & union of those 6 months passed but too soon."[22]

An important key to understand Mother Teresa's darkness in the years that follow is the fact that she had now reached union with Jesus, the state of contemplative prayer. In his book *The Fire Within*,[23] Fr. Thomas Dubay states that in this state of union, the person experiences consolation or the joy of union as well as moments of dryness and longing for even greater union. Exceptionally, Mother Teresa did not experience again the first characteristic, the consolation and joy of union (except for about a month in 1958), but she did experience both extreme dryness and an intense and even painful longing. The great Dominican theologian Father Reginald Garrigou-Lagrange sheds light on Mother Teresa's particular experience. He writes:

20. Kolodiejchuk, *Come Be My Light*, 28–29.
21. Kolodiejchuk, *Come Be My Light*, 96.
22. Kolodiejchuk, *Come Be My Light*, 210.
23. Thomas Dubay, *Fire Within: St. Teresa of Avila, St. John of the Cross, and the Gospel—On Prayer* (San Francisco: Ignatius Press, 1989).

The lives of some great servants of God especially dedicated to reparation, to immolation for the salvation of souls or to the apostolate by interior suffering, make one think, however, of a prolongation of the night of the spirit even after their entrance into the transforming union. In such cases, this trial would no longer be chiefly purificatory; it would be above all reparative.... The common opinion is that the servants of God are more particularly tried; ... following the example of our Lord, they must work by the same means as He used for a great spiritual cause, such as the foundation of a religious order or the salvation of many other souls.[24]

This is how Mother Teresa lived her union: paradoxically, being united to Jesus by not experiencing that union. Mother Teresa often stated that the greatest poverty in the world today is to be "unloved, unwanted, uncared for"[25]—and she was experiencing this with Jesus. At the same time, this very experience united her more closely to those she served, the poorest of the poor who are the most "unloved, unwanted, uncared [for]."

Even though Mother Teresa received many consolations from Jesus in the months following the call to be an MC (beginning with Inspiration Day, September 10, 1946[26]), he declared that her "vocation is to love and suffer and save souls" and that she and her sisters were to be "victims" of his love. He also challenged her: "if you are My own little Spouse—the Spouse of the Crucified Jesus—you will have to bear these torments on your heart."[27] Mother Teresa had no way of knowing at the time what exactly these words of Jesus meant and how much she would have to suffer to fulfill this vocation to be a "victim of love" and bear his "torments on [her] heart."

24. Father Reginald Garrigou-Lagrange, OP, *The Three Ages of Interior Life: Prelude of Eternal Life*, vol. 2, trans. Sr. M. Timothea Doyle, OP (St. Louis, MO: B. Herder, 1948; Rockford, IL: Tan Books, 1989), 503–4.

25. See, e.g., Kolodiejchuk, *Come Be My Light*, 292.

26. See Kolodiejchuk, *Come Be My Light*.

27. Kolodiejchuk, *Come Be My Light*, 49.

Mother Teresa's mission in the streets of Calcutta began in earnest in 1949–50. During this same time, she again is plunged into darkness: she feels a terrible sense of loss, great loneliness, and the torment of thinking she is not wanted by God; she feels no faith or love, and even more painful than this sense of loss is the pain of unfulfilled longing—"it is so painful to be lonely for God," she wrote.[28] We can try to imagine how terrible this experience is for someone so passionately in love with Jesus as to want to love him as he has never been loved before. In a letter to Jesuit Father Joseph Neuner, she expresses how difficult this is and her need for divine help to live it: "Pray for me—for the life within me is harder to live. To be in love & yet not to love, to live by faith and yet not to believe. To spend myself and yet be in total darkness—Pray for me."[29]

During the first years of this post-Inspiration experience of darkness, Mother Teresa was not able to grasp the nature or meaning of this suffering. For example, in 1955, she asks Archbishop Périer, her ecclesiastical superior as archbishop of Calcutta, "How long will Our Lord stay away?"[30]

A few years later, however, Mother Teresa's attitude has changed: she has come to accept the darkness as a way to express her love and begins to sense that her own suffering could be for the good of others:

In the call You said that I would have to suffer much.—Ten years— my Jesus. You have done to me according to Your will—and Jesus hear My prayer—if this pleases You—if my pain and suffering— my darkness and separation gives You a drop of consolation—my own Jesus, do with me as You wish—as long as You wish, without a single glance at my feelings and pain. I am Your own.—Imprint on my soul and life the sufferings of Your Heart. Don't mind my feelings.—Don't mind even, my pain. If my separation from You—

28. Kolodiejchuk, *Come Be My Light*, 222.
29. Kolodiejchuk, *Come Be My Light*, 248.
30. Kolodiejchuk, *Come Be My Light*, 158.

brings others to You and in their love and company You find joy
and pleasure—why Jesus, I am willing with all my heart to suffer
all that I suffer—not only now—but for all eternity—if this was
possible. Your happiness is all that I want.—For the rest—please do
not take the trouble—even if you see me faint with pain.—All this
is my will.—I want to satiate Your Thirst with every single drop of
blood that You can find in me.[31]

To understand this, we need to realize that for Mother Teresa the
thirst of Jesus is the unifying element of her vocation and religious
charism, her spirituality and mission. The thirst of Jesus had a tremendous impact on her heart, a heart so in love with him.

From the cross Jesus cried out, "I thirst." From the beginning of
her new mission, Mother Teresa understood this intense, "painful" (as
she described it often, following the Lord himself[32]) thirst of Jesus as
a thirst for love and for souls. She would quench Jesus's thirst *for love*
by her passionate love for him, by her intense desire to return love for
love. She would also quench Jesus's thirst *for souls* by, as she expressed
it, "laboring at the salvation and sanctification of the poorest of the
poor." Mother Teresa in this way joined "I thirst" (Jn 19:28), which
reflects her calling to satiate Jesus's thirst (her aim) and "you did it
to me" (Mt 25:40), which reflects the means of doing it. A brief word
about these two elements.

Pope Benedict gives us a beautiful portrayal of spousal love in his
encyclical letter *Deus Caritas Est*. The spouse, he writes, is more concerned with the beloved than with self: "in drawing near to the other,
it is less and less concerned with itself, increasingly seeks the happiness
of the other, is concerned more and more with the beloved, bestows
itself and wants to 'be there for' the other."[33]

31. Kolodiejchuk, *Come Be My Light*, 193–94.
32. See, e.g., Kolodiejchuk, *Come Be My Light*, 310.
33. Pope Benedict XVI, Encyclical Letter *Deus Caritas Est*, December 25, 2005,

An outstanding characteristic of Mother Teresa's spousal love for Jesus evidenced throughout her letters is precisely her intense longing to love Jesus, to please only him. To take but one example, she writes,

> I would not like for anything, not even for a second of a second to do the less pleasing. I want Him to have all the pleasure. His longing, His suffering on account of these little children, on account of the poor dying in sin, of the unhappiness of so many broken families is great. I feel so terribly helpless in front of all.—I, little nothing, long to take away all that from His Heart.[34]

Even when she feels completely rejected by God, her longing for God remains intense, and her desire to please Jesus continues firm:

> There is so much contradiction in my soul.—Such deep longing for God—so deep that it is painful—a suffering continual—and yet not wanted by God—repulsed—empty—no faith—no love—no zeal.— Souls hold no attraction—Heaven means nothing—to me it looks like an empty place—the thought of it means nothing to me and yet this torturing longing for God.—Pray for me please that I keep smiling at Him in spite of everything. For I am only His—so He has every right over me. I am perfectly happy to be nobody even to God.[35]

Blessed Columba Marmion wrote in one of his letters about the person undergoing such trials:

> She [the soul] *seems* to herself to have lost faith & love, for she *feels* nothing. It is pure naked faith. This longing for God is a most powerful & constant prayer; for God reads the inmost thoughts of our hearts; & this thirst of Him is a cry to His Father's heart … "Thy ear

http://w2.vatican.va/content/benedict-xvi/en/encyclicals/documents/hf_ben-xvi_ enc_20051225_deus-caritas-est.html, no. 7.

34. Pope Benedict XVI, Encyclical Letter *Deus Caritas Est*, no. 66.
35. Pope Benedict XVI, Encyclical Letter *Deus Caritas Est*, nos. 169–70.

hath heard the *desire of the poor*," & no one is poorer than those who are serving God in the trials of pure faith.[36]

Mother Teresa was so united to Jesus in will, thought, and sentiment—she had such strong faith, hope, and love—that he could share for so long and so intensely his most painful suffering—the torments of his heart (as he had said to her in 1946)—that he underwent during his agony in the Garden and then on the cross.

Besides being a way of satiating Jesus's thirst for love and living in union with him, the darkness was a way of satiating his thirst for souls. In 1961, Fr. Neuner was the channel of this key insight: the darkness is the "spiritual side of her work," a sharing in Christ's *redemptive* love. This is how Mother Teresa expressed her gratitude to him for this insight:

> I can't express in words—the gratitude I owe you for your kindness to me.—For the first time in this 11 years—I have come to love the darkness.—For I believe now that it is a part, a very, very small part of Jesus' darkness & pain on earth. You have taught me to accept it [as] a "spiritual side of 'your work'" as you wrote.—Today really I felt a deep joy—that Jesus can't go anymore through the agony—but that He wants to go through it in me.—More than ever I surrender myself to Him.—Yes—more than ever I will be at His disposal.[37]

As Mother Teresa's mission expanded to the West, she understood even more that the greatest poverty in the world today is interior: to be unloved, unwanted, lonely. In one of her letters, she connects her interior state of darkness with this type of poverty:

---

36. Columba Marmion, *The English Letters of Abbot Marmion, 1853–1923*, foreword by Amleto Cardinal Cicognani (Baltimore: Helicon Press, 1962), 79.

37. Marmion, *Letters of Abbot Marmion*, 214.

I have been reading "The Nun" St. Margaret Mary & the Sacred Heart by Margaret Trouner[38]—Her love for Jesus gave me such painful longing, to love as she loved Him. How cold—how empty —how painful is my heart.—Holy Communion—Holy Mass—all the holy things of spiritual life—of the life of Christ in me—are all so empty—so cold—so unwanted. The physical situation of my poor left in the streets unwanted, unloved unclaimed—are the true picture of my own spiritual life, of my love for Jesus.[39]

Precisely because Mother Teresa was so united to Jesus, she was able to identify so completely with the poorest of the poor, sharing their spiritual destitution.

A fundamental Catholic principle is that, in the Redemption, Jesus substitutes for us, stands in our place, sharing and suffering our interior separation from God, the tragic result of original sin and our own sins. Mother Teresa understood that united to Jesus, sharing in his redemptive love, we can have a part in this. We can help quench his love for souls, we can be in the place of others, suffer for others, and so obtain graces for others. Shortly after Fr. Neuner helped her grasp the connection between her darkness and Jesus's suffering and death, Mother Teresa gave the following instruction to her Sisters:

Try ... to increase your knowledge of this Mystery of Redemption. —This knowledge will lead you to love—and love will make you share through your sacrifices in the Passion of Christ.

My dear children—without our suffering, our work would just be social work, very good and helpful, but it would not be the work of Jesus Christ, not part of the redemption.—Jesus wanted to help us by sharing our life, our loneliness, our agony and death. All that He has taken upon Himself, and has carried it in the darkest night. Only by being one with us He has redeemed us. We are allowed to

38. The correct name is Margaret Trouncer, not Trouner.
39. Marmion, *Letters of Abbot Marmion*, 232.

do the same: all the desolation of the poor people, not only their material poverty, but their spiritual destitution must be redeemed, and we must have our share in it.—Pray thus when you find it hard—"I wish to live in this world which is so far from God, which has turned so much from the light of Jesus, to help them—to take upon me something of their suffering."—Yes, my dear children—let us share the sufferings—of our poor—for only by being one with them—we can redeem them, that is, bringing God into their lives and bringing them to God.[40]

To understand Mother Teresa's experience, what it was and what it was not, it is helpful to understand the experience of Jesus himself. St. John Paul II referred to this in his General Audience of November 30, 1988:

If Jesus feels abandoned by the Father, He knows, however, that this is not really so. He Himself said, "I and the Father are one" (Jn 10:30), and speaking of His future Passion He said; "I am not alone, for the Father is with me" (Jn 16:32). Dominant in His mind, Jesus has the clear vision of God and the certainty of His union with the Father. But in the sphere bordering on the senses, and therefore more subject to the impressions, emotions, and influence of the internal and external experiences of pain, Jesus' human soul is reduced to a waste land, and He no longer *feels* the presence of the Father.[41]

Mother Teresa possessed and lived each day by faith and charity, even if she did not feel them. In her writings, she speaks of her "unbroken union."[42] She observed: "my mind and heart is habitually with God."[43] Reflecting on her suffering, she said, "I know this is only feel-

---

40. Marmion, *Letters of Abbot Marmion*, 220.

41. Quoted in Father William Most, "Must Forgiveness Be Accepted?," Catholic Culture.org, accessed September 14, 2012, https://www.catholicculture.org/culture/library/most/getwork.cfm?worknum=77.

42. Kolodiejchuk, *Come Be My Light*, 223.

43. Kolodiejchuk, *Come Be My Light*, 203.

ings—for my will is steadfast bound to Jesus."[44] Even when the desire for felt union crept in, she would pull herself up and renew her surrender. In one of her letters she wrote, "I wish I could feel what they [the Sisters] feel.—Never mind—I am very happy & keep a big smile for all."[45]

A particularly beautiful expression of Mother Teresa's understanding of her experience, permeated with deep faith and spousal love, is found in one of her later letters:

> My love for Jesus keeps growing more simple and more, I think, personal.... I want Him to be at ease with me—not to mind my feelings—as long as He feels alright—not to mind even the darkness that surrounds Him in me—but that in spite of everything Jesus is all to me and that I love no one but only Jesus.[46]

Once the interior darkness of Mother Teresa became known, the constant joy Mother Teresa demonstrated is all the more astonishing. Mother Teresa lived her spousal and redemptive love in real joy, shown to us by her ready cheerfulness. "Today really I felt a deep joy—that Jesus can't go anymore through the agony—but that He wants to go through it in me."[47] As the saints have demonstrated, this spiritual joy is compatible with suffering, even the intense interior suffering that Mother Teresa experienced.

Mother Teresa's communion of will, thought, and sentiment with her spouse Jesus was the basis of her constant surrender to his loving will. This led to the serenity and joy visible in her—two fruits of the Holy Spirit indicating God's presence and action within her.

Mother Teresa spoke often of the joy of surrender and the joy of loving. For example, she used such expressions as "the joy of letting

---

44. Kolodiejchuk, *Come Be My Light*, 257.
45. Kolodiejchuk, *Come Be My Light*, 243.
46. Kolodiejchuk, *Come Be My Light*, 274.
47. Kolodiejchuk, *Come Be My Light*, 214.

God [be] free with me";[48] "to accept whatever He gives and to give whatever He takes with a big smile";[49] "keep the joy of Jesus as your strength";[50] and "let us keep the joy of loving Jesus in our hearts and share this joy with all we meet."[51]

Fr. Raniero Cantalamessa, OFM, preacher to the papal household, commenting on Mother Teresa's darkness, observed:

> It would be a grave mistake to think that such people's lives are nothing but gloomy suffering. In the depth of their souls, they enjoy a peace and a joy that are unknown to the rest of mankind, arising from the certainty—stronger in them than their doubts—that they are living according the will of God. Saint Catherine of Genoa compares the suffering of souls in this condition with that of Purgatory, and says that it "is so great that it can be compared only to that of Hell," but that there is in it a "tremendous contentment" that can be compared only to that of the saints in Paradise. The joy and serenity that radiated from Mother Teresa's face was not a mask, but rather the reflection of the profound union with God she experienced within her soul.[52]

CONCLUSION

I began this essay by suggesting that St. Teresa of Calcutta has something—and perhaps much—to share with the science of academic theology. One example of St. Teresa's lived theology is in her sharing in the mystery of Holy Saturday. In his book *Eschatology*, the future Pope Benedict notes how in the recent history of holiness "Hell" has taken on

48. Kolodiejchuk, *Come Be My Light*, 237.
49. Kolodiejchuk, *Come Be My Light*, 241.
50. Kolodiejchuk, *Come Be My Light*, 275.
51. Kolodiejchuk, *Come Be My Light*, 295.
52. Cantalamessa, "Mother Teresa, 'The Night' Accepted as a Gift."

a completely new meaning and form. For the Saints, "Hell" is not so much a threat to be hurled at other people but a challenge to oneself. It is a challenge to suffer in the dark night of faith, to experience communion with Christ in solidarity with his descent into the Night. One draws near to the Lord's radiance by sharing his darkness. One serves the salvation of the world by leaving one's own salvation behind for the sake of others in such piety, nothing of the dreadful reality of Hell is denied. Hell is so real that it reaches right into the existence of the Saints. Hope can take it on, only if one shares in the suffering of Hell's night by the side of the one who came to transform our night by suffering.

In his reflection after viewing the Shroud of Turin, Pope Benedict noted that

in our time, especially after having lived through the past century, humanity has become particularly sensitive to the mystery of Holy Saturday. The concealment of God is part of contemporary man's spirituality, in an existential almost subconscious manner, like a void in the heart that has continued to grow larger and larger.... After the two World Wars, the *lagers* and the *gulags*, Hiroshima and Nagasaki, our epoch has become increasingly a Holy Saturday: this day's darkness challenges all who are wondering about life and it challenges us believers in particular. We too have something to do with this darkness.[53]

Along with this negative aspect of Holy Saturday, the pope also suggests that there is a positive side to this mystery it is a "source of comfort and hope."[54] Like Jesus before her, Mother Teresa lived in "radical solidarity" with those who live in the poverty of a lack of hope

53. Pope Benedict XVI, "Veneration of the Holy Shroud," May 2, 2010, http://w2.vatican.va/content/benedict-xvi/en/speeches/2010/may/documents/hf_ben-xvi_spe_20100502_meditazione-torino.html.
54. Pope Benedict XVI, "Veneration of the Holy Shroud."

and especially the poverty of the lack of love, "where total abandonment reigns without any word of comfort: 'hell.'"[55] But again, like Jesus, while Mother Teresa was plunged into darkness, she also radiated
light, thereby fulfilling her vocation to be a light—his light.

Mother Teresa is, according to Fr. Cantalamessa, among "the
greatest Christian mystics,"[56] whose "exceptionally long … period of
interior dereliction is," says Fr. Egan, "unique in the Christian mystical
tradition."[57] In union with Jesus, she willingly and lovingly shared in
that "concealment of God"[58] out of love for our dark world. For love
of Jesus and the poor, she accepted "mystical martyrdom,"[59] the pain
of not experiencing God's love, of feeling unloved and unwanted by
him. As John Paul II said of Jesus, we can say of Mother Teresa: "that
lack of interior consolation was [her] greatest agony."

St. Teresa of Calcutta lived the double reality of Christian passion
as both an intense longing to love and be loved by Jesus and as suffering in union with Jesus because of that longing. As a compelling,
contemporary example of a mystic and expert in the "science of love,"
I believe she can be a rich resource for theologians today.

55. Pope Benedict XVI, "Veneration of the Holy Shroud."
56. Cantalamessa, "Mother Teresa, 'The Night' Accepted as a Gift."
57. Egan, Soundings, 370.
58. Pope Benedict XVI, "Veneration of the Holy Shroud."
59. Egan, Soundings, 370.

2

JOHN OF THE CROSS AND MOTHER TERESA

The Truth about Dark Nights

~

Ralph Martin, STD

Even though the main lines of Mother Teresa's experience of "darkness" had been known for several years, the full publication of her private letters drew worldwide media coverage.[1] *Time* magazine did a cover story on it. Prominent articles appeared in the *New York Times* and other major publications. There were many television and radio interviews.

Some secularists chose to interpret her talk of darkness as a sign of hypocrisy and even accused her of not really believing in God. Only a superficial and partial reading of these letters could have occasioned this interpretation. Some believers were disturbed and confused to hear of her prolonged experience of aridity or emptiness in her rela-

1. Brian Kolodiejchuk, ed., *Mother Teresa: Come Be My Light* (New York: Doubleday, 2007).

tionship with God. This has made some afraid to undertake the spiritual journey and the suffering it might entail, and has held some back from embracing wholeheartedly the call to holiness. Some thought the letters were so disturbing that it was a mistake to publish them. This last concern, while understandable, is unfounded, since the letters in question are part of the official record compiled in the process of canonization and are generally made public. And by now we must know that efforts to "edit" the life or writings of a saint (as the sisters of Thérèse of Lisieux tried to do in the case of their sister's writings) only detract from the awesome witness to holiness that is found, albeit in sometimes unexpected and disturbing ways. In the long run, this widespread media attention, even with its imperfections, to the publication of these letters will bear great fruit.

Having read the entire book when it first came out, and now having reread it for the purpose of this essay, I am left awestruck at the depth of Mother Teresa's holiness. Her faith and her heroic service were more profound than I ever imagined.

It is certainly true that while receiving remarkable communications from the Lord and deep spiritual/sensible consolation at the beginning of her mission, so much so that her spiritual director thought she was approaching the highest state of union, for almost fifty years Mother Teresa was left almost totally bereft of such consolation. She carried out her mission with almost no affective experience of God's love and presence. She could see the fruit that her work was producing. She could see that when she spoke to her Sisters and others that they came alive and grew in the experience of God's love, but she herself for the most part felt only emptiness. She often commented on the emptiness she felt behind her smile.

This experience of Mother Teresa is commonly referred to as her "dark night." But in order to understand more precisely what the meaning of this darkness could be and whether it should even properly be called a dark night, we need to examine its classic exposition in the writings of St. John of the Cross.[2]

John speaks of a first "dark night" that has its active and passive dimensions. This dark night happens in the beginning stages of the spiritual journey and is referred to as the "night of the senses." Its active dimension is our effort in reordering our life around the Lordship of Christ, and the passive dimension is the action of the Spirit in our soul enabling us to do so, helping "put our loves in order," as St. Bernard of Clairvaux describes it.

But John points out that this first purification or dark night is similar to the gardener cutting off the weeds in the garden at the surface of the soil—the garden is then in some real sense "in order," but under the surface, the roots survive and will continue to cause problems. The second and deeper purification, then, is the active and passive dark nights of the soul or spirit, because the wounds of sin are located deep within our spirits.

How does this second, more profound purification present itself in its most profound or passive dimension—God's action in the soul? The "presenting symptoms" are almost always a deep aridity or experience of emptiness, darkness, or lack of connection with God. Prayer is extremely difficult, and we don't think we are connecting in any way. We may be tempted to think that God has abandoned us or that what we previously experienced of his presence wasn't real. This may be accompanied by difficult external circumstances in our life: humiliation, failed relationships, financial setbacks, unemployment, illness, loneliness, and so on.

How does this deeper purification come about? Much like the initial purification, but in a deeper and more intense form. The very fallenness of the world, the flesh, and the devil are turned into means

2. Most of the material on the classic definitions of "dark night" is drawn from chapter 14 of my book *The Fulfillment of All Desire* (Steubenville, OH: Emmaus Road, 2006).

to draw us into deeper union with God. And God himself acts in the soul directly.

There is no transformation without the foundational biblical principle being observed: the grain of wheat must fall into the ground and die if it is to bear fruit (cf. Jn 12:24).

> The trials that those who are to reach this state [transforming union] suffer are threefold: trials, discomforts, fears, and temptations from the world; and these in many ways: temptations, aridities, and afflictions in the senses; and tribulations, darknesses, distress, abandonment, temptations, and other trials in the spirit.[3]

When we hear descriptions of the types of trials and depths of purification that we must undergo to be able to be fully united to God, this purification isn't optional. It's necessary. It's not a question of "if" but of "when." If the purification doesn't take place in this life, it will have to happen in purgatory if we are to be able to see God.

"Strive for that holiness without which no one will see God" (Heb 12:14). The sooner this purification takes place, the better—for us and for everyone else in our lives. The root of all our unhappiness is the result of sin and its effects. The sooner we are free from the distortions and crippling of sin, the sooner we will experience a fuller joy and freedom as sons and daughters of God, and be able more and more to be a blessing to others.

> Since unpurified souls must undergo the sufferings of fire in the next life to attain union with God in glory, so in this life they must undergo the fire of these sufferings to reach the union of perfection. This fire acts on some more vigorously than on others, and on some for a longer time than on others, according to the degree of union to which God wishes to raise them, and according to what they must be purged of.[4]

3. John of the Cross, *The Living Flame of Love*, stanza 2, nos. 24–25.
4. John of the Cross, *The Living Flame of Love*, stanza 2, nos. 24–25.

Fire is an important image of the purifying action of God's Spirit, both in Scripture and in the writing of the mystics. One of John's most illuminating descriptions of how this purifying action of God's Spirit works and what it accomplishes is based on his analogy of a burning log. He considers this a particularly useful analogy that "illustrates many of the things we are saying and will say."

> For the sake of further clarity in this matter, we ought to note that this purgative and loving knowledge, or divine light we are speaking of has the same effect on a soul that fire has on a log of wood. The soul is purged and prepared for union with the divine light just as the wood is prepared for transformation into the fire. Fire, when applied to wood, first dehumidifies it, dispelling all moisture and making it give off any water it contains. Then it gradually turns the wood black, makes it dark and ugly, and even causes it to emit a bad odor. By drying out the wood, the fire brings to light and expels all those ugly and dark accidents that are contrary to fire. Finally, by heating and enkindling it from without, the fire transforms the wood into itself and makes it as beautiful as it is itself.[5]

John explains how this analogy pertains to the purification of the soul.

> Similarly, we should philosophize about this divine, loving fire of contemplation. Before transforming the soul, it purges it of all contrary qualities. It produces blackness and darkness and brings to the fore the soul's ugliness; thus one seems worse than before and unsightly and abominable. This divine purge stirs up all the foul and vicious humors of which the soul was never before aware; never did it realize there was so much evil in itself, since these humors were so deeply rooted. And now that they may be expelled and annihilated they are brought to light and seen clearly through the illumination of this dark light of divine contemplation. Although the soul is no worse than before, either in itself or in its relationship with God, it

---

5. John of the Cross, *Dark Night*, book II, chap. 10, no. 1, 416.

feels clearly that it is so bad as to be not only unworthy that God sees it but deserving of his abhorrence. In fact, it feels that God now does abhor it.[6]

Let's examine now the nature of the purifying sufferings of this dark night, and the great fruit that they bring.

PURIFYING SUFFERINGS

First, the reality of the dark night of a deeper purification isn't an invention of John of the Cross. It's an observation, a discovery, of how God works with souls that many of the saints speak about using a variety of different terminologies. It's a reality that's spoken about directly in Scripture that the saints have been able to describe in some detail because of their experience and the gift of teaching that God has given some of them, most particularly the Doctors of the Church on whom we are focusing.

Many of the saints, especially John, make a point of explicitly relating their teaching to Scripture.

In speaking of this deeper purification that he calls the "dark night," John states: "So many are the scriptural passages we could cite that we would have neither the time nor the energy to put it all in writing."[7] John has analyzed this process of purification and developed a technical and poetic language to describe it perhaps better than anyone else, but there is a wide testimony to the reality and necessity of this purification.

Teresa categorizes the sufferings of this deeper purification—the

6. John of the Cross, *Dark Night*, book II, chap. 10, nos. 1–2, 416–17. All citations to John of the Cross's works are from *The Collected Works of St. John of the Cross*, trans. Kieran Kavanaugh and Otilio Rodriguez (Washington, DC: ICS Publications, 1991).

7. Some of the many passages that John cites to illumine what he means by the "dark night" include: Job 16:12–16; Lam 3:1–20; Ps 18:5–6, 55:15, 69:1–3, 88:8, 139:12, 143:304; Jon 2:1–3.

dark night of the spirit—into exterior and interior trials. She teaches that as we are drawing closer to union with God, he prepares the soul for deeper union by accelerating the process of preparation through gifts and graces, wounds of love, and also trials of all kinds.

EXTERIOR TRIALS

Teresa specifically names several exterior trials that she underwent: the harsh, judgmental criticism of others, the praise of others, the bad advice and lack of understanding by indecisive and inexperienced confessors, rejection by friends, and the suffering of physical illness.[8] The Apostle Paul likewise cites a long list of sufferings that tested and purified him: afflictions, hardships, constraints, beatings, imprisonments, riots, labors, vigils, fasts, dishonor, and insults (cf. 2 Cor 6:4–10).

Dark nights can be experienced intermittently or for more extended periods, and at varying levels of intensity. Thérèse talks of the anguish of waiting three days for her uncle to give approval for her to enter the convent as a "dark night." The profound trial of her father's mental deterioration, which lasted three years, was a deeper and longer-lasting dark night. She speaks of unbearable anguish, as the profound sorrow of her heart was soon joined by a deep aridity of her soul. Yet, as painful as it was, she wouldn't have traded it for the world. She knew the value of suffering. In the mysterious embrace of the cross of suffering, Thérèse knew that she and her Sisters were "flying" toward God.[9] The deepest night of all was not to come until the last year and a half of her life, when, while suffering from tuberculosis, she

8. Teresa of Avila, *The Interior Castle*, sect. VI, chap. 1, nos. 2–9, 360–64. All citations of Teresa of Avila are from *The Collected Works of St. Teresa of Avila*, trans. Kieran Kavanaugh and Otilio Rodriguez (Washington, DC: ICS Publications, 1987).

9. Thérèse of Lisieux, *Story of a Soul*, chap. 7, 156–57. All citations from Thérèse of Lisieux are from *The Autobiography of St. Thérèse of Lisieux: The Story of a Soul*, trans. John Clarke (Washington, DC: ICS Publications, 1996).

experienced acute and continuing temptations to abandon faith itself.

Teresa of Avila mentions that physical illnesses, when the pains are acute, are the greatest of the exterior trials because the pain of the body affects the soul "in such a way that it doesn't know what to do with itself … although they do not last long in this extreme form."[10]

The purpose of what might seem like overwhelmingly impossible trials is to purify and to lead us to a deeper trust in God and abandonment to his will, "supernaturalizing" our hopes and dreams. Paul remarks of his own afflictions experienced in Asia:

> We were so utterly, unbearably crushed that we despaired of life itself. Why, we felt that we had received the sentence of death; but that was to make us rely not on ourselves but on God who raises the dead. (2 Cor 1:8–9)

Teresa encourages us, as usual, and reminds us that "God gives no more than what can be endured and His Majesty gives patience first" (cf. 1 Cor 10:13).[11] She testifies that since she first began to experience the initial touches of the prayer of union when she was just twenty-two years old and only a few years in the convent—she was about sixty-two years old when she wrote this—she hadn't a day without some kind of physical illness and other trials of various kinds. She claims that this is because of her wretchedness and the fact that she deserved hell and that others, who hadn't offended the Lord as much, might be led by a different path.[12] While the external trials can be severe, particularly in the case of serious illness, both Teresa and John explain that the interior trials of this deeper purification are even more difficult.

---

10. Teresa of Avila, *Interior Castle*, sect. VI, chap. 1, no. 6, 362.

11. Teresa of Avila, *Interior Castle*, sect. VI, chap. 1, no. 6, 362.

12. Teresa of Avila, *Interior Castle*, sect. VI, chap. 1, no. 7, 362.

INTERIOR TRIALS

The most serious of the interior trials involves the suffering that comes from feeling that one has perhaps been abandoned by God or has seriously gotten off track. Sometimes the absence of feeling in prayer and in the overall relationship with God—aridity—combined with the tempting of the devil, can produce a hellish, agonizing experience of abandonment and almost hopeless condemnation.

Teresa of Avila explains that, as in the case of Job, the Lord sometimes gives permission for the devil to test the soul even to the point of thinking it is rejected and abandoned by God.[13] During these times of profound interior trial, she explains, the presence of grace is so hidden that not even a tiny spark of it is visible.

> The soul doesn't think that it has any love of God or that it ever had any, for if it has done some good, or His Majesty has granted it some favor, all of this seems to have been dreamed up or fancied. As for sins, it sees certainly that it has committed them.[14]

Nothing satisfies during these times. Solitude is unbearable, but so is being with other people. All kinds of prayer, vocal and mental, feel empty and useless. And even though the soul tries to maintain a positive disposition during this time, it finds it impossible to do so, and "goes about with a gloomy and ill-tempered mien that is externally very noticeable." It also suffers the added humiliation of everyone seeing how "down" it is.[15]

In this state, nothing seems to be able to relieve the soul's misery. Even if a spiritual director were to explain what one was experiencing and why—the dark night and how it would eventually lift—it proba-

---

13. Teresa of Avila, *Interior Castle*, sect. VI, chap. 1, no. 7, 364.
14. Teresa of Avila, *Interior Castle*, sect. VI, chap. 1, no. 11, 364–65.
15. Teresa of Avila, *Interior Castle*, sect. VI, chap. 1, no. 13, 365.

bly would not help. The reason is that this trial "comes from above and earthly things are of no avail in the matter. Our great God wants us to know our own misery and that He is king; and this is very important for what lies ahead."[16]

Teresa explains that, because this is a divine work, nothing we do can get rid of the trial, but a good way of enduring it "is to engage in external works of charity and to hope in the mercy of God who never fails those who hope in Him." In fact, she makes clear that "there is no remedy in this tempest but to wait for the mercy of God."[17]

The reason for the depth of this trial is so that we can know on a much deeper level our incapacity for union with God and our absolute need of his grace and mercy if we are to be able to love him and follow him. And then, when this phase of the preparation has been accomplished, "at an unexpected time, with one word alone or a chance happening," this great trial will be over. The soul will emerge, deeply humbled, and with great joy, delight, praise, and gratitude, having been made ready to enter the seventh mansion.[18]

John of the Cross makes clear that what we are undergoing is not just a trial, a suffering, or a temptation, but an actual work of God deep in the soul. He explains that in this passive night of the spirit, God infuses pure light and love into the soul ("dark contemplation"). It is only because of our limitations and sinfulness that what is in itself purely delightful is experienced by us, in our fallen condition, as painful and distressing.

> These proficients are still very lowly and natural in their communion with God and in their activity directed toward him.... Wishing to strip them in fact of this old self and clothe them with the new, which is created according to God in the newness

---

16. Teresa of Avila, *Interior Castle*, sect. VI, chap. 1, no. 12, 365.
17. Teresa of Avila, *Interior Castle*, sect. VI, chap. 1, no. 10, 13, 364–65.
18. Teresa of Avila, *Interior Castle*, sect. VI, chap. 1, no. 10, 15, 364, 366.

of sense, as the Apostle says [Col 3:9–10, Eph 4:22–24, Rom 12:2], God divests the faculties, affections, and senses, both spiritual and sensory, interior and exterior. He leaves the intellect in darkness, the will in aridity, the memory in emptiness, and the affections in supreme affliction, bitterness, and anguish by depriving the soul of the feeling and satisfaction it previously obtained from spiritual blessings.... The Lord works all of this in the soul by means of a pure and dark contemplation.[19]

John is eager, as always, to show the scriptural foundation for what he is teaching. He is attempting to "unpack" the dense layers of meaning contained in what Scripture describes in more succinct terms. Besides the New Testament passages speaking of complete transformation that John often cites, he also discerns the same "passive night of the spirit" in the profound testing and trials that great figures of the Old Testament underwent. In this regard, he often cites the experiences of Job, Jonah, David, Joseph, Abraham, and Jeremiah as illuminative of what he is calling, in his poetic language, a "dark night."[20]

Job is almost a prototype of the dark night of purification. Besides the experience of abandonment by God, John points out that Job felt a lack of understanding and rejection from those close to him, for "such persons also feel forsaken and despised by creatures, particularly by their friends."[21]

As with the story of Job, so also Psalm 88 provides a striking description of many of the elements of the dark night.[22] It speaks of apparent abandonment by God, rejection by friends, anguish of soul and

19. John of the Cross, *Dark Night*, book II, chap. 3, no. 3, 399.
20. It's remarkable to read some of these references in light of John's interpretation: Job 7:20, 12:22, 16:12–16, 23:6; Jon 2:1–7; Ps 18:5–6, 55:15, 69:1–3, 88:4–8, 139:12, 142:3–4; Lam 3:1–20; Ezek 24:10–11.
21. John of the Cross, *Dark Night*, book II, chap. 6, no. 3, 404.
22. See also Psalms 6 and 38 for particularly vivid descriptions that speak of the dark night.

body, darkness of understanding, temptations against faith and trust. It can be rightly called a "psalm for the dark night."

These themes of profound affliction and the experiential absence of God surface in much of the Scripture, most notably in Jesus's recitation of Psalm 22 in his own agony on the cross. No matter how deep the darkness and agony may seem, despair never wins; faith and trust amid darkness remain the only light, and ultimately lead to the glory of the Resurrection and the beatific vision. Jesus is our leader, and we have only to follow him through the darkness.

> In the days of his flesh, Jesus offered up prayers and supplications, with loud cries and tears, to him who was able to save him from death, and he was heard for his godly fear. Although he was a Son, he learned obedience through what he suffered; and being made perfect he became the source of eternal salvation to all who obey him. (Heb 5:7–9)

The dark night calls from us in the deepest part of our being a deeper and purer faith, hope, and love. In the dark night, God is giving us the grace to believe (cf. Ps 116:10) even when afflicted. To believe without seeing or experiencing, to hope without possessing, and to love without experiencing love in return either from God or even from people. He is lovingly guiding us on our way even when there is no perception of his presence. Even though we are in darkness, we are not to focus on the darkness, as perhaps some non-Christian forms of meditation might suggest, but we need to focus on Jesus, who remains the "pioneer and perfecter" (Heb 12:2) of our faith. If we do, the darkness will eventually turn into an immense light. Another secret of the spiritual life is the need to just "keep showing up." Mother Teresa always showed up for Mass and prayer before the Blessed Sacrament even when she felt absolutely nothing or dead inside.

And I will lead the blind in a way that they know not,
  in paths that they have not known I will guide them.
I will turn the darkness before them into light, the rough places into
  level ground.
These are the things I will do, and I will not forsake them. (Is 42:16)

Although we "go forth weeping," we shall "come back rejoicing" at the fruitfulness that has been revealed, as we persevere in faith, hope, and love (Ps 126:6). John also explains clearly that everything that comes from God is good; this "dark contemplation" that comes into the soul is experienced as painful only because of our unclean, untransformed condition.

> When this pure light strikes in order to expel all impurity, persons feel so unclean and wretched that it seems God is against them and they are against God....
>
> The soul understands distinctly that it is worthy neither of God nor of any creature. And what most grieves it is that it thinks it will never be worthy, and there are no more blessings for it. This divine and dark light causes deep immersion of the mind in the knowledge and feeling of one's own miseries and evils; it brings all these miseries into relief so the soul sees clearly that of itself it will never possess anything else....
>
> Persons suffer affliction ... because of their natural, moral and spiritual weakness. Since this divine contemplation assails them somewhat forcibly in order to subdue and strengthen their soul, they suffer so much in their weakness that they almost die, particularly at times when the light is more powerful. Both the sense and the spirit, as though under an immense and dark load, undergo such agony and pain that the soul would consider death a relief.[23]

23. John of the Cross, *Dark Night*, book II, chap. 5, nos. 5–6, 402–3.

Teresa mentions that this desire to die and have it all done with, which is characteristic of this phase of purification, gives way in the seventh mansion to a peaceful love of God's will—so much so that even if Jesus wanted us to spend another thousand years on earth undergoing extraordinary sufferings, we would be delighted to do so out of love for him and his will.

In the meantime, however, the soul undergoes a deep purification, and John vividly describes the feelings that accompany it.

> And the soul not only suffers the void and suspension of these natural supports and apprehensions, which is a terrible anguish (like hanging in midair unable to breathe), but it is also purged by this contemplation. As fire consumes the tarnish and rust of metal, this contemplation annihilates, empties, and consumes all the affections and imperfect habits the soul contracted throughout its life. Since these imperfections are deeply rooted in the substance of the soul, in addition to this poverty, this natural and spiritual emptiness, it usually suffers an oppressive undoing and an inner torment.... For the prophet [Ezek 24:10–11] asserts that in order to burn away the rust of the affections the soul must, as it were, be annihilated and undone in the measure that these passions and imperfections are connatural to it.[24]

Everything unclean must go. Everything twisted and bent as a result of sin must be straightened. Everything crippled and sick in the depths of our soul must be healed, and everything out of its proper order must be put into order. Every attachment that is not to the Lord and in the Lord must be broken. The illness we suffer from is grave and life-threatening; the medicine to cure this "sickness unto death" must itself be strong to be effective.

What must "die," "be crucified," or, in the language of John of the

---

24. John of the Cross, *Dark Night*, book II, chap. 6, no. 5, 405.

Cross, "be annihilated" is not the human personality or even the body, but the distortions that sin has worked in the depth of the human person. This must happen in order for each of us, body and soul, to truly live as we were created to live, beginning on this earth and continuing in fullness when we live with risen bodies. Oh, blessed death! Oh, blessed crucifixion! Oh, blessed annihilation!

Catherine of Siena also speaks of the intensity of this purification, but without using the terminology of "dark night." In speaking about the intensity of trials, temptations, and dryness in prayer that a soul trying to make progress encounters, the Father gives Catherine the answer to a question that all of us have surely asked: Why must we undergo this trial? The answer is in harmony with what Teresa, Bernard, and John have explained.

> And why do I keep this soul, surrounded by so many enemies, in such pain and distress? Not for her to be captured and lose the wealth of grace, but to show her my providence, so that she will trust not in herself but in me. Then she will rise up from her carelessness and her concern will make her run for protection to me her defender, her kind Father, the provider of her salvation. I want her to be humble, to see that of herself she is nothing and to recognize that her existence and every gift beyond that comes from me, that I am her life. She will recognize this life and my providence when she is liberated through these struggles, for I do not let these things last forever. They come and go as I see necessary for her. Sometimes she will think she is in hell, and then, through no effort of her own, she will be relieved and will have a taste of eternal life. The soul is left serene. What she sees seems to cry out that God is all-aflame with loving fire, as she now contemplates my providence. For she sees that she has come safely out of this great flood not by any effort of her own. The light came unforeseen. It was not her effort but my immeasurable charity, which wanted to

provide for her in time of need when she could scarcely take anymore.[25]

We hear the same message: this purification is necessary for humility to deepen and to know our total dependence on God. It is not an end in itself but raises us to a higher level of union with God. God will not let us be tested beyond our strength, even though sometimes it will seem like we are. The revelation of our weaknesses, mistakes, sins, or failures in our relationships or work may all be means that God makes use of to draw us more radically to him.

John of the Cross also notes that purification varies in intensity and does not last forever. Depending on how God deems best to work with each individual soul, it may come in intervals, alternating with consolations.

> God humbles the soul greatly in order to exalt it greatly afterward. And if he did not ordain that these feelings, when quickened in the soul, be soon put to sleep again, a person would die in a few days. Only at intervals is one aware of these feelings in all their intensity. Sometimes that experience is so vivid that it seems to the soul that it sees hell and perdition open before it. These are the ones who go down into hell alive (Ps 55:15), since their purgation on earth is similar to what takes place there.[26]

Here John is talking about the purifying process of "purgatory," not the eternal damnation of hell. He then makes the remarkable statement, which is echoed by many saints, that the more purification that can be undergone here on earth, the better.

---

25. Catherine of Siena, *The Dialogue*, chap. 144, 301. All citations from Catherine of Siena are from *Catherine of Siena: The Dialogue*, trans. Suzanne Noffke (New York: Paulist Press, 1980).

26. John of the Cross, *Dark Night*, book II, chap. 6, no. 6, 405–6.

For this purgation is what would have to be undergone there. The soul that endures it here on earth either does not enter that place, or is detained there for only a short while. It gains more in one hour here on earth by this purgation than it would in many there.[27]

The sooner the purification can happen and the more advanced it can become, the better for us and everyone else. The more we are purified and conformed to God's will and image, the happier we will be and the better able to truly love God and everyone else in our life, and to live our life in a way that's a blessing for others.

As John explains, what an individual will experience in this purification will vary greatly, depending on how much needs to be purified and to what degree of union God is leading the person. Both Teresa and John try to include everything in their descriptions that they believe people could possibly experience, while knowing that what an individual will actually experience will vary considerably and that few, if any, will experience everything of which they speak.[28]

Francis de Sales also talks of this deep purification. He describes how St. Francis of Assisi went through such a time of intense purification.

> The glorious father of whom we speak was himself once assailed and disturbed by such deep spiritual melancholy that he could not help showing it in his conduct. If he wanted to talk with his religious he could not do so; if he withdrew from their company it was worse. Abstinence and bodily mortification weighed him down and prayer gave him no relief. He went on in this way for two years so that he seemed completely abandoned by God. Finally, after he had humbly endured this violent storm, the Savior in a single instant restored him to a happy calm.[29]

27. John of the Cross, *Dark Night*, book II, chap. 6, no. 6, 406.
28. John of the Cross, *The Living Flame of Love*, stanza 1, no. 24, 651.
29. Francis de Sales, *Introduction to the Devout Life*, trans. John K. Ryan (New York: Doubleday, 1989), Part IV, chap. 15, 269–70.

Francis de Sales's conclusion is that if even the greatest of saints had to undergo such purification, then we should not be astonished that we lesser servants have to undergo purification in some measure also.

In commenting on the purification of Job and of the apostles, Francis links such purifications to the unique and mysterious sufferings of Jesus.

> In like manner our divine Savior was incomparably afflicted in his civil life, being condemned as guilty of treason against God and man; beaten, scourged, reviled, and tormented with extraordinary ignominy; in his natural life, dying in the most cruel and sensible torments that heart could conceive; in his spiritual life enduring sorrows, fears, terrors, anguish, abandonment, interior oppressions, such as never had, nor shall have their like.... So in the sea of passions by which Our Lord was overwhelmed, all the faculties of his soul were, so to say, swallowed up and buried in the whirlpool of so many pains, excepting only the point of his spirit, which, exempt from all trouble, remained bright and resplendent with glory and felicity.[30]

Just as Jesus at the "point of his spirit" maintained the experience of the beatific vision, although all else was darkness, Francis indicates that when we are going through the most intense of purifications, so too will the "heights of the spirit" of our souls maintain some perception, however obscure, of the link with God.

John makes the same point when speaking about the experience of abandonment of Jesus on the cross. Even though Jesus's whole being experienced the desolation of crucifixion in all its sensory and spiritual dimensions, the "higher" part of his soul remained in the peace of the beatific vision.

---

30. Francis de Sales, *Treatise on the Love of God,* trans. Henry Benedict Mackey (Rockford, IL: Tan Books, 1997), book IX, chap. 5, 376–77.

EMPTIED IN ORDER TO BE FILLED

Trials, temptations, sufferings, and purifications are not ends in themselves. They are means to a positive end. They are preparing us for union. They are enlarging the capacity of our soul so that we can "grasp fully, with all the holy ones, the breadth and length and height and depth of Christ's love, and experience this love which surpasses all knowledge, so that you may attain to the fullness of God himself" (Eph 3:18–19).

In retrospect, it is possible to see the great grace of this deeper purification. In John's words:

> I departed from my low manner of understanding, and my feeble way of loving, and my poor and limited method of finding satisfaction in God.... This was great happiness and a sheer grace for me, because through the annihilation and calming of my faculties, passions, appetites, and affections, by which my experience and satisfaction in God were base, I went out from my human operation and way of acting to God's operation and way of acting....
>
> My intellect departed from itself, changing from human and natural to divine. For united with God through this purgation, it no longer understands by means of its natural vigor and light, but by means of the divine wisdom to which it was united. And my will departed from itself and became divine. United with the divine love, it no longer loves in a lowly manner, with its natural strength, but with the strength and purity of the Holy Spirit....
>
> The memory, too, was changed into eternal apprehensions of glory. And finally, all the strength and affections of the soul, by means of this night and purgation of the old self, are renewed with divine qualities and delights.[31]

---

31. John of the Cross, *Dark Night*, book II, chap. 4, nos. 1–5.

Every aspect of the purification is an expression of the great mercy of God. Every painful aspect of the transformation is rooted in God's immense desire to make us capable of sharing in the fullness of his joy. Every suffering is temporary, making us capable of an eternal weight of glory.

> Even though this happy night darkens the spirit, it does so only to impart light concerning all things; and even though it humbles individuals and reveals their miseries, it does so only to exalt them; and even though it impoverishes and empties them of all possessions and natural affection, it does so only that they may reach out divinely to the enjoyment of all earthly and heavenly things with a general freedom of spirit in them all.[32]

The process of letting go of inordinate attachments (this clinging to the things and people of this world out of fear or greed) once the purification has been completed paradoxically leads to the ability to love and enjoy the things and people of this world in a much greater measure of love and in great freedom of spirit.

In summary, John prays,

> For you, O divine life, never kill unless to give life, never wound unless to heal. When you chastise your touch is gentle, but it is enough to destroy the world.... You have wounded me in order to cure me, O divine hand, and you have put to death in me what made me lifeless, what deprived me of God's life in which I now see myself live.... And your only begotten Son, O merciful hand of the Father, is the delicate touch by which you touched me with the force of your cautery and wounded me.[33]

But perhaps we've spent more than enough time talking about the great Doctors' explication of the dark night and it is time to briefly

---

32. John of the Cross, *Dark Night*, book II, chap. 9, no. 1, 412.
33. John of the Cross, *The Living Flame of Love*, stanza 2, no. 16, 663–64.

summarize some of the additional points that they make, which are relevant to our goal of coming to some understanding about the nature of Mother Teresa's darkness.

In brief, John of the Cross teaches that there are three reasons why someone may experience deep aridity, emptiness, or darkness in their prayer or relationship with God. One reason is "lukewarmness" or infidelity in "doing our part" in sustaining our relationship with God. We may become careless about regular prayer and spiritual reading, we may not frequent the Eucharist and Sacrament of Reconciliation, we may fill our minds and hearts with worldly entertainment, we may not be diligent in rejecting temptation, we may not develop relationships with others who desire to follow the Lord. Such carelessness and infidelity lessen our hunger for God and desire to be with him and produce lukewarmness and repugnance for things of the spirit. This is not a purifying darkness but rather the result of laxity, and the only solution is to repent and take up the spiritual practices that dispose us for union with God.

A second reason is physical or emotional illness. The advice of the saints is to try to get better, pray for healing, go to the doctor, but keep on as best one can in living a fervent Christian life. And if one is not healed, it's an invitation to join our suffering with the suffering of Jesus and offer it as reparation for our own sins and as intercessory prayer for others.

A third reason why such darkness or aridity may be present is that we are ready to move to a deeper level of faith, hope, and love and that God purposely removes the experience of his love, presence, or favor—but not their reality—in order to give us a chance to believe, hope, and love more deeply and purely. This true "dark night" may be intense and last for a long period of time, or it may happen intermittently, interspersed with times of sensible consolation. A true dark night is accompanied by deep, painful longing for God. Even though what Mother Teresa experienced isn't a typical dark night, this longing is acutely present in her. One sign that it is an authentic dark night is that we don't in our aridity try to fill the emptiness with worldly or fleshly consolations but remain faithful in seeking God even in the pain of his apparent absence.

But the point that we need to clearly understand from these great teachers of the purifying action of God is that dark nights are not ends in themselves, and they are not usually a life-long state. (Fr. Kolodiejchuk notes that only St. Paul of the Cross seemed to experience something approaching a life-long darkness, and is it not significant in understanding his experience as the founder of the Passionists.) In the classical teaching of St. John of the Cross and other great Doctors, dark nights give way to an immense joy, freedom, experience of God's presence, insight into the mysteries of the faith, and great apostolic fruitfulness. Not that suffering or purification ever entirely cease, but they are now lived in a state of remarkable habitual and constant awareness of the presence of God and being held in a stable embrace of his love. Suffering now is not primarily about purification but about sharing in the sufferings of Christ as reparation for sin and the conversion of sinners. This allows us, then, to consider what has been called Mother Teresa's dark night.

During the first ten years of this "darkness," she was deeply troubled by it and sought to understand what was happening by consulting a few trusted priests. She wondered whether this prolonged darkness was a sign of her great sinfulness and imperfection. Some of the advice she received was helpful, but it wasn't until she met Fr. Neuner, a Jesuit working in India, that she came to grasp some of the special meaning of her suffering. He explained to her that this wasn't the typical "dark night" as described by St. John of the Cross, that it wasn't just for her own purification, but that it was a special gift that God was giving her to participate in the sufferings of Christ, particularly in Jesus's own sense of abandonment in his agony in the garden of Gethsemane before his crucifixion. She was forever grateful:

> I can't express in words the gratitude I owe you for your kindness to me. For the first time in these 11 years I have come to love the darkness. For I believe now that it is a part, a very, very small part of Jesus' darkness and pain on earth. You have taught me to accept it as a "spiritual side of 'your work'" as you wrote. Today really I felt a deep joy; that Jesus can't go anymore through the agony but that He wants to go through it in me. More than ever I surrender myself to Him. Yes, more than ever I will be at His disposal.[34]

In fact, Mother Teresa had prayed for just such a participation in the agony of Christ years previously! It was not unlike the prayer that St. Thérèse "found herself praying" that led to the last year and a half of her life being a suffering of darkness and trials of faith in solidarity with the atheism of nineteenth-century France.

As a young woman, she had resolved "to drink the chalice to the last drop." After the founding of the Missionaries of Charity, she again resolved "to drink only from His chalice of pain and to give Mother Church real saints."[35]

The understanding she received from Fr. Neuner gave her a measure of peace and even joy, although it didn't take away the pain of not being able to experience the sensible/spiritual consolation of God's love and favor, which often seemed on the verge of being unbearable.

Mother Teresa, although she claimed she couldn't profit from spiritual books, did profit from reading St. John of the Cross and wrote to Fr. Neuner about how moved she was at John's writings about God. As Fr. Kolodiejchuk puts it:

---

34. Kolodiejchuk, *Come Be My Light*, 241.
35. Kolodiejchuk, *Come Be My Light*, 141.

Though familiar with the Carmelite saint's thought, she did not label her own suffering as a "dark night." She had the intuition and now a confirmation from her spiritual director that, though the sufferings were similar, their purpose was different.[36]

Mother Teresa gave one of her most explicit statements of faith about the darkness. The darkness was not just "her darkness: it was "*His* darkness"; she was sharing in *Jesus's* pain.[37] At times, though, she perhaps wavered.

In humility, Mother Teresa continued to think that she still needed purification from her imperfections. In reality, her agonizing and interminable darkness was reparatory rather than purgative. It was a participation in the mission of saving souls; she was following the example of Jesus her Master, and of his Blessed Mother, who suffered immensely not to be purified from sin, but to save sinners.[38]

Fr. Raniero Cantalamessa in his Advent Meditations given in 2003 to the Holy Father and the papal household summed up well the reasons why God led Mother Teresa by this unusual path, and the full text of the letters and the commentary of Fr. Kolodiejchuk confirms this interpretation.[39]

Because the Lord knew that the remarkable mission that Mother Teresa was undertaking would be blessed greatly and that the whole world would come to admire it, it was important that the special gift of acute "spiritual poverty" be given to Mother Teresa as a protection against pride. The experience of her "nothingness" and "emptiness" was a gift that God gave to protect her from the adulation she would receive, including the reception of the Nobel Peace Prize in 1979.

---

36. Kolodiejchuk, *Come Be My Light*, 218.

37. Kolodiejchuk, *Come Be My Light*, 224.

38. Kolodiejchuk, *Come Be My Light*, 254.

39. Ralph Martin, *The Fulfillment of All Desire* (Steubenville, OH: Emmaus Road, 2006), 431–33. See also my article "The 'Dark Night' of Mother Teresa," in *Mosaic* (Fall 2016): 8–11.

Also, because of the specific nature of the mission he was calling her to, he gave her the gift of knowing in the depth of her being what it was like for those she was serving: people who had been abandoned by their families, rejected, unwanted, left alone to die on the streets of Calcutta, or children abandoned by their parents. She understood and felt deep compassion for these abandoned ones in part because of her own experience of "darkness" and abandonment.

And, finally, she was being given to a remarkable degree the gift of being one with Jesus in his passion, out of which comes so much redemptive power. A gift she had asked for on more than one occasion.

Yes, she experienced temptations to give up, to despair, even temptations to blasphemy and unbelief, but to be tempted is not to sin. Her heroic perseverance in the face of such interior suffering is truly awe-inspiring. What an example to us in our need to persevere no matter what the difficulties, no matter what we experience or don't experience.

On the other hand, there are dangers in misunderstanding Mother Teresa's unusually sustained experience of darkness. It was because of her special vocation that this darkness accompanied her for so long. It is not the normal purifying "dark nights" that John of the Cross speaks of, neither for beginners or the more advanced. Nor is every experience of aridity, emptiness, or darkness a purifying or redemptive dark night. It is helpful to avail ourselves of the wisdom of our spiritual tradition to understand this better. Mother Teresa, pray for us!

3

THE DISTRESSING DISGUISE

St. Teresa of Calcutta and Touching Jesus Today

~

David Vincent Meconi, SJ

This collection of essays seeks to rehabilitate and renew three unpopular areas of contemporary academic theology: mysticism, spirituality, and the thought of St. Teresa of Calcutta. This is a most fitting convergence, as most work available on Mother Teresa seems to be collected for one of two polarized purposes. On one hand, we receive snippets but nothing sustained—prayerful and beautiful quotes, perhaps, but a life as long and as involved as Mother's cannot be captured in soundbites. On the other hand, her detractors are those adversaries who turn to the Missionaries of Charity only to defame and slander the goodness therein. Charlatans (like Christopher Hitchens) are all too well known—supposed scholars who have turned to her work in the hope of uncovering grave inconsistencies or simply detracting from a woman who challenges their own complacency and anti-Catholic biases. While Mother has not proven standard fare for academic discourse hitherto, one of my hopes in writing this essay is to show how Teresa of Calcutta is best understood in a long line of Christian saints and theologians whose work is motivated by a robust and orthodox understanding of the Mystical Body.

This essay accordingly proceeds in three main movements: the first will be to define and dissect what Christians since the time of Paul the Apostle have meant by the Body of Christ. The second section takes up St. Teresa's own reflections on this notion that Christ is to be met in his followers, in the "distressing disguise," as she most often calls this meeting Jesus in the other. Here I also show how Teresa's theology of the Mystical Body combats a "stern-minded" Christianity in which all self and all love are relegated to the divine in such an unhealthy way that God alone is to be cherished with creatures counting ultimately for naught. In the third and final section, I turn to the Eucharistic Lord to understand how Mother Teresa found the source of loving Christ in and as others. I use this intimate union in her life to show how Teresa's so-called dark night was effected precisely because of this union and her inability to perceive the Lord with the normal capacities of human cognition and experience.

MYSTICAL BODY

The foundation of the Christian Mystical Body is that Christ and Christian make up one individual. This is a nonliteral and participatory union between the only begotten Son of God and those adopted sons and daughters whom Christ incorporates into his own well-being. Made members of his own body, Christ offers the faithful an emblematic union that simultaneously makes them a literal extension of Christ as well as a symbolic representative of his divine presence and mission. This union is thus at once a literal appropriation of our humanity into Christ's own divine personhood—he now lives in us—while also being a representational participation in that no creature actually becomes divine in and of himself. Mystical union is therefore both factual as well as figurative, perhaps the way a golden crown in Britain can both truly stand in for the monarchy while never being confused as a strict identification with the queen herself.

For example, Cyril of Jerusalem teaches his recently baptized neophytes that they now share in Christ and, through the grace of God, can thus be "appropriately called 'Christs.'"[1] They, in turn, are surely instructed and understand that while they now enjoy the Lord's indwelling, none of them are to be equated with the Messiah himself. It is the language of the body that ensures the head is always united but never identified with the needier, more dependent members— what is known collectively as the body. The incarnation establishes an analogy: as God becomes human, humans in Christ can now become divine. The elect are now able to share in realities like love and everlasting life no mere creature can conjure for him- or herself. Moreover, as the Son's kenosis did not annihilate his divine nature, a Christian's incorporation into Christ's body does not eradicate his or her humanity. As iron is cold and hard alone and apart from a flame, in that fire the iron shares in a nature not its own—it becomes warm, aglow, and malleable—but yet it never ceases to be iron; in Christ, the human person shares in qualities not human but divine. Yet because the human person is made de facto in the divine image and likeness (Gn 1:26–27), such union, far from obliterating one's humanity, fulfills and perfects it.

When we turn to the origins of this Mystical Body, we first hear the Lord telling his listeners that whatever they do to the least of his, they do unto him as well; we receive images of vine and branches and consuming his body and blood; we also hear Jesus cry from the heav-

---

1. Cyril of Jerusalem, *Catechetical Mysteries* 3.1 (PG 33, 1088A), quoted in the *Catechism of the Catholic Church* (CCC) §2782.

ens to the Teacher of the Law turned Christian persecutor, "Saul, Saul, Why do you persecute me?" (Acts 9:4, 22:7). For it is the Lord himself who realizes how love unites and transforms the lover and beloved. No longer Saul, the Apostle Paul translates this insight (and personal experience!) into language of Head and Body. Paul, immersed in the culture and intellectual atmosphere of Hellenic Roman culture, surely knew how the body was a metaphor around the pagan Mediterranean for not only civic cohesion but also as the means by which ideals were transmitted between otherwise disparate individuals.

The various workings and intersections of disparate parts brought into a unified whole makes the body a natural image with which to stress unity, concord, and even the needed hierarchy that ensures proper function. Take the fable on "The Stomach and the Body" from the ancient storyteller Aesop as an early example, used as a warning against generals and foot soldiers on how all members of a body politic must listen to one another and emerge with some level of harmony if any level of survival is to be realized:

> The stomach and the feet were arguing over their strength. The feet constantly alleged that they were much superior in strength because they carried the stomach. To this the stomach replied: "But, my friends, if I don't provide you with nourishment, you won't be able to carry me."[2]

Such imagery abounded in other early writers, the most influential perhaps being Plato's likening the city-state, his *Republic*, to the human soul, realizing that the reflection and magnification of each our own individual selves are precisely what the body politic is.

Yet surely by Paul's time in the first century of Christ's time, the most popular image of the body is found in a speech by Menenius

2. Fable no. 66 (no. 130 per Melvin Perry's standard numbering) in *Aesop's Fables*, trans. Laura Gibbs (Oxford: Oxford University Press, 2002), 35.

Agrippa—Roman consul in 503 BC—that was reported and replayed by many influential writers of Paul's day, like Xenophon, Cicero, Dionysius of Halicarnassus (d. circa 7 AD) and Livy (d. 17 AD), from whom the following excerpt comes. In his extensive work on the history of Rome, Livy tells us about a particular division between the army and its leaders causing great fear in the senators who lived in constant threat of conspiracies and assassination attempts. The senators thus sent one of their own, Agrippa Menenius, eloquent statesman, one loved by the plebs as one of their own by birth. Having gathered the masses together, then, Agrippa Menenius tells them this story:

> In the days when man's members did not all agree amongst themselves, as is now the case, but had each its own ideas and a voice of its own, the other parts thought it unfair that they should have the worry and the trouble and the labor of providing everything for the belly, while the belly remained quietly in their midst with nothing to do but to enjoy the good things which they bestowed upon it; they therefore conspired together that the hands should carry no food to the mouth, nor the mouth accept anything that was given it, nor the teeth grind up what they received. While they sought in this angry spirit to starve the belly into submission, the members themselves and the whole body were reduced to the utmost weakness ... [and a bit later, Livy concludes] Drawing a parallel from this to show how like was the internal dissension of the bodily members to the anger of the plebs against the Fathers, he prevailed upon the minds of his hearers.[3]

If this was one of the stories influencing first-century intellectual life in general and political theory in particular, is it any surprise that the erudite, Rabbinically trained Saul (Acts 22:3) should have had such a

---

3. Livy, *Ab Urbe Condita* 2.16.33; T. J. Luce, trans., *Livy, The Rise of Rome: Books One to Five* (Oxford: Oxford University Press, 1988), 104; the same apologue is found in Xenophon, *Mem.* II. iii. 18; Cicero, *Off.* III. v. 22; and St. Paul, *Cor.* I. xii. 12.

similar narrative in his arsenal when he was called later in life to lead the Body of Christ?

We cannot know what of the Greco-Roman world St. Paul read, but we see a similar warning against bodily discord in his first letter to the Corinthians (12:12–20), surely the most Hellenic and learned of all of his addressees:

> As a body is one though it has many parts, and all the parts of the body, though many, are one body, so also Christ. For in one Spirit we were all baptized into one body, whether Jews or Greeks, slaves or free persons, and we were all given to drink of one Spirit. Now the body is not a single part, but many. If a foot should say, "Because I am not a hand I do not belong to the body," it does not for this reason belong any less to the body. Or if an ear should say, "Because I am not an eye I do not belong to the body," it does not for this reason belong any less to the body. If the whole body were an eye, where would the hearing be? If the whole body were hearing, where would the sense of smell be? But as it is, God placed the parts, each one of them, in the body as he intended. If they were all one part, where would the body be? But as it is, there are many parts, yet one body.

As a Christian, Paul now knew that division means death but love and unity were synonymous. Love melds lover and beloved into the type of whole that perfects individuality, whereas sin is what defaces and depersonalizes, and charity consummates our personhood and transforms us into the Christified communal creatures we are each made to be—or, back to Paul's own language, "It is no longer I who live but Christ who lives in me" (Gal 2:20).

The Christian theology of the Mystical Body is founded on the reality that love not only moves toward the other but also in a way becomes the other. Eros may begin in ecstasy, one's leaving oneself to enter into the life of another, but eros ends in transfiguration, wherein the lover nonliterally but really becomes the beloved as well. Such a commitment to the transformative power of love forces everyone to ask, "What ought I love?" because this is the query that will also eventually determine the answer to the question "Who will I forever become?" It is what great poets like Shakespeare knew:

> For all that beauty that doth cover thee
> Is but the seemly raiment of my heart,
> Which in thy breast doth live, as thine in me.

It is the oblation of the Inklings' Charles Williams to Mary Wall when doubting his mindfulness of her, "Love you? I am you."[4] It is Catherine's confirmation to Nelly in *Wuthering Heights* that her care for Heathcliff has changed her forever and although,

> My love for Linton is like the foliage in the woods: time will change it, I'm well aware, as winter changes the trees. My love for Heathcliff resembles the eternal rocks beneath: a source of little visible delight, but necessary. Nelly, I *am* Heathcliff! He's always, always in my mind: not as a pleasure, any more than I am always a pleasure to myself, but as my own being. So don't talk of our separation again: it is impracticable.[5]

This yearning for union is not a uniquely Christian concept; every lover has known the "sweetbitter" nature of eros, a love that begins usually in the allure and attraction of pleasure but leads to the carrying of the cross.[6] Yet only Christianity both provides the tools with which to order our loves properly and also gives the only source by which this love can be known truly, the kenosis of the Christ.

For Christians, the Mystical Body is therefore a foundational way

---

4. C. S. Lewis, *The Four Loves* (New York: Houghton Mifflin Harcourt [1960] 1991), 95.

5. Emily Brontë, *Wuthering Heights* (Hertfordshire: Wordsworth, 1992), 59.

6. This taxonomical reversal works in the Greek: whereas modern English speakers use "bittersweet," the ancients had in mind a more realistic attraction that began in the pleasant but often ended in pain, γλυκύπικρον; for more here, see Ann Carson, *Eros: The Bittersweet* (Princeton, NJ: Princeton University Press, 1998).

of describing Christ's sharing his life with his followers, stressing the organic unity and how love not only melds lovers together but also ecstatically allows them to share an identity. Such a mutual indwelling thus enables shared experiences and expectations: it is how mortals are able to receive God's own life—becoming "sharers in the divine nature" as 2 Peter 1:4 expresses it—while also being the same place where Christ continues humbly to identify his fullest self with his members. Here head and body are one, dependent upon one another, albeit in diverse ways: the body necessarily needy by nature, the head hungry out of assumed humility. The dependency is therefore different in type and degree, but both head and body in fact necessitate the presence of the other in order that both head and body may be fully realized—the branches otherwise desiccated without the vine, but the vine, too, remaining fruitless without the branches.

This is why the Mystical Body is a uniquely Christian concept: whereas other cultures naturally enough used the image of a body to talk about harmony and the need for a common mission, only the kenotic Son of God who empties himself into the hands of sinners could make himself the head dependent upon a body, the shepherd in search of his strays, the hungry bridegroom setting out to woo his bride. All other rulers rely on their subjects for their own gain as well as the welfare of the body politic, but no ruler empties himself into the hands of his subordinates. Only love can effect that great exchange, in which the lowly are elevated by the Sovereign's descent. Mother thus instructed her sisters in this way:

> When you take care of him, say with prayers, "Lord, You in the disguise of this child, be with me now and forever. Thank You, Lord, that You are my son, as I am a son to you. Thank You, Lord, for I can serve You, as You served us all. Thank You, Lord, for I can love You as You loved us all. Thank You, for today You depend on me, as I always depend on You. Thank You, Lord, when you keep Your

sleepy head on me, for I too rest on you forever ... Thank You, Lord, as so dearly You have come as my son."[7]

Once again, Teresa of Calcutta echoes the ancient theologies of the Mystical Body. Her instincts are accurate, and her insights truly Catholic. For she has the same imagery and message as one of the oldest homilies in Christianity, as a second-century bishop tells his congregation on Holy Saturday evening that in his harrowing of hell,

The Lord approached [Adam and Eve], bearing the cross, the weapon that had won him the victory. At the sight of the him Adam, the first man he had created, struck his breast in terror and cried out: "The Lord be with you." Christ answered him, "And with your spirit." He then took him by the hand and raised him up, saying, "Sleeper, awake, and rise from the dead, and Christ will give you light. Out of love for you and for your descendants I now by my own authority command all who are held in bondage to come forth, all who are in darkness to be enlightened, all who are sleeping: Arise! I order you, O sleeper, awake! I did not create you to be held a prisoner in hell. Rise from the dead, for I am the life of the dead. Rise up, work of my hands, you who were created in my image. Rise, let us leave this place, for you are in me and I am in you, and together we form only one person and we can never again be separated."[8]

This is the Christ for whom Teresa of Calcutta lived her life, the Christ who united himself with those trapped in hell, in the poorest of the poor. Let us now turn to Mother's Christology in order to understand better the lowly Christ who was present in nearly every thought, word, and deed of her eighty-seven-year-long life.

7. Mother Teresa, *A Call to Mercy: Hearts to Love, Hands to Serve* (New York: Crown, 2016), 291–92.

8. Slightly adjusted from Christopher Howse, ed., *Best Sermons Ever* (New York: Continuum, 2001), 11–12; this ancient homily is also available as "The Lord's Descent into Hell," website of the Holy See, accessed December 19, 2017, http://www.vatican.va/spirit/documents/spirit_20010414_omelia-sabato-santo_en.html.

MOTHER TERESA ON THE MYSTICAL BODY

If a theology of the Mystical Body informed Teresa's consecration and service, it should not surprise us to learn that one of her favorite terms for the Christian life is the *distressing disguise*, an image she links directly with her missionary life: "Dear Lord, help me to understand now what wholehearted service means ... the meaning of distressing disguise."[9] For Mother, Christ's love for all disguised him in the most distressed, and his longing to be united with every human person allowed him to become one with those in need of wholeness. This is the first of two points in St. Teresa of Calcutta's writings, namely, that the Lord's incarnation is continued today in those the faithful meet. He is to be recognized in those whom Christians encounter because, out of perfect love for all humanity, the Lord continues to make himself incarnationally available. Because of this, Mother Teresa never lets love compete with love: we love our neighbor because our neighbor is in a nonliteral but truly real way Christ to and for us. The second aspect of Mother's thought, then, is how the Eucharist is the originative yet complementary source of this sacred presence in the human.

First, the Holy One of Israel was never some arcane memory or figure stuck in the annals of history for Mother Teresa. The historical Jesus is also the Mystical Messiah whose divine life transcends time and space, enabling him to live even now. This is the new man, one so open to the Father that he is totally available to all the Father's children, not just those who happened to live in the rather limited plains of Galilee in the first third of the first century. This is what the Belgian Augustinian friar and patristics scholar Tarsicius van Bavel calls the *seconde pauvreté*.[10] It is the second emptying of the Son of God: first

9. Mother Teresa, *Where There Is Love, There Is God* (New York: Doubleday Religion, 2010), 158.

10. Tarcisius van Bavel, OSA, *Recherches sur la Christologie de Saint Augustin, l'humain et le divin dans le Christ d'après Augustin*, Paradosis X (Fribourg, Switzerland:

in the womb of our Lady as the Logos humbly received the fullness of the human condition, and second as the man Jesus Christ transfers his same divinely human presence into his pilgrim Body on earth.

This transferrable continuation of Christ into others fulfills the Lord's promise to be with his people always (Mt 28:20) and never to leave us orphans (Jn 14:18). It is also what graced Teresa to find him in whatever face she gazed:

> Hungry for love, He looks at you.
> Thirsty for kindness, He begs from you.
> Naked for loyalty, he hopes in you.
> Sick and imprisoned for friendship, He wants from you.
> Homeless for shelter in your heart, He asks of you.
> Will you be that one to Him?[11]

Present in each, Christ can be encountered and embraced today, but the last inviting question is key. "Will you be that one to Him?" Love never forces itself on another but always stands apart and offers itself; love never demands but invitingly delights and awaits a free response. As such, Mother ends this prayer by subtly asking if those who read this might be the ones that day who offer Christ their hunger, their thirst, their barrenness, their heart?

The free consent of our Lady thus continues to those willing to let Christ enter themselves: "May it be done unto me according to your word" (Lk 1:38). So, while the Incarnation is of course literally an utterly once and for all event, it can be said to continue even today. Like the Mystical Body, this reality is at once both factual—God became human—and figurative—God continues to use our humanity in order

---

Éditions Universitaires, 1954), 113: "L'Incarnation constitue le premier mode de notre inclusion dans le Christ et cette inclusion est plutôt physique, car elle a pour base l'unité de la nature humaine du Christ avec la nôtre. Mais voilà que le Christ a voulu ajouter une seconde pauvreté à son premier abaissement."

11. Becky Benante and Joseph Durepos, eds., *No Greater Love* (Novato, CA: New World Library, 2002), 86.

to extend his incarnation. He uses both body and soul, and both were the loci of Mother Teresa's love.

This is no doubt why Fr. Kolodiejchuk, MC, arranged his wonderful collection of Mother's writings by way of the traditional almsdeeds, *A Call to Mercy: Hearts to Love, Hands to Serve.* In her special love of the indigent and undignified, she saw this Christ most especially in the poor and needy, but never constricted that need to body or soul. Nor did Mother ever relegate the almsdeeds to the supererogatory but knew, as found in Aquinas, that these are matters of justice. That is, burying the dead and feeding the hungry are not the special privileges of the Christian but are in fact the duty of every well-functioning human person. What Mother added to this demand was to name the grace that allowed Christians the special means with which to fulfill this call.

She lived in Calcutta long enough to know the dire deprivations of a life without proper sanitation, without food that nourishes, and without the comforts that make life bearable, but she was also enough of a Westerner to know true loneliness, the misgivings that bombard the doubting, and the grievances that haunt the hurt. Her life of service was never that of a psychologist or a welfare worker in opposition. She knew that just as the Son of God stood in humble need of Mary's human flesh and blood, he assumes and thus uses our human lives to continue and extend his incarnation still. In this way, we freely become the disguise that Christ asks all people to wear, to dress up as him so that the world may know he is still alive. He is encountered spiritually as we pray for one another, counsel and guide each other, and met in the body as we genuflect, but also clothe the naked and give drink to the thirsty.

This is what is beautiful for God, a life of body and soul striving in every opportunity to know and love him in his world.

May we never forget that in the service to the poor we are offered a magnificent opportunity to do something beautiful for God. In fact, when we give ourselves with all our hearts to the poor, it is Christ whom we are serving in their disfigured faces. For He Himself said, "You did it for me."[12]

It is intriguing to hear that we serve Christ as we serve Christ's brothers and sisters with no real qualification regarding chosen creed or sacramental status. The faithful are called to serve others because Christ impels them to see him in the needy and alone, not because these poor ones already happen to belong to him.

It is to her fellow Christians that Mother writes: "We have the home for the dying in many places.... We must love them not by feeling pity for them. We love them because it is Jesus in the distressing disguise of the poor. They are our brothers and sisters. They are—all people, those lepers, those dying, those hungry, those naked—they are Jesus."[13]

This is an essential aspect of Mother's thought: that love is one and cannot be separated. The Christian mandate is to love God and neighbor and in so doing to love oneself. Here we begin to see the awesome prospect of Christian charity. It is, literally, all or nothing: either we love rightly with the very love who is God, or we eventually realize that what we had called "love" was in fact something else all along.

Because our Teresa was graced to see the same love for Christ as she had for the poor of the streets, we should see how she reflected on the dual commands to love God and to love one's neighbor as oneself. Amuse me and listen to a somewhat lurid fifth-century hagiographical tale. It is an account I recall often because it points to an unfortunate thread of Christian discipleship that demands exclusivizing the love of God, which is proven by how little one is attached to the things

12. Benante and Durepos, *No Greater Love*, 73.
13. Mother Teresa, *Where There Is Love*, 184–85.

of God, even God's people. John Cassian, St. Cassian in the East, was born around 360 AD near where Romania and Bulgaria meet today. Drawn to the holy legends of the great Christian saints, he too left home and traveled to the Egyptian desert in order to chronicle the feats he had heard so much about since his youth. His *Institutes* gathered these stories and sought to hold them up as exemplars of holy Christian lives, the qualities any serious Christian should strive to have.

One of his more memorable accounts immortalizes a man we know only as Patermutus (literally, "the silent father," supposedly for his unwillingness to speak against the local abbot) who arrives at one of the most celebrated cenobia in the lower Egyptian desert (most probably at Thmuis) with his eight-year-old son in tow. To test how obedient Patermutus might be, Abba John berates and even physically abuses the little boy, taunting him and slapping him across the face. Cassian therewith praises the father for never flinching, even appearing glad to suffer "unmoved" by his son's cheeks "streaking with the dry traces of tears," telling us that only "out of Patermutus' love for Christ" could any biological father endure such a scene. Either frustrated or consoled by Patermutus's eerie impassiveness, the abbot orders the final test and has his monks throw the boy off the monastery walls into the Nile River many meters below. Other monks were stationed below to keep the boy from drowning, and Patermutus's "faith and devotion were so acceptable to God that they were immediately confirmed by divine testimony."[14] Such testimony is not infrequent in patristic and medieval piety, appearing in subtle and unexpected ways.

This unfortunate strand in Christian thought falsely maintains that if one is going to love God, one must curb, if not kill, love for

---

14. Cassian, *Institutes* 4.27; Boniface Ramsey, trans., *The Institutes* (New York: Paulist Press, 2000), 92–93.

anything that is not God. This is a position of thought that commits itself to the belief that love of God and love of neighbor are actually opposed, that charity is a zero-sum reality that is diminished when distributed. This was not at all Mother Teresa's way, and in her understanding of how Christ dwells in each face we encounter, she teaches us that love must not be separated and that the only way to love a God-made human is truly to love the human before you.

Yet throughout the history of the Christian faith, some holy men and women have so emphasized the love and service of God that they have neglected the integrity and transformation of the human creature. The love of God in such a system tends not to convert but annihilate the heart, bordering on a form of Buddhism that judges the individuality and the desires of the human heart as negligible and in need of extinguishing. Take, for example, advice St. Francis de Sales (1567–1622) gives the Baronne de Chantal in a letter penned from Annecy, dated February 18, 1605. Whereas de Sales is usually the least "stern minded" of all the early moderns, almost always filled with sage advice and love for sinners as well as patience for the gradualness of human conversion, he too can at times fall back into a certain unhealthy denial of one's own self. In a letter exhorting St. Jane Francis de Chantal to carry her cross in life and to accept her burdens with the trust of a beloved daughter, she is introduced to a God who "wants you to serve him without joy, without feeling, with repugnance and revulsion of spirit. Such service gives you no satisfaction, but it pleases him; it is not according to your liking, but according to his."[15] This is one small but significant instance, for in such lines part of the Christian tradition has felt it necessary to extirpate all affection for creatures if their love of the Creator would go unchallenged. At first glance this may even make sense: the Almighty is certainly worthy

15. St. Francis de Sales, "Letter 9," in *Selected Letters*, ed. Elisabeth Stopp (New York: Harper and Brothers, 1960), 84.

of a love that assumes all of our mind, all of our soul, and surely with all of our hearts (Mt 22:37). And if Christ demands that we love God with "all" of ourselves, what could be left for any other object of love? This is where spiritualities that stress "God alone" arise and where we sometimes receive the advice to check our love for creatures.

While never explicitly resorting to the thought of St. Augustine of Hippo, Teresa resonates his theology of the Mystical Body. For Augustine's theology of the *totus Christus* was exactly how Mother Teresa lived. Developed first while composing his lengthy *Expositions of the Psalms* in the mid-390s, Augustine coined this term "the whole Christ" because he was looking for a way to describe how it is really Christ singing the words of Israel's songs—for he alone offers words of true healing and true absolution. This is why in the Christian tradition it is the Lord Jesus who ultimately prays Israel's hymns of praise and lament. For he has come to unite us with himself, and even in the most perplexing psalm, as he cries from the cross, "My God, my God, why have you forsaken me?" (Ps 22:1), we receive dominical assurance that still, at that moment, the Lord is near. This is how Augustine can preach that

> Uniting us into one body with himself and making us his members, so that in him we too are Christ (*in illo et nos Christus essemus*) ... In him all of us belong to Christ, but we too are Christ because in some sense (*quodammodo*) the *whole Christ* (*totus Christus*) is both Head and body.[16]

This *totus Christus* assumes a mutual indwelling that allows Christ to live our lives and graces us to live his. In him we are all now one, and in us he now is still made visible. The beautiful thing about this exchange is that it gives Augustine the pastoral framework to invite his flock into witnessing their truest identities.

16. *En. Ps.* 26, exp. 2.2; Maria Boulding, trans., *Expositions of the Psalms 1–32* (Hyde Park, NY: New City Press, 2000), 275.

The whole Christ thus provides a mirror for who the human person truly is; it is not sin or imperfection that best measures those made in God's image, but God's only Son is the one in whom we should see who we are:

> Now, however, I wonder if we shouldn't have a look at ourselves, if we shouldn't think about his body, because he is also us (*quia et nos ipse est*). After all, if we weren't him, this wouldn't be true: *When you did it for one of the least of mine, you did it for me* (Mt 25:40). If we weren't him, this wouldn't be true: *Saul, Saul, why are you persecuting me?* (Acts 9:4). So we too are him, because we are his organs, because we are his body, because he is our head, because the whole Christ (*totus Christus*) is both head and body.[17]

The Augustinian "whole Christ" is another way of saying that the New Adam has recapitulated all men and women into a new head, a new family, a new way of being human after the Fall altered and skewed reality as God intended. This is why Augustine's congregations would have heard Christ tell them that "they too are he himself," or that "we too are he" (*nos ipse essemus*).

Teresa too sees in Christ's perfect charity an openness that gathers a lover and a beloved into one:

> We are surprised how the people hurt Jesus: they slapped Him, spat on him. What we thrown in the drain, we throw on Jesus. And Jesus—not a word. Each time, when we say ugly things, uncharitable words, we are doing the same thing to Jesus—"You did it to me" (Mt 25:40). Terrible … throwing, spitting—that's where

---

17. s. 133.8; Hill, *Sermons* (III/4) 338: "Iam uero si nos ipsos attendamus, si corpus eius cogitemus, quia et nos ipse est. Nam etsi nos ipse non essemus, non esset uerum, *Cum uni ex minimis meis fecistis, mihi fecistis* (Mt 25:40). Si nos ipse non essemus, non esset uerum, *Saule, Saule, quid me persequeris* (Acts 9:4)? Ergo et nos ipse, quia nos membra eius, quia nos corpus eius, quia ipse caput nostrum (Eph 1:22), quia totus Christus caput et corpus"; PL 38.742. For more, see my *The One Christ: St. Augustine's Theology of Deification* (Washington, DC: Catholic University of America Press, 2013).

Veronica came in and wiped His face. Spitting on Our Lord—"You did it to me." When? Now. We think that what they did, we are not responsible; it is exactly what they did to Him [that] we are doing now.[18]

This is a mutual indwelling, Christ and Christian, that allows the Lord to be constantly encountered as he is born, hungers, and cries out still today. This is the most humbling aspect of true love: not embarrassed to be identified with the most broken of humans.

See, our poor people have to suffer so much; we are the only ones who can help them. Offer your pain to Jesus for them. Share in His pain, humiliation, Passion. Nobody ever has gone through more pain and humiliations than Jesus, all for you.[19]

Mother Teresa reveals a person who realizes that one's love of Jesus is in no way diminished by one's love for other persons. It is precisely the love of neighbor that becomes both a prerequisite and a measure for one's love for Christ. Or, in the words of the Evangelist, "If anyone says, 'I love God,' but hates his brother, he is a liar; for whoever does not love a brother whom he has seen cannot love God whom he has not seen" (1 Jn 4:20). By loving those humans God puts into our paths, we love Christ, but only because the converse is true as well. Only by loving Jesus are we truly able to love our neighbor, for without that love of Christ, any other kind of outreach or connection is not really love but some fabrication of our own hunger, pride, lust, or desire to control. To see that Jesus is truly present in those visible faces before us is to enter into this dynamism of charity wherein Christ leads us outward, and the love of others leads us always back to the love of Christ. Mother Teresa can accordingly ask her sisters:

---

18. Mother Teresa, *Where There Is Love*, 78.
19. Mother Teresa, *Call to Mercy*, 232.

Can I in sincerity say: "Jesus is really living in me now?" Have I
come to know Jesus in reality, not only in imagination? Externally
I might be very recollected and prayerful, but this counts for nothing, Sisters, unless deep down you can see that Jesus is really there.[20]

And again, we hear her plea when others had dismissed a lonely looking pilgrim in an airport one day; for only Teresa had noticed the for-
lorn woman sitting alone scowling at the missionaries: "Sisters, see
how is it that Mother sees and you do not see? Please learn to see Jesus
in the people."[21]

This second section has argued that through loving one another,
by entering into the lives of one another, not only our love for neighbor grows but also our love for Christ. It is in service of neighbor that
affection for the Lord ripens and matures, and this is why Mother
Teresa's love for the poor is inextricably linked to her spiritual and
liturgical life. True charity is always the fruit of years of silence, patience and prayer, Eucharistic worship and communion, and so on.
To see how this played out in Teresa's life, let us now turn to the third
section in order to understand better the connection in her mind between the Eucharist and the marginalized.

THE EUCHARIST COMMITS US TO THE POOR

In a letter to her sisters, Mother pleadingly reaches out to them
to teach how,

For us MCs, we cannot say that we love Jesus in the Eucharist but
that we have no time for the poor. If you really love Jesus in the
Eucharist, you will naturally want to put that love into action. We
cannot separate these two things—the Eucharist and the poor.[22]

20. Mother Teresa, *Where There Is Love*, 73; cf. Benante and Durepos, *No Greater
Love*, 54.
21. Mother Teresa, *Call to Mercy*, 293.
22. Mother Teresa, *Where There Is Love*, 54.

The liturgy does not cease at the chapel door for the Missionaries of Charity. From their founding, they have learned how Jesus thirsts not only at Holy Communion but also throughout the human condition. The Eucharist is the focal point of this thirst, of this yearning for wholeness, for it is the Eucharist that equips this world to encounter a God-made flesh:

> Our life is linked to the Eucharist. Through faith in and love of the body of Christ under the appearance of bread, we take Christ literally: "I was hungry and you gave me food. I was a stranger and you welcomed me, naked and you clothed me." The Eucharist is connected with the passion. I was giving Communion this morning—my two fingers were holding Jesus. Try to realize that Jesus allows Himself to be broken. The Eucharist involves more than receiving; it also involves satisfying the hunger of Christ. He says, "Come to me." He is hungry for souls.[23]

Mother's active life found its life in the Eucharistic Lord. Just as he stripped himself of all glory to come to us under bread and wine, she found in the inglorious the very substances of a new liturgy always pleasing to God.

The body of the historical Christ, the body of the Eucharistic Lord, and the body of the leper dying in Calcutta were all held in harmonic unison by the saintly eyes and heart of Teresa:

> Our sisters had to go to the home for the dying. And before they went, I said to them, "See, you are going there; during Mass"—we always have Mass and Holy Communion in the morning before we go—and I said, "You saw during Holy Mass with what tenderness, with what love, father was touching the Body of Christ. Make sure, it is the same body in the poor that you will be touching."[24]

---

23. Benante and Durepos, *No Greater Love*, 115.
24. Mother Teresa, *Where There Is Love*, 167.

Her altar was the street and her offertory were the lame and dying, eternal oblations in whom Jesus lives. She surely would have enjoyed the new translation of the *Second Eucharistic Prayer*, in which the people of God thank him for being able to "Stand in your presence and minister to you."[25] Teresa was uniquely empowered to embrace how those gathered in prayer are able to minister to a God who has chosen to identify himself with those oppressed, with those who are marginalized and in need of service. We minister to the incarnate God as we minister to his people, as his other-centered charity always includes his people's well-being with his own.

This is why, under the teaching on the "Sacrament of the Eucharist," the *Catechism of the Catholic Church* invokes the great Bishop of Constantinople St. John Chrysostom to remind us all how

> The Eucharist commits us to the poor. To receive in truth the Body and Blood of Christ given up for us, we must recognize Christ in the poorest, his brethren: "You have tasted the Blood of the Lord, yet you do not recognize your brother. . . . You dishonor this table when you do not judge worthy of sharing your food someone judged worthy to take part in this meal. . . . God freed you from all your sins and invited you here, but you have not become more merciful."[26]

What a challenge such a homily would be, what a call Teresa sought to answer: to recognize Christ not simply in the sanctuary but in the street too, not just on the rather safe and satiny linens of Mass but in the messiness and ambiguities of raw human living as well. While never doubting the Catholic teaching that the Eucharist is the preeminent sacrament of grace, Teresa lived to amplify that presence outward. She took the consecration just as seriously as the dismissal, as she became

25. *The Roman Missal*, 3rd typical ed. (Chicago: Liturgy Training, 2011), 648.
26. *CCC* §1397, quoting St. John Chrysostom, *Hom. in 1 Cor.* 27:4, PG 61, 229–30; cf. Mt 25:40.

increasingly assimilated to that Host she loved, returning to the world divinized and able to receive the same communion in others.

If union between head and body was the foundational theological image propelling Teresa of Calcutta's outward actions, this essay concludes by proposing it was this very union that also brought about her internal darkness. Who was not shocked when the Missionary of Charity was revealed to be also the Saint of Darkness?[27] In *Come Be My Light*, millions around the world learned of Teresa's decades of spiritual dryness and emotional aridity. This was not desolation in the strictest sense, in that it was not an active movement away from faith, hope, and charity. It was, in my opinion, an eternal uniting of this communion to which the Lord called Teresa.

We see this in her constant advice to her Sisters, not to deny themselves per se but to create the space in their spiritually poor hearts for Christ to live. At times the rhetoric may be strong, but Mother Teresa was not "stern minded" in her desire to reduce the individuality and the intricacies of another human to meaninglessness—she wanted each person to recognize that alone each was not even human. Made in God's own image and likeness, Teresa knew that a human is fully so only when in union with the divine. On this score, she echoes the French School of Spirituality, a movement from the late seventeenth to the nineteenth century encouraging Christians to offer their lives in such freedom that Christ enters and lives their lives for them. It stressed a consecration of conversion, empowering the baptized to see their own lives as always reflections and instruments of Christ's own embodiment. Mother accordingly teaches her sisters to offer the Father their very selves in order that Jesus can continue his "yes" in them:

27. Brian Kolodiejchuk, MC, ed., *Mother Teresa: Come Be My Light* (New York: Doubleday, 2007).

Your "Yes" is the beginning of being or becoming empty. It is not
how much we really 'have' to give but how empty we are, so that we
can receive [Him] fully in our life and let Him live his life in us. In
you today He wants to relive His complete submission to the Father.
Allow Him to do so. [It] does not matter what you feel, as long as
He feels all right in you.[28]

Yet if union with Christ caused her ardor, could it not also account for
her aridity? Imagine it this way: when we humans encounter another,
we need three things. First, we must have properly functioning recep-
tacles with which to receive that other—an ear for hearing, sensitive
skin for touching, an eye for seeing, and so on; second, there must be
an object capable of being beholden; and third, the medium through
which the other is able to be encountered, how sound demands air,
and sight some distance.

If God had truly abandoned Mother Teresa and set her out on
her way alone, either he would be a moral monster or she would have
suffered from the ancient temptation of Pelagianism, that heresy ar-
guing we can do good works without grace. But Teresa did more than
"good works"—she served Christ as she became evermore one with
him, as him. This was not because the divine had become distant; it
was possible only because the divine drew so near that Teresa's natural
human capacities failed. The medium was overcome—there was no
space between her natural abilities and the person of Christ, who was
now truly one with her.

We began by seeing love this way, the transformation of lover into
beloved. This is what every poet knows, what every saint lives, but
Teresa received such union that she began to lose the ability to recognize the other as he evermore grew into the very soul and sinews
of Mother's being. This is a union lovers know, how constant contact

28. Mother Teresa, *Call to Mercy*, 283; cf. Benante and Durepos, *No Greater Love*, 11.

of the flesh renders the other over time unrecognizable and in perfect tandem with one's own movements:

> I love you without knowing how, or when, or from where.
> I love you straightforwardly, without complexities or pride;
> so I love you because I know no other way
> than this: where I does not exist, nor you,
> so close that your hand on my chest is my hand,
> so close that your eyes close as I fall asleep.[29]

Just as the Eucharistic Lord cannot be given until he is broken, Mother Teresa was called to that same brokenness—a breaking not of one's being, good and made in God's own likeness, but a breaking of one's fallen temptation to act without Christ and to be and to serve the human alone. For in her service of Christ in the distressed disguise, Mother herself became evermore another Christ.

CONCLUSION

How often St. Teresa of Calcutta cried, "Lord, you are in the disguise of this child."[30] She was a woman unique in her perception of the heavenly on earth and did more than most to highlight the plight of the poor. But perhaps even more lastingly, she modeled for the world a truthful challenge: these poor are Christ, as he is the poor. "I heard the call to give up all and follow him into the slums to serve him among the poorest of the poor."[31] Here is where Christian charity must therefore be fostered and increased. The faces before her were always the face of Christ, the face of his Blessed Mother, the "distressing disguise"

---

29. Pablo Neruda, *100 Love Sonnets (Cien Sonetos de Amor)*, trans. Stephen Tapscott (Austin: University of Texas Press, 1986), 39.

30. Mother Teresa, *Call to Mercy*, 291.

31. Malcolm Muggeridge, *Something Beautiful for God: Mother Teresa of Calcutta* (New York: Image Books, 1977), 62.

of how God continues to meet those looking for him. Such a union forbids us from dividing our love into a sacred and a secular, into a beatitudinal and a biological love—all love is ultimately divine, as all love is ultimately where God is present.

In the fourth century, Evagrius of Pontus commented, "If you are a theologian, you will pray truly, and if you pray truly, you will be a theologian."[32] As such, Mother Teresa, St. Teresa of Calcutta, counts as a theologian, and this volume honors her well as such. She combined central insights of many of the Church Fathers and Medieval Doctors, and she not only prayed and reflected, but also loved. In her contemplation in action, she showed the world how close God can come to his creatures, sometimes even seemingly obliterating the distance between him and his beloved. This is the "distressing disguise," and this is where Teresa calls each of us to meet her, to meet Christ.

In such a worldview and way of life, nothing in creation is inherently opposed to the divine: all things call forth the God who made them, and all things invite a free return. Those made in God's own image and likeness are missioned with a call to union, to seek and to find God in all things (cf. 1 Cor 15:28), especially in his privileged poor. This is why she lived the life she did; this is why generations following must turn to her writings—to thank her, to pray in communion with her, and to grow in our awareness of how God relies on each of our lives to touch those most tenderly his own.

32. Evagrius Ponticus, *On Prayer* §61; A. M. Casiday, trans., *Evagrius Ponticus*, Early Church Fathers Series (London: Routledge, 2006), 192.

4

AUGUSTINE, AQUINAS, THÉRÈSE, AND THE MYSTICISM OF MOTHER TERESA'S FIVE-FINGER GOSPEL

~

Andrew Hofer, OP

The word "mystical" comes from the Greek word *mystikos*, an adjective for the mysteries, especially those celebrated by the initiated, and refers to something secret or hidden.[1] Early Christians borrowed and transformed the term from pagan Greeks for their own liturgical celebrations and approach to God. For example, the early sixth-century writer who wrote under the name of Dionysius the Areopagite, the name of a man in Athens converted by Paul the Apostle as recorded in Acts 17, wrote a brief and highly dense treatise titled *Mystical Theology*.[2] When in the twelfth century John Sarracenus translated from Greek to Latin this *Mystical Theology*, he wrote a prologue where he

---

1. See *Greek-English Lexicon*, s.v. "*mysteriazô*" and "*mystikos*," 1156.
2. An English translation is in Colm Luibheid, trans., *Pseudo-Dionysius: The Complete Works*, Classics of Western Spirituality (New York: Paulist Press, 1987), 135–41.

explains the title in this way: "It is clearly called 'mystical' because it is hidden and closed."[3] In the thirteenth century, St. Albert the Great, commenting on the *Mystical Theology*, uses as his *thema* the scriptural verse that sets the tone for the entire commentary, Isaiah 45:15: "Truly God of Israel, the Savior, you are a hidden God."[4] St. Albert thus accentuates this ancient sense that the mystical involves that which cannot be seen, ultimately, God himself. For, as we read elsewhere in Scripture, "No one has ever seen God" (Jn 1:18) and "He dwells in unapproachable light and no human being has seen him or can see him" (1 Tm 6:16).[5] Even in the Incarnation, God remains hidden, as few who saw Jesus came to believe in him as Lord. His preaching, in fact, emphasizes the hiddenness of the Kingdom of God: like treasure hidden in a field (Mt 13:44) or yeast hidden by a woman in three measures of flour (Mt 13:33). Essential to the Gospel, the mystical is always something hidden at work in the lives of the saints.

Considering St. Teresa of Calcutta in the mystical tradition for the renewal of our spiritual theology, we can emphasize her awareness of the hiddenness of the Lord in her life. In Mother Teresa's life, this hiddenness of Jesus's presence can be appreciated in a number of ways, especially these three: in the Holy Eucharist, in her soul's darkness, and in the poor, where he is in distressing disguise. Again, Mother Teresa could not literally see Jesus in the Eucharist, in her soul, or in the poor, and yet she held by a persistent faith that he was present—even paradoxically when some part of her wondered where he was, or felt, in prayer to God, as if she had no faith. Her life was transformed by

---

3. See translation in Albert the Great's quotation of John Sarracenus at the beginning of his commentary on Dionysius's *Mystical Theology* in Simon Tugwell, OP, trans., *Albert and Thomas: Selected Writings*, Classics of Western Spirituality (New York: Paulist Press, 1988), 134.

4. Commentary on Dionysius's *Mystical Theology*, chap. 1, in Tugwell, *Albert and Thomas*, 134.

5. Cf. Commentary on Dionysius's *Mystical Theology*, chap. 1, in Tugwell, *Albert and Thomas*, 135.

that hidden presence or present hiddenness, and she became one of the great mystics of the Christian faith of all times.

These three forms of Jesus's hidden presence/present hiddenness are related in Mother Teresa's life, as the Jesus who came to Mother Teresa's soul through receiving the Blessed Sacrament was also loved by her in the poor. From the darkness of her soul, she could say with her Sisters in Eucharistic adoration the addition of the Missionaries of Charity to the familiar Divine Praises at the time of Benediction: "Blessed be Jesus in the poorest of the poor." This essay contributes to our appreciation of Mother Teresa's mysticism by focusing on just one of these three forms of the hidden Jesus in her life. Dominican Father Paul Murray, who knew Mother Teresa quite well, recounts this story:

> I remember, on one occasion, Mother Teresa taking my hand and, with her forefinger, spelling out this message on my fingers. "The entire mystery," she said, "is here, Father Paul, in this one sentence: 'You—did—it—to—me.'" Then she took my hand a second time and repeated the exercise, this time with an even greater emphasis: "You—did—it—to—me." Twice—I think she must have realized I was a slow learner![6]

This can be called the five-finger Gospel, and it summarizes our Lord's last act of preaching before the Passion Narrative in St. Matthew's account of the Gospel. We do not see Jesus in the poor, but we are called to know of his presence now so as to love him and serve him in the poor. In Matthew 25:31–46, we learn that if we give food to the hungry, give drink to the thirsty, welcome the stranger, clothe the naked, visit the sick and the imprisoned, Jesus will say on Judgment Day: "You did it to me." The Gospel can thus be summarized in those five words, and

---

6. Paul Murray, OP, *The Hail Mary: On the Threshold of Grace* (Liguori, MO: Liguori Publications, 2010), 36.

so our very hands, which are meant to be at the service of our neighbor, can remind us and enact the five-finger Gospel.

Mother Teresa's message has a piercing simplicity to it, and it can be studied theologically in the tradition's reception of Matthew 25:31–46. This essay, before examining Mother Teresa's emphasis in the five-finger Gospel at greater length, considers first select aspects of teachings from St. Augustine of Hippo, St. Thomas Aquinas, and St. Thérèse of Lisieux as related to this Gospel passage. Each of these four saints gives a remarkable teaching about the mysticism, the heightened awareness of the hiddenness, of Jesus present in the poor. With Augustine, it is through the preaching of a bishop from his episcopal cathedra for the sake of his North African people in late antiquity. With Aquinas, it is through the teaching of a thirteenth-century Dominican friar in an academic setting. With Thérèse, it is through the contemplative insight of a young cloistered Carmelite nun in the second half of the nineteenth century. With Mother Teresa, it is through the practice of a religious foundress in the second half of the twentieth century who loved Jesus in the poorest of the poor on the streets. Augustine, Aquinas, and Thérèse are Doctors of the Universal Church, and their teaching can help us situate Mother Teresa's teaching within the Western tradition. In fact, Augustine and Aquinas are recognized as two of the most influential teachers on mystical theology, and indeed on many theological topics, in all Christian history.[7] Their teachings are usually not associated with the simplicity that radiates Mother Teresa's few words. St. Thérèse, on the other hand, was claimed by Mother Teresa as her patroness, and Mother Teresa translated her cloistered patroness's spirituality to be that of a Missionary

---

7. For overviews of Augustine and Aquinas in the history of Western mysticism, see esp. Bernard McGinn's series *The Presence of God: A History of Western Christian Mysticism*. For Augustine, chap. 7 in vol. 1, *The Foundations of Mysticism: Origins to the Fifth Century* (New York: Crossroad, 1995), 228–62; for Thomas Aquinas (with Albert the Great), chap. 1 in vol. 4, *The Harvest of Mysticism in Medieval Germany* (New York: Crossroad, 2005), 11–47.

of Charity in the world.[8] It is natural for there to be the most affinity between Thérèse and Mother Teresa, but one should not discount the usefulness of referring to Augustine and Aquinas as touchstones for comparison. In each of these four figures, we glimpse that which is mystical, the hidden God at work in the lives of his saints.

ST. AUGUSTINE OF HIPPO

Known as the Doctor of Grace, Augustine frequently returns in his writings to the double-love command, loving the Lord our God with our whole heart, soul, and strength, and loving our neighbors as ourselves. Augustine ties together these two commandments in his hermeneutic of charity in reading Scripture.[9] He makes concrete for his people what this love means. For example, he preaches on 1 John 4:12, "No one has ever seen God" in this way. God "is an invisible reality; he must be sought not with the eye but with the heart," says Augustine.[10] He later continues, "This is what you should think of if you want to see God: *God is love*. What sort of countenance does love have? What sort of shape does it have? What sort of height does it have? What sort of feet does it have? What sort of hands does it have?" Augustine then answers: "No one can say. Yet it has feet, for they lead to the Church. It has hands, for they stretch out to the poor person."[11] Notice what love's hands do: they are extended to the poor. As such, they make visible the God whom no one can see.

Augustine had a special devotion to Matthew 25:31–46, with its

8. For a helpful comparison of these two figures, see Jacques Gauthier, *I Thirst: Saint Thérèse of Lisieux and Mother Teresa of Calcutta*, trans. Alexandra Plettenberg-Serban (Staten Island: Society of St. Paul, 2005).

9. See examples of the double love command's prominence in book 1 of Augustine, *On Christian Doctrine* 1.26.27, 1.35.39, and 1.36.40.

10. Augustine, *Tractatus in Epistolam Joannis ad Parthos*, Homily 7.10, in *Homilies on the First Epistle of John*, trans. Boniface Ramsey (Hyde Park, NY: New City Press, 2008), 111.

11. Homily 7.10 in Ramsey, *Homilies on the First Epistle of John*, 111.

emphasis on Judgment Day of having our hands outstretched to the poor. He cites this Gospel passage more than 275 times in his works.[12] In a moment of revealing how he was personally affected by the words "When you did it to one of my least ones, you did it to me," he says, "I confess that in God's Scripture this has moved me the most."[13] Here are two immediate examples of how Augustine preached on this Gospel passage to move his audience to care for Christ hidden in the poor.

In one sermon, Augustine quotes "you did it to me" (Mt 25:40), and then says to his people, "There, that's who you're giving to. He is the nourisher, and he goes hungry for your sake; he is the benefactor, and he's destitute. When he's the benefactor, you are willing to receive; when he's destitute, you are not willing to give. Christ is destitute when any poor person is destitute. He was ready to give eternal life to all who are his own, and he is pleased to receive temporal help in every single poor person."[14] Augustine is here emphasizing the humility and generosity of the Lord. The Lord identifies himself with every poor person and wants to give eternal life to those who care for the poor. In another sermon, Augustine recalls the Gospel passage of Zacchaeus and that wealthy tax collector's great fortune, after climbing up a tree to see Jesus, of welcoming Christ into his home (Lk 19:1–10). Augustine finds that his congregation would all love to welcome Christ, and then he says, "you are not cheated of Christ's presence."

12. Tarcisius J. van Bavel, OSA, "The Double Face of Love in Augustine," *Augustinian Studies* 17 (1986): 169–81, at 180.

13. In Augustine's Latin Bible, the verse is: "cum uni ex minimis meis fecistis, mihi fecistis." Augustine said: "me fateor in scriptura dei plurimum mouit." The Latin text of Sermon 389 is edited by C. Lambot in *Revue Bénédictine* 58 (1948): 43–52; see 49 for excerpt in Sermon 389.5. Tarcisius van Bavel translates "the passage in Holy Scripture which has made the deepest impression" on him. See van Bavel, "Double Face of Love in Augustine," 180. Allan Fitzgerald comments about this influence on Augustine: "a passage that moved him deeply." See Allan A. Fitzgerald, OSA, *Augustine through the Ages: An Encyclopedia*, s.v. "Mercy, Works of Mercy," 557–61.

14. Augustine, Sermon 38.8, trans. Edmund Hill, OP, in *Sermons II (20–50) on the Old Testament*, Works of Saint Augustine: A Translation for the 21st Century (Brooklyn, NY: New City Press, 1990), 213.

Augustine cites Matthew 25:40 and comments: "You are all looking forward to greeting Christ seated in heaven. Attend to him lying under the arches, attend to him hungry, attend to him shivering with cold, attend to him needy, attend to him a foreigner."[15] Augustine thus shows how the desire of his people to welcome Christ can be fulfilled by caring for him as the poor and needy. Christ remains on this earth.

The third example of Augustine's preaching on this Gospel passage is better developed and taken from his expansive *Expositions of the Psalms*, wherein he commented on all 150 Psalms, some of them multiple times.[16] Quoting Matthew 25:31–46 over ninety times in these Psalm expositions, he used this Gospel passage as a "rule" for interpreting the psalter.[17] Guided by his understanding that Christ is both head and body, Augustine knows that "you did it to me" is the voice of Christ that shows the unity of head and body.[18] For Augustine, we are to hear the *vox totius Christi*, the voice of the whole Christ, head and body, throughout the psalter. Let us listen to how he develops Psalm 40/41, concerning its verse: "Blessed is the one who understands about the needy and poor one; the Lord will free him on the evil day."[19]

For Augustine, "the needy and poor one" is Christ himself. Referring to 2 Corinthians 8:9, "although he was rich, he became poor, so that by his poverty you might be enriched," Augustine wants his people to understand about Christ himself. Too often people dismiss

15. Augustine, Sermon 25.8, trans. Edmund Hill, OP, in *Sermons II (20–50) on the Old Testament*, 86.

16. The English translation of this work by Augustine appears in six volumes. See *Expositions of the Psalms*, 6 vols., trans. Maria Boulding, OSB, Works of Saint Augustine: A Translation for the 21st Century (Hyde Park, NY: New City Press, 2000).

17. See Andrew Hofer, OP, "Matthew 25:31–46 as an Hermeneutical Rule in Augustine's *Enarrationes in Psalmos*," *Downside Review* 126 (2008): 285–300.

18. For an excellent overview of Augustine's understanding of Christ's unity and for the theological context of his teaching on divinization, see David Vincent Meconi, SJ, *The One Christ: St. Augustine's Theology of Deification* (Washington, DC: Catholic University of America Press, 2013).

19. In Augustine's Latin Bible, he reads for the beginning of Psalm 40: "Beatus qui intellegit super egenum et pauperem, in die mala liberabit eum Dominus."

him as only a man, and they miss the reality of how Christ "emp-
tied himself and took the form of a slave" (Phil 2:7). Christ is both
rich as God and poor as human. Augustine preaches: "Understand
that where weakness is displayed before your eyes, there godhead lies
hidden. He is rich, because that is what he is, but poor, because that
was what you were. His poverty is our wealth, just as his weakness is
our strength, his foolishness our wisdom, and his mortality our im-
mortality."[20] Appealing to Colossians 2:3, "in him are hidden all the
treasures of wisdom and knowledge," Augustine wants his people to
realize how the riches are hidden in Christ seen as a poor man. Augustine repeats several times the Psalm verse, "Blessed is the one who
understands about the needy and poor one," throughout this portion
of his sermon and then makes the application:

> Keep in mind all the poor, needy, hungry and thirsty people,
> travelers far from home, the ill-clad, the sick, the prisoners. Try to
> understand about a poor person of this sort, because if you do, you
> will understand about him who said, "I was hungry, I was thirsty,
> naked, a stranger, sick and in prison." Then on that fateful day the
> Lord will pluck you out of danger.[21]

Augustine's preaching on Christ's hidden presence in the poor mo-
tivates his people to understand that presence and show their love.

ST. THOMAS AQUINAS

As master of the sacred page, St. Thomas had as a principal duty
the reading and commenting on Sacred Scripture. One of his tasks
during his second regency period in Paris was commenting on the
Gospel according to St. Matthew.[22] Thomas's *reportatio*, a commen-

---

20. *Expositions of the Psalms* 40.1, trans. Boulding, 2:226.
21. *Expositions of the Psalms* 40.2, trans. Boulding, 2:227.
22. For the historical setting of Thomas's work on Matthew, see Jean-Pierre

tary taken down by scribes, was done after he had compiled comments from the Fathers of the Church in his *Catena Aurea*, the Golden Chain of patristic comments, on that Gospel account. By studying Aquinas on Matthew, we study the Common Doctor of the Church, who had learned extensively from previous Doctors. Here we pause at three places of the Gospel passage with Aquinas, hearing his interpretation in this commentary. Afterward, I attend to a few of his systematic teachings related to Matthew 25:31–46: on mercy/giving alms and Christ's authorization of the voluntary poor to share in his judicial authority on Judgment Day.

In studying Aquinas's comments on this passage from Matthew 25, we first consider with him how the Son of Man begins his address on the last day with these words to those gathered at his right: "Come, you blessed by my Father." This line can be considered in its two constitutive parts: an invitation and a recognition of those who are invited. Thomas begins with that recognition. The blessing here denotes the grace of God at work in the lives of those who ministered to the poor. Matthew 25:31–46 is primarily a Gospel of grace, not a Gospel of works. Aquinas writes: "It is because the invitation will not be according to our merits, but according to the fact that we are strengthened by Christ's merits."[23] One of the scriptural quotations to show that is Luke 22:29: "Behold, I dispose to you, as my Father has disposed to me, a kingdom." When giving attention to that word "Come," Aquinas sees the invitation as a conformity that changes the state of people. In other words, the blessing preceded the works of mercy, and now the invitation shows the changes that occur in the transition of the blessed to heaven. During this life on earth, people are joined to God by an incomplete charity and by a dark, or obscure, faith. Then, on

Torrell, OP, *Saint Thomas Aquinas*, vol. 1, *The Person and his Work*, rev. ed., trans. Robert Royal (Washington, DC: Catholic University of America Press, 2005), 55–57, 197, and 339.

23. On Matthew 25:34, in Thomas Aquinas, *Commentary on the Gospel of St. Matthew*, trans. Paul M. Kimball (Camillus, NY: Dolorosa Press, 2012), 833.

the last day, the blessed will have a full charity, and there will be no more darkness. Although St. Thomas will at times call faith a light, he has a perception that faith, by its very nature here on this earth, has an obscurity or darkness. He writes elsewhere: "The obscurity of faith does not pertain to the impurity of sin, but rather to the natural defect of the human intellect, according to the present state of life."[24]

Second, Aquinas comments on the significance of the corporal works of mercy. He corrects those who think that all of salvation hinges upon these particular works, so that if one does them, one goes to heaven, and if one omits them, one is damned. Aquinas can say this because he reads the passage within the biblical canon, and he knows that Paul states that those who do certain sins shall not inherit the kingdom of God (Gal 5:6 and Rom 1:32). And yet Aquinas catches himself and cites how someone could stop sinning, repent, and give alms—and so be freed from sin. Thus these works of mercy can be precisely the path for a sinner to reject sin and enter the kingdom of God by grace. Aquinas furthermore asks why these corporal works are mentioned. Aquinas follows Gregory the Great and speaks about how these works are minimal: "for if they do not do these works, which nature suggests, nor will they do other, much greater, works."[25] In other words, these corporal works of mercy are rather simple and relatively easy to do— intelligible as good things to do even to those unaware of the higher spiritual works of mercy, such as instructing the ignorant about the faith, forgiving injuries, and praying for the living and the dead.[26]

Third, Aquinas gives a teaching on humility: both the humility of those who show mercy and their reward as well as the humility of the

---

24. *Summa theologiae* (*ST*) II-II, q. 7, a. 2, ad 3; cf. *De Veritate* q. 18, a. 3, ad 1. The translation of the *Summa theologiae* used is that of the Fathers of the English Dominican Province, revised edition in 1920, and now available in multiple print and Internet publications.

25. On Matthew 25:35, in *Commentary on the Gospel of St. Matthew*, 835.

26. See *ST* II-II, q. 32, a. 3.

least of Christ's brethren. Supported by Luke 17:10's reference to "we are unprofitable servants," and with Romans 8:18's acknowledgment that "the sufferings of this time are not worthy to be compared to the glory to come," Aquinas says: "It is characteristic of good souls to consider the things that they do for God to be little."[27] Those who do the works of mercy think their acts are small and are astonished by their reward. God, in turn, exalts the humble and praises those who belittle themselves. Now, as for the humility of those who receive the alms, they are called "least of my brethren." Aquinas thinks that we should give alms to all, both good and wicked alike, as all are the Lord's brethren, some only by nature, but others also by grace. Following a scriptural tradition, Aquinas thinks that it is better to give alms to the good, who are the "little ones" (Mt 11:25) favored by God and who are considered the least by worldly people.

Turning to some pertinent passages in his more systematic theology of the *Summa theologiae*'s treatment of charity, we find that Aquinas considers mercy to be an interior effect of charity. Following Augustine, Aquinas defines mercy as heartfelt sympathy for another's distress; one with mercy (*misericordia*) takes another's misery into the heart (*cor*).[28] When asking whether mercy is the greatest of virtues, Aquinas affirms the primacy of charity in loving God. Yet he does acknowledge a preeminence in mercy when carrying out love of neighbor: "of all the virtues which relate to our neighbor, mercy is the greatest, even as its act surpasses all others, since it belongs to one who is higher and better to supply the defect of another, in so far as the latter is deficient."[29]

Just as mercy is an interior effect of charity, so almsgiving is an exterior effect of charity. For Aquinas, almsgiving is a matter of pre-

27. On Matthew 25:37, in *Commentary on the Gospel of St. Matthew*, 836.
28. *ST* II-II, q. 30, a. 1; cf. Augustine, *City of God* 9.5.
29. *ST* II-II, q. 30, a. 4.

cept. He provides Matthew 25:31–46 as his authority and comments that some are punished eternally for not giving alms.[30] He explains that one sins mortally by not giving alms in two considerations: on the recipient's part, when someone's need is particularly urgent, and on the giver's part, when someone has a surplus and does not give from that surplus to help those in need.[31] Aquinas gives a long quotation from Basil the Great's preaching in support of this position, including this thought: "It is the hungry man's bread that you withhold, the naked man's cloak that you have stored away, the shoe of the barefoot that you have left to rot, the money of the needy that you have buried underground: and so you injure as many as you might help."[32]

For a final systematic pertinent consideration from Aquinas, we turn to his pondering the mystery of the General Judgment. Aquinas thinks that Christ shares his judiciary power with the voluntary poor who have left all things to follow Christ, in accordance with Job 36:6's saying that God gives judgment to the poor.[33] For Aquinas, this means not only that the poor will receive justice from God, but also that they will judge with Christ on the last day. The least ones, who identified with Christ in his own poverty, are especially fitting to do this for three reasons. The first is that they have despised worldly things and cleave to Christ, and so they are not swayed against divine justice. Second, they merit the reward of judging others on account of their humility in life, as God lifts up the lowly. Third, Aquinas considers that poverty especially disposes one's heart to the manner of judging.

Aquinas thus shows the power of this Gospel passage within the totality of the Christian revelation, which is to be accepted during this

---

30. *ST* II-II, q. 32, a. 5, sed contra.

31. *ST* II-II, q. 32, a. 5.

32. *ST* II-II, q. 32, a. 5 ad 2; cf. Basil the Great, Homily 6, on Lk 12:18.

33. *ST Supplementum*, q. 89, a. 2. This *Supplementum*, compiled after his death on March 7, 1274, takes up St. Thomas's earlier teaching found in his *Scriptum* on Peter Lombard's Four Books of the Sentences.

time of the darkness or obscurity of faith. As a friar in a mendicant order dedicated to preaching the Gospel, he also communicates by his life a union with Christ hidden in beggars.

ST. THÉRÈSE OF LISIEUX

Turning now to our third Doctor of the Church, we come to someone who lived a hidden life within a cloister. St. Thérèse of the Child Jesus and the Holy Face entered the Carmel of Lisieux, France, as a postulant on April 9, 1888, at the age of fifteen, and found her vocation to be love at the heart of the Church. Before her death on September 30, 1897, at the age of twenty-four, she experienced profound darkness in her soul. On one day, she was able to see through the window among the trees a hole and commented to Mother Agnes: "I am in a hole just like that, body and soul. Ah! What darkness!"[34] Several teachings from Thérèse are pertinent to the hiddenness of Jesus in the poor, but I focus on her interpretation of Matthew 25:31–46 as expressed in two texts. Whereas we do not know how extensively Mother Teresa knew the teachings of Augustine and Aquinas on this Gospel passage, she assuredly knew the teachings of Thérèse. Not only was Thérèse considered her lifelong inspiration and namesake, but Mother Teresa also heard a portion of the following letter during a homily by Fr. Paul Murray.[35]

On August 2, 1893, Thérèse wrote her sister Céline a priceless letter that gives insight to Thérèse's thinking about our topic. She begins by referencing the path that Céline walks as the same path traced by Jesus himself. In the Song of Songs, the lover and the beloved do not

34. From the epilogue in Thérèse of Lisieux, *Story of a Soul: The Autobiography of St. Thérèse of Lisieux*, third edition, John Clarke, OCD (Washington, DC: Institute of Carmelite Studies, 1996), 266.

35. Paul Murray, OP, *I Loved Jesus in the Night: Teresa of Calcutta, A Secret Revealed* (Brewster, MA: Paraclete Press, 2008), 83.

find each other in the repose of the bed. Thérèse writes, "Jesus does not will that we find his adorable presence in repose; he hides himself; he wraps himself in darkness."[36] During his earthly ministry, Jesus would charm the weak souls of great crowds with his words in order to make them strong for the day of trial. His friends were quite few "when he was SILENT before his judges!" She comments, "Oh! What a melody for my heart is this silence of Jesus.... He made himself poor that we might be able to give him love."[37]

Here Thérèse communicates how Christ initiates this encounter by begging for our love. She explains:

> He holds out his hand to us like a *beggar* so that on the radiant day of judgment when he will appear in his glory, he may have us hear those sweet words: "Come, blessed of my Father, for I was hungry and you gave me to eat; I was thirsty, and you gave me to drink; I did not know where to lodge, and you gave me a home. I was in prison, sick, and you helped me." It is Jesus himself who spoke these words; it is he who wants our love, who *begs* for it.[38]

Thérèse then finds how the Lord wants to be the recipient of our mercy: "He places himself, so to speak, at our mercy; he does not want to take anything unless we give it to him, and the smallest thing is precious in his divine eyes."[39]

Asking Céline to take delight in this beautiful way of giving to Jesus, she then emphasizes, "Jesus is a *hidden* treasure, an inestimable good which few souls can find, for it is *hidden*, and the world loves what sparkles!"[40] Thérèse goes on to comment about how Jesus does

36. Thérèse of Lisieux, *Letters of St. Thérèse of Lisieux*, vol. 2, *1890–1897*, general correspondence translated from the original manuscripts by John Clarke, OCD (Washington, DC: Institute of Carmelite Studies, 1988), 808. The emphases of italics and all caps are reproduced as they appear in the texts.

37. Thérèse of Lisieux, *Letters* 2:808.

38. Thérèse of Lisieux, *Letters* 2:808.

39. Thérèse of Lisieux, *Letters* 2:808.

40. Thérèse of Lisieux, *Letters* 2:808–9.

not want to be loved for his gifts, but for himself, who is meant to be our reward. She instructs: "To find a hidden thing one must hide oneself; our life must then be a *mystery*. We must be like Jesus, Jesus whose *face was hidden*."[41]

After referencing the late medieval classic *Imitation of Christ*, Thérèse concludes her letter by consoling Céline: "Jesus loves you with a love so great that, if you were to see it, you would be in an ecstasy of happiness that would cause your death, but you do not see it, and you are suffering." She then closes the letter with a cry for Jesus's manifestation: "*Soon* Jesus will stand up to save all the meek and humble of the earth!"[42]

The other document for our consideration from this Carmelite doctor's life is from her autobiography, *Story of a Soul*. Near the end of her life, Thérèse recounts an act of charity that God inspired her to perform for the elderly and infirm Sister St. Pierre. Thérèse writes, "It was only a very small thing, but *our Father who sees in secret* and who looks more upon the intention than upon the greatness of the act *has already rewarded me* without my having to wait for the next life."[43] The older Sister was not easy to please, and she suffered much from her various Sister caretakers. Thérèse says that she did not want "to lose such a beautiful opportunity for exercising charity, remembering the words of Jesus: 'Whatever you do to the least of my brothers, you do to me.'" She then remarks in her reflection: "I offered myself very humbly to lead her, and it was with a great deal of trouble that I succeeded in having my services accepted!"[44]

This "very small thing" exemplifies Thérèse's "Little Way," her doctrine of charity of doing little deeds with great love. Thérèse did not have access to perform acts of charity for the poor on the streets, but

41. Thérèse of Lisieux, *Letters* 2:809.
42. Thérèse of Lisieux, *Letters* 2:809.
43. Thérèse of Lisieux, *Story of a Soul*, 247.
44. Thérèse of Lisieux, *Story of a Soul*, 247.

she did regularly perform such acts for those who lived with her. Motivated ultimately by a daily life of charity for Jesus alone, she became a great witness to the hidden presence of Jesus in those around us.

ST. TERESA OF CALCUTTA

When Mother Teresa was only eighteen years old and leaving her homeland to become a religious Sister, her mother said to her about Jesus: "Put your hand in His hand, and walk alone with Him. Walk ahead, because if you look back you will go back."[45] Mother Teresa came to learn the meaning of walking alone with Jesus. After she heard the Lord call to be his light and do his work of founding the Missionaries of Charity, she discovered the hidden Jesus in the "dirty and dark holes of the street beggars."[46] Then her soul itself became a sort of dark hole, as became known with the publication of her private letters years after her death. She thought of Jesus wanting her to give to him from this darkness. She had heard him repeatedly ask, "Wilt thou refuse?"[47] She knew that Jesus asked for her love, begged for it, and she did not refuse his request. During this long darkness in her own life, Mother Teresa spoke frequently about Jesus in the distressing disguise of the poor. She spoke from her experience, and she wanted others to experience the hidden Jesus.

Perhaps most famous among Mother Teresa's addresses were those on the occasion of winning the 1979 Nobel Peace Prize. In that year, she gave both an acceptance speech on December 10 and a Nobel lecture on December 11. In her acceptance speech, she emphasized how we are to love one another, and that we see Jesus in each other.

45. From Mother Teresa's Instructions to the Sisters, May 24, 1984, quoted in Brian Kolodiejchuk, MC, ed., *Mother Teresa: Come Be My Light* (New York: Doubleday, 2007), 13.

46. This description of "dark holes" is repeated by Mother Teresa through the years. See the example of her rules for her society, as proposed to Archbishop Ferdinand Périer, Feast of Corpus Christi, 1947, quoted in Kolodiejchuk, *Come Be My Light*, 74.

47. Kolodiejchuk, *Come Be My Light*, 48–49.

She quotes the beatitude "Blessed are the clean of heart, for they shall see God." Then she explains:

> And to make sure that we understand what he means, he said that at the hour of death we are going to be judged on what we have been to the poor, to the hungry, naked, the homeless, and he makes himself that hungry one, that naked one, that homeless one, not only hungry for bread, but hungry for love, not only naked for a piece of cloth, but naked of that human dignity, not only homeless for a room to live, but homeless for that being forgotten, been unloved, uncared, being nobody to nobody, having forgotten what is human love, what is human touch, what is to be loved by somebody, and he says: Whatever you did to the least of these my brethren, you did it to me.[48]

Mother Teresa continues about how holiness is not a luxury of the few, but a simple duty for each one to love. She then says about the reason for accepting the Nobel Prize:

> To this love for one another and today when I have received this reward, I personally am most unworthy, and I having avowed poverty to be able to understand the poor, I choose the poverty of our people. But I am grateful and I am very happy to receive it in the name of the hungry, of the naked, of the homeless, of the crippled, of the blind, of the leprous, of all those people who feel unwanted, unloved, uncared, thrown away of the society, people who have become a burden to the society, and are ashamed by everybody.[49]

Again, she wanted to "understand the poor," something that can remind us of the beginning of Psalm 41, and she urged others to practice the simplicity of the Gospel.

The next day, when she gave her Nobel lecture, Mother Teresa

---

48. Mother Teresa, "Acceptance Speech," NobelPrize.org, accessed July 27, 2017, https://www.nobelprize.org/nobel_prizes/peace/laureates/1979/teresa-acceptance_en.html.

49. Mother Teresa, "Acceptance Speech."

twice cited Matthew 25:31–46. The first time was in the context of understanding the meaning of love. Following 1 John 4:20, Mother Teresa explained that we cannot love the unseen God if we do not love the neighbor we see. For Mother, loving has to hurt, just as it hurt Christ to love. She said:

> We have been created to love and be loved, and then he has become man to make it possible for us to love as he loved us. He makes himself the hungry one—the naked one—the homeless one—the sick one—the one in prison—the lonely one—the unwanted one—and he says: You did it to me. Hungry for our love, and this is the hunger of our poor people. This is the hunger that you and I must find, it may be in our own home.[50]

Notice how Mother Teresa emphasizes that we may find Christ hungry for our love "in our own home." Mother Teresa also cited our Matthean Gospel passage within the context of testimonies of two dying, destitute persons she and her Sisters cared for. Mother Teresa picked up one woman dying on the streets and brought her to a bed. Rather than complaining, the woman simply smiled, took hold of Mother's hand, and said, "Thank you." She then died. A man who had been half-eaten by worms was brought to the home of the Missionaries of Charity. He said to the Sisters, "I have lived like an animal in the street, but I am going to die like an angel, loved and cared for." Mother Teresa commented after relating these two personal stories: "Like an angel—this is the greatness of our people. And that is why we believe what Jesus had said: I was hungry—I was naked—I was homeless—I was unwanted, unloved, uncared for—and you did it to me."[51]

On March 25, 1993, Mother wrote a letter to her "Dearest Children, Sisters, Brothers, and Fathers" in her society as an extended

---

50. Mother Teresa, "Nobel Lecture," NobelPrize.org, accessed July 27, 2017, https://nobelprize.org/nobel_prizes/peace/laureates/1979/teresa-lecture.html.
51. Mother Teresa, "Nobel Lecture."

commentary on the meaning of "I thirst," Jesus's cry from the cross, for the Missionaries of Charity. In the letter she says:

> The heart and soul of MC is only this—the thirst of Jesus' Heart, hidden in the poor. This is the source of every part of MC life.... "I Thirst" and "You did it to me"—Remember always to connect the two, the means with the Aim. What God has joined together let no one split apart. Do not underestimate our practical means—the work for the poor, no matter how small or humble—that make our life something beautiful for God. They are the most precious gifts of God to our Society—Jesus' hidden presence so near, so able to touch.[52]

In every Missionary of Charity chapel, next to the crucifix, one finds the words "I THIRST." Here in this emblematic letter of her society's spirituality, she says that it is "the thirst of Jesus' Heart, hidden in the poor." The five-finger Gospel of "You did it to me" comes after Jesus, hidden in the poor, says, "I was thirsty, and you gave me to drink." Moreover, that hidden presence is "so near, so able to touch." Mother Teresa never tired of sharing her insight that all are called to recognize Jesus's hidden presence in the poor. Paul Murray writes that Mother Teresa had "almost an obsession" with the idea that God begs and pleads: "She believed, and with an intense and living faith, that it was not only in the broken Host we see before us on the altar, but also in the person whom we see to be afflicted or in great need that Jesus *thirsts* for our love, begs for our attention."[53]

Again, we listen to Mother Teresa's words about Matthew 25:31–46, this time with her special attention to meriting a reward at the universal judgment and the poor as the hope of humanity:

---

52. Michael Collopy, *Works of Love Are Works of Peace: Mother Teresa of Calcutta and the Missionaries of Charity*, quotes and spiritual counsel by Mother Teresa with the daily prayers of the Missionaries of Charity (San Francisco: Ignatius Press, 1996), 198.

53. Murray, *I Loved Jesus in the Night*, 84–85.

In order to help us deserve heaven, Christ set a condition: At the
moment of our death, you and I, whoever we might have been or
wherever we have lived, Christians and non-Christians alike, every
human being who has been created by the loving hand of God in
His own image, shall stand in His presence and be judged according
to what we have been for the poor, what we have done for them.
Here a beautiful standard of judgment presents itself. We have to
become increasingly aware that the poor are the hope of humanity,
for we will be judged by how we have treated the poor. We will have
to face this reality when we are summoned before the throne of
God: "For I was hungry. I was naked. I was homeless. And whatever
you did to the least of my brethren, you did it to me."[54]

Mother Teresa here emphasizes the importance of judgment, and that
the poor are "the hope of humanity." We will face this reality, she says,
and be judged by our love for Christ in the poor on the last day.

CONCLUSION

The meaning of "mystical" goes back to an ancient Greek sense of
"hidden." Mother Teresa adds a distinctive and important contribution to the Christian mystical tradition in numerous ways. This essay
has focused on the mysticism of her five-finger Gospel by considering
it in relation to three Doctors of the Church: Augustine of Hippo,
Thomas Aquinas, and Thérèse of Lisieux. All the saints have com-
monality in Christ, and one could certainly benefit from considering how St. Teresa of Calcutta stands in comparison with additional
saints, including more Doctors of the Church, on Matthew 25:31–46.[55]

54. Mother Teresa, *No Greater Love*, foreword by Thomas Moore, ed. Becky
Benenate and Joseph Durepos (Novato, CA: New World Library), 103.

55. Among the Doctors of the Church, St. John of the Cross, that mystical doctor
of darkness, certainly has great significance for understanding St. Teresa of Calcutta's
mysticism of living out the mystery of Mt 25:31–46, a passage that expresses, in St. John

Each of these three featured Doctors and Mother Teresa can be found among those who instructed others in goodness. They shine like the stars for all eternity. Mother Teresa's mystical teaching on Matthew 25:31–46 elucidates the hidden power of Jesus, received in Holy Communion, and at work in the darkness of her soul. Here are some results from our work in the mystical tradition on Christ's hiddenness in the poor, with attention to how Mother Teresa compares to each of the selected Doctors of the Church.

Like Augustine, who was most moved by this scriptural passage in all the Bible, Mother Teresa considered Matthew 25:31–46 to be of greatest prominence. She pairs this passage with Jesus's cry from the cross, "I thirst," as of the utmost significance for Missionary of Charity spirituality. Augustine, who developed a hermeneutic of charity to read all of the Bible and who found Christ's voice everywhere in the Psalter, provides a theological framework for the charism of the Missionaries of Charity received by Mother Teresa on the distressing disguise of Jesus in the poor. Simply put, we are to love him.

Aquinas both considered mercy to be the greatest actualization of love of neighbor and emphasized that the corporal works of mercy were of lesser significance than the spiritual works. Aquinas thinks that those who choose to be poor will share with Christ in his judgment on all peoples. Mother Teresa also emphasized how common and available these acts are. For her, you did not need to go to Calcutta to give food to the hungry and drink to the thirsty, you could do works of mercy wherever you live. For her, the poor are our hope on Judgment Day, and so we are to care for them now.

What St. Thérèse was, who by her charity became patroness of foreign missionaries, St. Teresa of Calcutta in some ways became as the foundress of the Missionaries of Charity. She shows the action on

---

of the Cross's saying, "At the evening of life, we shall be judged on our love." See John of the Cross, *Dichos 64*, quoted in *Catechism of the Catholic Church* §1022.

the streets of her patroness's cloistered spirituality. Thérèse considered Jesus himself to be begging for our love, and she knew that he still wanted her love in the midst of her darkness of faith before she died. Mother Teresa profoundly experienced a similar darkness, and all the while continued to give to Jesus the beggar on the streets.

When some Christians hear of the "mystical," they think of something quite abstruse and foreign to their capability and experience. Mother Teresa's life reminds us that the Christian tradition of the mystical is one of the Lord's hiddenness in ways that include what is available to all moved by grace. The five-finger Gospel for her is so simple; just look at your hand and recall what Jesus, hidden in the poor today, will say on the last day to those who helped the needy: "You did it to me." Then do acts of love, works of mercy, for Jesus hidden in the poor. She teaches that because Jesus mystically asks for our love now. He begs it.

5

MOTHER TO MOTHER

The Mystical Intimacy of Mother Teresa
with the Mother of God

~

Mark Miravalle

Consider the following extraordinary Mariological statements:

"Nothing is impossible for all who call Mary Mother."[1]

"With Mary, we make more progress in the love of Jesus in one month than we make in years while living less united to this good Mother."[2]

"No Mary, no Jesus."[3]

Outside of the context of this volume, who would you venture to guess to be the author of these superlatively maximalistic statements about the Mother of Jesus? St. Bernard of Clairvaux? St. Lawrence

1. Joseph Langford, *Mother Teresa: In the Shadow of Our Lady* (Huntington, IN: Our Sunday Visitor, 2007), jacket copy.

2. Original Rule Explanation no. 4, quoted by Langford, *Mother Teresa*, 75–76.

3. Common expression of St. Teresa, as confirmed in correspondence from James Towey, longtime personal lawyer and friend, January 4, 2017.

of Brindisi? St. Louis Marie de Montfort? St. Maximilian Kolbe? In fact, it is the humble little Albanian sister we call "Mother." Not only is St. Teresa of Calcutta the source and articulator of these sublimely Marian truths, but also her person and life have been repeatedly referred to by Catholic, Protestant, and even Hindu coworkers as the very "embodiment of Mary." President James Towey of Ave Maria University, in his twelve years as personal attorney and close friend to Mother, describes her as the "most Mary-like person since Mary herself."[4] What type of union of hearts, of mystical intimacy between Mother Teresa and the Mother of God, could result in such an astonishing Marian identification and "presence" in our saintly Champion of the Poor?

I identify at least seven foundations of the mystical intimacy between the Mother of Calcutta and the Mother of God, an intimacy that is in fact at the very core of one of the greatest satiatings of the divine thirst of Christ for his neglected poor that has been witnessed in human history.

Please permit me two preliminary notes. First, as the Gospel provides the *kerygma* of Jesus, upon which all later *didache* must necessarily depend, I recognize and offer due praise for the masterful text of Fr. Joseph Langford, MC, cofounder of Missionaries of Charity Priests, *Mother Teresa: In the Shadow of Our Lady*, which provides the "gospel of Mary with Mother Teresa." Fr. Langford's text is extensively quoted here, and I believe all authentic teachings of this sublime union of these two Mothers should be based upon it.

Second, the subtitle of this book, *Toward a Renewal of Spiritual Theology*, likewise merits recognition. The noble task of this meeting is to lead minds to a better appreciation of spirituality of St. Teresa through proper theological categorization and analysis, as is the proper task of spiritual theology in general in the service of great spiritual-

---

4. Correspondence with James Towey, January 4, 2017.

ities. If spiritual theology has perhaps received a "bad name" in some theological circles,[5] it is because certain spiritual theological works so theologized, structuralized, and jargonized various spiritualities that their original "beauty in simplicity" were consequently lost, or at least drastically obscured. Like an inferior stain on a superior piece of wood, certain attempts of spiritual theology resulted in dulling the original beauty of the spirituality, rather than illuminating and vivifying the fine inherent grains of a particular charism. Garrigou-Lagrange refers to this undesirable effect within the ranks of spiritual theology as the "cult of the detail," which consequently usurps the "contemplation of divine things."[6]

It is therefore my hope and prayer that in this humble effort to offer a theological synthesis of some of the spiritual foundations of the Marian mysticism of Mother Teresa that this in no way will dull or dissipate the anointed profundity in simplicity contained within the mystical union of these two sublime Mothers. To better serve this goal, St. Teresa's actual quotes are provided and accentuated whenever possible, as well as the most valuable primordial commentary by Mother's cofounder and companion, Fr. Langford.

FOUNDATION 1: OUR LADY IN THE INITIATION OF ST. TERESA'S MISSION

It is now well known that the mission of Mother Teresa, who received her "call within a call" to form Missionaries of Charity, was revealed to her in a series of graces and visions that began during her 1946 train ride to Darjeeling and continued with the monumental

5. For a sample contemporary reference, cf. P. Willey, P. de Cointet, and B. Morgan, *The Catechism of the Catholic Church and the Craft of Catechesis* (San Francisco: Ignatius Press, 2008), 131n3.

6. R. Garrigou-Lagrange, *The Three Ages of the Interior Life: Prelude of Eternal Life* (Charlotte, NC: TAN Books, 1989), 1:8–9.

tripartite vision of 1947. To quote Fr. Langford: "Many have understood, in the wake of that vision, that Mother Teresa was serving her crucified Lord in serving the sick, the poor, the dying, and the outcast. *But few have known that the idea and initiative of the whole of it belonged to Our Lady.*"[7] Her threefold vision in 1947 summarized and concretized all that Jesus had revealed to her and was asking of her during this year and a half of private revelations.

In the first scene of her historic vision, Jesus reveals the horrific material poverty of the poor, and even more painful, their interior anguish. In this vision, a "great crowd of poor of all ages, were asking Mother to save them, and to bring them to Jesus, and then ending with the crucified Jesus in their midst."[8] In the second vision, the same crowd of agonizing poor were present, but now Mother could see the great sorrow and suffering on their faces. This time, Our Lady was present, and Mother was kneeling at Our Lady's side. Mother was turned toward the suffering impoverished. She could not see Our Lady's face but immediately heard her words:

> Take care of them—they are mine!—Bring them to Jesus—carry Jesus to them.—Fear not. Teach them to say the Rosary—the family Rosary and all will be well.—Fear not—Jesus and I will be with you and your children.[9]

In the third scene of the vision, the same crowd, now covered in some form of darkness, were present, and Jesus, upon the cross, was in their midst. Our Lady was also there, "at a little distance," facing the cross with Mother Teresa, who was as present in the vision as a "little child." Our Lady's left hand was on Mother's left shoulder, supporting her,

---

7. Langford, *Mother Teresa*, 19.

8. Brian Kolodiejchuk, MC, *Mother Teresa: Come Be My Light* (New York: Doubleday, 2007), 99. Quoted by Langford, *Mother Teresa*, 20.

9. Kolodiejchuk, *Come Be My Light*, 99. Quoted by Langford, *Mother Teresa*, 20 (grammatical form as in original).

and her right hand, holding Mother's right hand, outstretched toward the crucified Jesus. Jesus then speaks:

> I have asked you. They have asked you, and she, my mother has asked you. Will you refuse to do this for me—to take care of them, to bring them to me?[10]

Fr. Langford offers the following Marian narrative regarding this monumental vision:

> It is through Our Lady's presence, as portrayed in this final scene, that Mother Teresa will find the grace and the courage to stand at the Calvaries of the world, knowing, with the same faith that sustained Our Lady at that darkest hour, that beneath this mystery was hidden the presence of the Son of God. In carrying out this difficult mission, Our Lady will be Mother Teresa's constant reference, model, and support....[11] Our Lady becomes the bridge between the poor and Mother Teresa, as well as between the poor and the crucified Jesus who thirsts for them.[12]
>
> Here, Our Lady acts as the Mediatrix [mesitis = "go-between"] between Mother Teresa and the poor, which then empowers Mother Teresa in turn to become a secondary mediatrix between the poor and the crucified Lord. Thus, through Our Lady's intercession, Mother Teresa shares in the spiritual motherhood of Mary for the poor, whom the Mediatrix of all graces declares to St. Teresa, "are mine!" St. Teresa consequently participates in the motherly mediation of Our Lady, who uniquely shares in the one mediation of Jesus (1 Tm 2:5). We see here the rich Catholic ecclesial experience of subordinate mediation in the one mediation of Jesus by both Mothers on their respective levels of participation. Yet it is a mystical and familial participation without competition, all for the

10. Kolodiejchuk, *Come Be My Light*, 99. Quoted by Langford, *Mother Teresa*, 20.
11. Langford, *Mother Teresa*, 23.
12. Langford, *Mother Teresa*, 22–23.

glory of God and, in this case, the historic spiritual and material care for the poor.

Mother would comment in 1996 in preparation for the fiftieth anniversary of Mother's Inspiration Day that "If Our Lady had not been there with me that day, I never would have known what Jesus meant when he said, 'I thirst.'"[13] President Towey confirms: "It was at the begging of Our Lady that Mother started the Missionaries of Charities [MC]."[14]

So central is the presence and influence of the Immaculate One in the heart of Mother Teresa that, from the very outset, Our Lady, along with the Crucified Jesus and the poor, constitutes one of the three quintessential elements in the life and mission of Mother Teresa.

FOUNDATION 2: THE "EMBODIMENT OF MARY" IN OUR MIDST

Common testimony and descriptions of St. Teresa by those around her, including from Catholics, Protestants, and Hindus alike, referred to her as the "embodiment" of Our Lady. Again from Father Langford:

When I was with her I had the sense—one shared by many others, and not only Christians—of being before one whom Mother Teresa simply called "Our Lady"; of *encountering a representation in human flesh* of her whom painters and poets sought for centuries to capture by their art. But here was more than a painting or a poem, much more than a figure in oil or in words ... during the thirty years that I knew her, Mother Teresa became the book on Our Lady that I could never put down, one that continues to teach me....[15] "Our Lady, noted by all who lived with her, was not a side-light, not a

13. Langford, *Mother Teresa*, 40.
14. Correspondence with James Towey, January 14, 2017.
15. Langford, *Mother Teresa*, 11.

peripheral devotion in her inner world, but an integral part of her spirituality and mission. And it was even more: Our Lady—her mystery, her grace, and her role—came to define Mother Teresa. Our Lady was the unseen foundation for all that Mother Teresa would accomplish in the Church and in the world."[16]

How is this possible—to be so united with the Immaculate Mother of God that others, many others, profoundly and consistently sensed Our Lady's presence when in the presence of St. Teresa? Such an external identification is only possible through *an extraordinary interior and mystical union.* This is analogous to a central principle of Pope St. John Paul II's *Theology of the Body,* aptly captured in the maxim "the body expresses the person." This phenomenon of Marian identification cannot be obtained simply through a type of external or modeling or mimicking, but rather as an outward expression of an internal transformation and union that can only come through an authentic "exchange of hearts," a mystical marriage of souls, that will consequently effect a perpetual conformity of wills. The external result of this interior union between Mother Teresa and the Mother of God is precisely the spiritual and aesthetical beauty we call sanctity, but with a clear Marian power and presence. According to Langford, this "hidden but powerful interior union made of Mother Teresa a kind of extension of Our Lady's presence."[17] Our Lady became the "spiritual atmosphere" in which Mother Teresa lived and worked, prayed, and loved."[18] This "unity of life" between these two Mothers was made possible only through a unity of hearts.

16. Langford, *Mother Teresa,* 17.
17. Langford, *Mother Teresa,* 49.
18. Langford, *Mother Teresa,* 49.

FOUNDATION 3: ENTERING INTO
THE IMMACULATE HEART

Mother Teresa profoundly and perpetually experienced an intimate communion with the person and grace of Our Lady. For the extremely challenging mission given her by Jesus, Mother Teresa placed
her unreserved confidence in the Immaculate Heart of Mary for its
fulfillment.[19]

Who and what was the Immaculate Heart of Mary in the mind of
St. Teresa? According to Mother, the Immaculate Heart constituted
Mary's soul and interiority whereupon one found the "Full of Grace."
The Immaculate Heart was the seat of the perfection of Mary's love.
St. Teresa would often speak of the goal of giving an "undivided love"
to God and neighbor, but only in Mary's heart could such love be
found. Therefore Mother directed the Missionaries of Charity to fly
to this Immaculate Heart, in order to love as we should with the virtues unique to her heart: poverty of spirit, humility, silence, thought-
fulness, and haste in service.[20] The Immaculate Heart points not only
to what Mary did, but also to the love with which she did everything.

Ultimately, and in union with these other attributes, the Immaculate Heart of Mary was still something more, and quintessentially
so: it was a "sacred place in which to dwell and to hear the voice of her
Crucified Lord."[21] The maternal Heart of Mary became a mystical
place for Mother Teresa to dwell, to hear more completely the inspirations and directives of her Jesus on the cross in the carrying out
of her mission, and her refuge of motherly peace and protection. As
Langford describes:

19. Langford, *Mother Teresa*, 61.
20. Langford, *Mother Teresa*, 41.
21. Langford, *Mother Teresa*, 47.

Our Lady's inner world, and her intimate experience of her Son, lived on Calvary and continued from heaven, became ever more the sacred place in which Mother Teresa lived. She referred to this mystery simply as "Our Lady's Heart." It was the spiritual atmosphere in which she would live and pray and serve. It was there she would find her place at the foot of the Cross, and her place in the Church.[22]

It is little wonder, then, why Mother Teresa chose the feast of the Immaculate Heart of Mary as the patronal feast of the Missionaries of Charity.[23] In order to follow the path of Mother in loving Jesus and the poor, Fr. Langford makes the following observation about the necessity of giving ourselves entirely and with full confidence to the Immaculate Heart:

> This is the first step. We won't get further in following Mother Teresa if we don't take this one. This is what divides Mother Teresa and her holiness from the struggles and failures of so many who admire and seek to imitate her, even among those who are members of her own religious order. So many have the same love for the poor; they work night and day, they spend the same amount of time in prayer, *but they don't have her relationship with Our Lady*. Because of that, they don't share in the depth of her relationship with Jesus crucified.[24]

FOUNDATION 4: LIVING IN THE SPIRIT OF MARY

In the time following her train experience and ensuing tripartite visions, Mother began to experience a new direction of grace, which she recognized was coming from the Mediatrix of all graces. St. Teresa also became aware that Our Lady desired to share this sacred place of her Immaculate Heart as a personal gift to others, and consequently

22. Langford, *Mother Teresa*, 40.
23. Langford, *Mother Teresa*, 77.
24. Langford, *Mother Teresa*, 48.

began to pray for two things: first, that Our Lady would "keep her in her Heart,"[25] and second, that Our Lady would "lend her, her Heart," and thus to enable the Saint of the Poor to "love her Lord and her neighbor the way Mary did."[26]

Eventually, Mother was able to more clearly and concretely articulate this new direction of grace: it was precisely Our Lady keeping her promise to those who took these two steps of seeking mystical intimacy with the Mother of Jesus by giving our hearts to Our Lady, and then subsequently by asking our Lady to lend us her heart, thereby being empowered to live in the very spirit of Mary. When asked about this "lending us of Mary's heart," Mother responded that it was not some type of abstract, pietistic notion, but rather a "concrete, lived reality."[27] She proceeded to designate this day-by-day living in the spirit of Mary as the foundational "Spirit of the Missionaries of Charity Society" and articulated this new grace as the following "three states of the soul": (1) loving trust, (2) total surrender, and (3) cheerful giving. Mother presented this threefold spirit "as an extension of and participation in Our Lady's spirit":

> If we stand with Our Lady, she will give us her spirit of loving trust, total surrender, and cheerfulness. . . .[28] He [Jesus] has given us Our Lady's spirit to be the Spirit of our Society . . . loving trust and total surrender made Our Lady say "yes" to the message of the angel, and cheerfulness made her run in haste to serve her cousin Elizabeth. This is so much our life—saying yes to Jesus and running in haste to serve Him in the poorest of the poor. Let us keep close to Our Lady and she will make that same spirit grow in each one of us.[29]

25. Langford, *Mother Teresa*, 47.

26. Langford, *Mother Teresa*, 47.

27. Langford, *Mother Teresa*, 48.

28. Mother Teresa to the MC Sisters, July 31, 1996. Quoted by Langford, *Mother Teresa*, 51.

29. Mother Teresa to the MC Sisters, September 5, 1997. Quoted by Langford, *Mother Teresa*, 52.

This sublime participation in the spirit of Mary is encapsulated in two brief prayers Mother taught her sisters: "Keep us in your most pure heart"[30] and "Immaculate Heart of Mary, cause of our joy, bless your own Missionaries of Charity. Help us to do all the good we can. Keep us in your most pure Heart, so that we may please Jesus through you, in you, and with you."[31]

Entering into and living in the Immaculate Heart of Mary was the air breathed by Mother Teresa and the Marian atmosphere she sought to provide for her spiritual children, in order that they may in turn provide for the poor. It is not surprising, therefore, that Mother named her first and most beloved home for the dying in Calcutta (once a Kali Temple dedicated to the Hindu goddess of death and destruction) the "Nirmal Hriday," that is, "Place of the Pure Heart,"[32] so that manifest fruit of living in the spirit of Mary's Heart—desperately poor people who lived like animals—could "die like angels."[33] As Mother instructed her sisters:

> That the society may more easily attain its end, let each sister choose the Immaculate Queen of Heaven for her Mother. She must not only love and venerate her, but fly to her with child-like confidence in all her joys and sorrows....[34] We must imitate her virtues and abandoned ourselves completely into her hands.... "Beg our Lady to keep us in her most pure heart so that we may love Jesus with an undivided love and immaculate love like hers."[35]

30. Langford, *Mother Teresa*, 41.
31. Missionaries of Charity, *Prayerbook*, quoted by Langford, *Mother Teresa*, 72.
32. Langford, *Mother Teresa*, 43.
33. Langford, *Mother Teresa*, 42.
34. Original Rule Explanation no. 4, quoted by Langford, *Mother Teresa*, 39.
35. Mother Teresa to the MC Sisters, July 31, 1996, quoted by Langford, *Mother Teresa*, 39.

FOUNDATION 5: COVENANT CONSECRATION
TO OUR LADY

According to Mother Teresa, Marian Consecration constitutes the lifetime resolution to enter the Immaculate Heart of Mary and to remain there. Mother explains, "Our consecration can be summarized in this way: it is the resolution to remain always in her heart, carefree, without attachments or worries, in constant prayer of heart and docility of will,"[36] and further, "Let us not think that we are working along with her if we only say a few prayers in her honor. We must live habitually with her."[37]

Mother directed all Missionaries of Charity to do the standard Marian consecration associated with St. Louis Marie Grignion de Montfort. According to Langford:

> Mother encouraged us to make in the Total Consecration to our Lady with the 30 days preparation according to St. Louis de Montfort. We do that very faithfully and renew our total consecration to Our Lady every year.... Mother taught us that when we go to our Lady with childlike confidence, everything becomes easy. Mother always led us to Our Lady and continually gave our Lady as an example for everything.[38]

Beyond the classic de Monfortian model of consecration, St. Teresa specifically accentuated Marian consecration as a "covenant." Again from Fr. Langford:

> The way that we "cling to Our Lady," in Mother Teresa's mind, is by establishing a personal covenant of life with her. This was the kind of

36. Mother Teresa to the MC Sisters, November 15, 1996, quoted by Langford, *Mother Teresa*, 74.
37. Mother Teresa to the MC Sisters, November 15, 1996.
38. Langford, *Mother Teresa*, 34.

covenant Jesus himself established between his mother and St. John on Calvary, when he said to John, "She will be your mother and you will be her son" (cf. Jn 19:26–27). Our covenant relationship with Our Lady is a kind of consecration by which we entrust ourselves and our whole lives entirely to her, and become and thereby "particularly her own." Consecration to our Lady is not a matter of words; it is rather a covenant of life shared with her in the service of her Son.[39]

Biblically, covenants entail both a complete gift of people over things and an exchange of duties over materials. In Mother's concept of covenant consecration, clearly nothing is withheld of body, soul, goods, duties, merits, life. Within the spirit and teachings of St. Teresa, Fr. Langford will identify seven components of an authentic covenant consecration with Our Lady in the spirit of Mother Teresa: total confidence, presence, absolute trust, abandonment, self-gift, entering her heart, and sharing her mission; as well as twelve duties of the consecration covenant on Our Lady's part and on the individual's part,[40] all of which manifest the radically unconditional nature of this self-donation, which leads to the Marian sanctification for life. In her words, "Let us all together consecrate our lives totally to her … so that through her guidance and help each of us may become the true spouse of Jesus crucified, a true Missionary of Charity."[41]

FOUNDATION 6: THE ROSARY AND
THE MIRACULOUS MEDAL

In light of the depth of Mariological elements such as the "mystical exchange of hearts" witnessed in other aspects of Mother's Marian

39. Original Rule Explanation no. 4, quoted by Langford, *Mother Teresa*, 73.
40. Langford, *Mother Teresa*, 78.
41. Langford, *Mother Teresa*, 78n35; Mother Teresa to the MC Sisters, November 15, 1996.

spirituality, some might see the simple prayer of the Rosary as something of more minor importance and efficacy. This would indicate a serious misjudgment as of the supernatural power of Rosary, not only in itself, but also in the mind of Mother Teresa. Mother identified the Rosary (precisely as did Pope St. John Paul II) as her "favorite prayer." Fr. Langford confirms: "Mother Teresa's favorite and most frequent prayer as she practiced union with Our Lady was, without doubt, the Rosary."[42] It was the particular efficacy of the Rosary that was the cord of grace that daily led Mother back to that sacred place of the Immaculate Heart and kept her there.

It must also be underscored that of all possible prayers and devotions within the Church, the prayer specified by Our Lady from the beginning of the granting of the MC charism was the Rosary. We hear once again from that 1947 vision: "Take care of them—they are mine.—Bring them to Jesus—carry Jesus to them—Fear not. Teach them to pray the Rosary—the family Rosary and all will be well."[43] What an extraordinary testimony to power of the Rosary and to its diversity—an archetypal prayer specified by Heaven for a ministry specially directed to the care of the poor!

The daily praying of the Rosary can indeed be a mystical prayer of union with Mary that keeps us aware of her presence and the execution of her desires. It certainly was for St. Teresa.

All who had any experience of being in Mother's presence can testify to fact that Mother forever held the Rosary in her hands, both to "hold on" to Our Lady's hand, and to "hold on" to the first vision and charism of the Missionaries of Charity. I personally recall some twenty-five years ago seeing Mother giving a talk in Rome with the Rosary in her hands, and I suddenly felt convicted to do the same. I have striven to do so ever since. That little, hunched-over woman

42. Langford, Mother Teresa, 60.
43. Langford, Mother Teresa, 20 and 60.

touched everyone who came even remotely into her anointed presence!

The Miraculous Medal was likewise for Mother a concrete sign of Marian identification, union, and confidence. Our Lady's simple promise at Rue du Bac in 1830 was that "All who wear it will receive great graces."[44] Mother Teresa believed this, and witnessed its power firsthand.

During one of our Marian conversations in Calcutta, Mother was discussing the power of the Miraculous Medal and said to me, "Whenever I need a building for my Sisters, I put Miraculous Medals around the building, and [leaning forward to me with a half smile], within a few days, it's mine!"[45]

On another occasion, Mother had requested a presentation on the solemn definition of Our Lady's Spiritual Motherhood in her original home for the dying, but it happened to be August 15, which is Independence Day in India, and reports of rioting were taking place in downtown Calcutta. A few of Mother's senior Sisters, fearing the potential violence, discouraged Mother from sending me for the talk. Mother thought for a moment, went over to the counter near her cell, grabbed a handful of Miraculous Medals, placed them in my hand, and peacefully instructed me, "Go with these—you will be fine!"[46] I did—and I was.

Mother's Marian mysticism never kept her from concrete reality, and her profound love and confidence in the likewise simple and humble Rosary and Miraculous Medal manifested this beautiful, incarnational balance of the Saint of the Poor.

44. Cf. Joseph Dirvin, CM, *St. Catherine Laboure of the Miraculous Medal* (Charlotte, NC: TAN Books, 2015), 77.

45. M. Miravalle, conversation with Mother Teresa, Calcutta, India, August 14, 1993.

46. M. Miravalle, conversation with Mother Teresa, Calcutta, India, August 15, 1993.

FOUNDATION 7: ST. TERESA AND
MARY CO-REDEMPTRIX

To comprehend properly the importance of this final Marian foundation, let us return to the initial visions of 1947. We see Mary at the foot of the cross, along with Mother Teresa represented as a child, both facing the cross of the crucified Jesus. Our Lady's hand is on Mother's shoulder and her other hand is next to Mother's, as if to direct everything to the Crucified Lord. This sublimely portrays the doctrine of Mary Co-redemptrix, which honors the Immaculate Virgin's unique cooperation in the Redemption accomplished by Jesus Christ, both by bearing the Redeemer, and also by suffering with the Redeemer, as the New Eve with the New Adam, in order to obtain the graces of human salvation. Mother Teresa well understood the message of the vision: that to accomplish her mission, which would include great suffering, Our Lady Co-redemptrix would be at her side through it all, as she was at the side of Jesus in the accomplishment of his mission.

In my first conversation with Mother in discussing Our Lady, I asked if she believed that Mary was the Co-redemptrix. She responded, "Of course, she is the Co-redemptrix! She gave Jesus his body, and the offering of his body is what saved us."[47] I retorted to Mother: "This is the difference between saints from theologians—it takes you 30 seconds to say what it takes us books to write."

Mother further explains how Our Lady's co-redemptive faith at Calvary brings forth the greatest miracle of the Resurrection:

> At the foot of the Cross, Our Lady saw only pain and suffering—
> and when they closed the tomb, she could not even see the Body of
> Jesus. But it was then that Our Lady's faith, her loving trust in total

47. M. Miravalle, conversation with Mother Teresa, August 14, 1993.

surrender, were greatest. We know that before, in Nazareth, Jesus could not work any miracles because they have no faith. Now, to work his greatest miracle—the Resurrection—He asks for the greatest faith from His own Mother. And because she belonged completely to God in loving trust and total surrender, he could bring to us the joy of the Resurrection, and Mary would be the Cause of our Joy.[48]

Is it any wonder, then, that Mother would feel a mystical camaraderie with the truth and the presence of Mary Co-redemptrix? Who else could best bring St. Teresa through the cross of her own mystical darkness, and guide the way to transforming the darkness into mystical light and sanctity than the Woman at the Cross? Langford explains:

The brilliant light that came to Mother Teresa wrapped in darkness was uncovered for her by Our Lady. It was Our Lady who taught her to see in the darkness, Our Lady who had seen through it first, and at its worst, as her Son struggled for his last breath. It was Our Lady whose faith bolstered and directed Mother Teresa's faith, and brought her to stand and not waiver, despite the darkness, at the cross planted in her own soul. And because Mother Teresa's long night made of this cross such familiar ground, she was able to recognize and stand in unfazed service at the crosses of the poor scattered across the globe, on Calvaries that bear no name, but where he who bears "the name which is above every other name" (Phil 2:9) is ever waiting to embrace, and save, and raise up.[49]

On August 14, 1993, Mother authored the following letter in support of the papal definition of Our Lady as Co-redemptrix, Mediatrix, and Advocate:

48. Mother Teresa to the MC Sisters, July 31, 1996. Quoted by Langford, *Mother Teresa*, 54.
49. Langford, *Mother Teresa*, 17.

Mary is the Co-redemptrix. She gave Jesus his body and suffered with him at the foot of the Cross.

Mary is the Mediatrix of all graces. She gave Jesus to us. As our Mother she obtains for us all his graces.

Mary is our Advocate who prays to Jesus for us. It is only through the Heart of Mary that we come to the Eucharistic Heart of Jesus.

The papal definition of Mary as Co-redemptrix, Mediatrix, and Advocate will bring great graces to the Church.

All for Jesus through Mary.

God bless you,

Mother Teresa M.C.[50]

Mother also requested that materials and petitions for the proclamation of this fifth potential Marian dogma would be sent to her seven hundred MC houses throughout the world.[51] I am confident that St. Teresa looked down from heaven with a smile of approval when her successor, Sr. M. Prema, the present Mother Superior of the Missionaries of Charity, sent to Vox Populi Mariae Mediatrici (the international movement seeking the papal definition of Our Lady's Spiritual Motherhood), the following in a letter dated October 1, 2016: "Thank you for all you are doing for this movement for the good of the Church and the world. May our own Mother's canonization give this proposed and important dogma a push forward!"

CONCLUSION

A few months before Mother's death, I called her at her MC house in Rome to ask whether she would be willing to assist in another proj-

---

50. Letter of Mother Teresa of Calcutta for Fifth Marian Dogma, August 14, 1993, Vox Populi Mariae Mediatrici Archives, Steubenville, Ohio.

51. M. Miravalle, conversation with Mother Teresa, August 14, 1993.

ect for the proclamation of the fifth Marian Dogma, for which she kindly and always gave her joyful "fiat." She ended the conversation with the words that I have always stuck in my heart: "Pray that I do not get in the way of God's designs." Here was the world's greatest living saint (along with Pope St. John Paul II) seriously requesting prayers that her will would not get in the way of God's—even in these final days of her historically holy life!

Surely, this was the final effect of the Heart of Our Lady in the Heart of Mother Teresa, with a manifest humility that made it clear that she simply did not know who she was, which is precisely what made her who she was. May the powerful intercession of these two humble and glorious Mothers bring each one of us ever closer to the Crucified Jesus in the proper fulfillment of our individual vocations for the Church and for the world.

6

SAINTED MOTHER TERESA OF CALCUTTA

A Witness to the Universality of God's Love
and the Natural Law

~

Matthew L. Lamb†

Sainted Mother Teresa of Calcutta, in her love and service of the poorest of the poor, illustrates the importance of the universality of human reason gifted to all by God. Mother Teresa often affirmed that she and her Missionaries of Charity were caring for the poorest of the poor, no matter what their religious affiliation or lack thereof. All in need were welcomed into the care of the Sisters and Brothers whether they were Christian, Hindu, Buddhist, Muslim, atheist, agnostic, or whatever. The sainted Mother simply affirmed that all in need should be welcomed into their care.

Mother kept insisting, at the same time, that she was ministering to Jesus in the poorest of the poor. The revelation she had of Jesus calling her to attend to the poorest of the poor emphasized that he thirsted for souls. In her spiritual conferences and letters, she would state how ministering to the poor was ministering to Jesus. She would quote the Gospel of Matthew, on the last judgment when Jesus commands care for the hungry, thirsty, stranger, naked, sick, or imprisoned. To those who did any of these, astonished that they did so to him, he responds: "Truly, I say to you, as you did it to one of the least of these my brethren, you did it to me" (Mt 25:40).

To those who came to her hospice, Mother would say:

the Sisters and volunteers serve the poorest of the poor with so much tender love and compassion without being concerned as to religion, nationality, caste or color. The sick may be Hindu, Muslim or Christian—all receive the care and love they need.[1]

To her Missionaries of Charity, she would enfold their devotion to the real presence of Jesus in the Eucharist, and the hours spent in adoration before the Tabernacle, to the presence of Jesus in the poor and destitute:

How privileged we are to have been chosen to be 24 hours in the presence of Jesus in the distressing disguise. Unless our hearts are clean and free from all uncharitable words, thoughts and deeds we will never be able to see Jesus in the distressing disguise of the poorest of the poor … Our work for the Poor is so real so beautiful because if our heart is Pure we can see we can touch—Jesus— 24 hours because He has made it so clear: "Whatever you do to the least of my Brethren—You—did—it—to—Me." The Gospel in our five Fingers—that is why we need that deep life of prayer—that will help us to grow in that intimate and personal love for Jesus and complete attachment to Him—so that our Sisters & our Poor can see Jesus in us, His love, His compassion.[2]

Seeking the face of God in everything, everyone, all the time, and

1. Brian Kolodiejchuk, MC, ed., *Mother Teresa: Come Be My Light* (New York: Doubleday, 2007), 300–304.
2. Charism and message of Mother Teresa.

his hand in every happening; This is what it means to be contemplative in the heart of the world. Seeing and adoring the presence of Jesus, especially in the lowly appearance of bread, and in the distressing disguise of the poor.[3]

The sainted Mother and her missionaries understood this identification of Jesus with the poor and needy from within their vibrant faith in Christ Jesus and his revelation as the Son of God. Yet the witness of their care for the neglected poor evoked admiration and esteem among millions who are not Christians.

In order to understand the profound theological significance of Mother Teresa's witness, it is necessary to show how the universality of God's love for each and every human being is bound up with the very nature of human beings. Mother Teresa's mysticism manifests the importance of nature and the natural law in Catholic teachings.

Mother's special friendship with St. John Paul II drew upon his insistence that Christianity has always held that the "image of God" is the immortal rational soul of each human being. This constitutes, the pope declared, "the immutable foundation of all Christian anthropology."[4] Karol Wojtyła turned to St. Thomas Aquinas to understand more fully this foundation.[5] Wojtyła wrote that a genuinely human act has a specific

interpretation found in the philosophies of Aristotle and St. Thomas Aquinas. This interpretation is realistic and objectivistic as well as metaphysical. It issues from the whole conception of being, and more directly from the conception of … the changeable and simultaneously dynamic nature of being.[6]

3. Mother Teresa, *In the Heart of the World: Thoughts, Stories, and Prayers* (Novato, CA: New World Library, 2010).

4. John Paul II, *Mulieris Dignitatem*, no. 6.

5. Cf. Matthew Lamb, "St. John Paul II's Thomism: Why St. Thomas Aquinas Is a Teacher of Humanity," in *Thomas Aquinas: Teacher of Humanity*, ed. John Hittinger and Daniel Wagner (Cambridge: Cambridge Scholars, 2015), 17–40.

6. Cf. Karol Wojtyła, *The Acting Person*, trans. Andrzej Potocki (Boston: D. Reidel,

St. John Paul II saw two key elements in Aquinas's later theology that help us understand the witness of Mother Teresa's mission to live out the universality of the natural law of God's love. One is his analysis of the three levels of the "image of God in man," and the other is his clear distinction between the virtue of religion and the theological virtue of charity. Both indicate the importance of the universality of God's love in all of nature and the natural law.

All human beings are created in the *imago Dei*, even though most of them may never know that they are such images of God. To understand this, it is important to turn to St. Thomas Aquinas, who succinctly states in *Summa theologiae (ST)* I, q. 93, a. 4c:

> Since man is said to be the image of God by reason of his intellectual nature, he is the most perfectly like God according to that in which he can best imitate God in his intellectual nature. Now the intellectual nature imitates God chiefly in this, that God understands and loves Himself. Wherefore we see that the image of God is in man in three ways.
>
> First, inasmuch *as man possesses a natural aptitude* for understanding and loving God; and this aptitude consists in the very nature of the mind, which is common to all men.
>
> Secondly, inasmuch *as man actually and habitually* knows and loves God, though *imperfectly*; and this image consists in the conformity of grace.

1997); this translation is poor, and I am drawing upon the better German translation from the Polish by Herbert Springer, *Person und Tat* (Freiburg: Herder, 1982), 33. Joseph P. Rice has drawn upon the Polish original and emphasizes, as I do, Wojtyła's transcendental approach, which breaks through the dichotomies between subjectivity and objectivity. See his "Consciousness, Conscience, and Persons: A Reflection on Wojtyła's 'Trans-Phenomenological' Approach to Subjectivity and Intersubjectivity," presented at the 2012 Fellowship of Catholic Scholars Conference, Washington, DC. See also Rocco Buttiglione, *Karol Wojtyła: The Thought of the Man Who Became Pope John Paul II*, trans. Paolo Guitti and Francesca Murphy (Grand Rapids, MI: Eerdmans, 1997). As Vincent Potter, SJ, points out, it would be futile to oppose Wojtyła to Thomas Aquinas; in this regard, Potter sees that Bernard Lonergan, SJ, adopts a similar way of seeing a key to human experience in Aquinas. Cf. John McDermott, SJ, ed., *The Thought of Pope John Paul II* (Rome: Gregoriana, 1993) 205ff.

Thirdly, inasmuch *as man knows and loves God perfectly*; and this image consists in the likeness of glory.

Wherefore on the words, "The light of Thy countenance, O Lord, is signed upon us" (Ps 4:7), the gloss distinguishes a threefold image of "creation," of "re-creation," and of "likeness." The first is found in all men, the second only in the just, the third only in the blessed.[7]

Every human being is endowed with reason from the moment of conception. It may take years for one to exercise or use his or her reason, but by the fact of having the rational faculties of intellect and will, each is created in the image of God. While minerals, plants, and animals have "traces" (*vestigia*) of God, only intellectual creatures (humans and angels) are by their intellect and will images of God. God infinitely knows and loves himself, so rational creatures image the Divine Nature in their faculties of knowing and loving.

Mother Teresa realized that the real presence of Jesus in the Eucharist means that presence must move from senses and imagination to the spiritual presencing of intelligence. Only then would love be properly ordered to God's infinite good. All men have, as Aquinas states, a natural aptitude to know and love God by the very fact of having a rational soul. The Roman Catholic Church upholds the classical, ancient, and Thomist understanding of natural law. The whole

---

7. *ST* I, q. 93, a. 4c: "Respondeo dicendum quod, cum homo secundum intellectualem naturam ad imaginem Dei esse dicatur, secundum hoc est maxime ad imaginem Dei, secundum quod intellectualis natura Deum maxime imitari potest. Imitatur autem intellectualis natura maxime Deum quantum ad hoc, quod Deus seipsum intelligit et amat. Unde imago Dei tripliciter potest considerari in homine. Uno quidem modo, secundum quod homo habet aptitudinem naturalem ad intelligendum et amandum Deum, et haec aptitudo consistit in ipsa natura mentis, quae est communis omnibus hominibus. Alio modo, secundum quod homo actu vel habitu Deum cognoscit et amat, sed tamen imperfecte, et haec est imago per conformitatem gratiae. Tertio modo, secundum quod homo Deum actu cognoscit et amat perfecte, et sic attenditur imago secundum similitudinem gloriae. Unde super illud Psalmi IV, *signatum est super nos lumen vultus tui, domine*, Glossa distinguit triplicem imaginem, scilicet creationis, recreationis et similitudinis. Prima ergo imago invenitur in omnibus hominibus; secunda in iustis tantum; tertia vero solum in beatis."

of creation has a God-given order that embraces all material and all spiritual beings. The key, as Mother knew from her studies and her readings of Pope John Paul II, was to *discover* the God-given order *not to impose* any arbitrary order that distorts the natural order and law.

The friendship between the pope and Mother Teresa was profound. The pope saw Mother as a "person-message" who communicated to the world how the Gift of God's love is engraved in human nature.[8] Mother Teresa drew deeply from the teachings of Vatican II, as had Pope John Paul II. As Weigel observes:

> Part of John Paul II's comprehensive program to implement the Second Vatican Council is by a method of *Ressourcement,* the recovery of foundational theological themes from the Bible, the theology of the first Christian centuries, and medieval scholarship. *Veritatis Splendor* is just such an exercise in retrieval, reclaiming the venerable notion of freedom as linked to truth and goodness that had gotten lost in the fourteenth and fifteenth centuries under the influence of the philosophy called "nominalism" and its equation of freedom with raw willpower.[9]

Within months of Mother Teresa's death, Pope John Paul II offered a strong injunction that went to the heart of Mother Teresa's living out the reality of presence:

> Know Yourself... In both East and West, we may trace a journey that has led humanity down the centuries to meet and engage truth more and more deeply. It is a journey that has unfolded—as it must—within the horizon of personal self-consciousness: the more human beings know reality and the world, the more they know themselves in their uniqueness, with the question of the meaning of

8. George Weigel, *Witness to Hope: The Biography of Pope John Paul II* (New York: Harper Collins, 1999), 513. See also Brian Kolodiejchuk, MC, ed., *Where There Is Love, There Is God: Mother Teresa* (New York: Image, 2010).

9. Weigel, *Witness to Hope,* 694.

things and of their very existence becoming ever more pressing. This is why all that is the object of our knowledge becomes a part of our life.[10]

Mother Teresa took to heart the admonition of John Paul II that the best way to prepare for the future is to enliven the Church's memory with insights from the treasuries of wisdom, intelligence, and holiness in the past millennia.[11]

To clarify the difference between the natural image of God common to all humans and the graced image, Aquinas differentiates the acquired virtue of religion from the infused virtue of charity. Following Aristotle, Aquinas states that the natural virtue of religion is the principal potential part of justice. In *ST* II-II, q. 81, a. 5, Thomas explains why the virtue of religion cannot be considered a theological virtue. The very *object* of a theological virtue, he says, is the ultimate end (i.e., the vision of the divine essence). The objects of the virtue of religion are the acts that man does as an admittedly inadequate response to God's magnificence and magnanimity. God comes into this structure as the end toward which these acts are directed, but religion itself is primarily in its proper acts. Thomas states:

> Due worship is offered to God in as much as certain acts, by which God is worshipped, are performed in reverence of him, for instance, offerings of sacrifices and other such things. Thus it is apparent that God is related to the virtue of religion not as material or object but

10. John Paul II, *Fides et Ratio*, para. 1.

11. John Paul II again emphasized this in *Tertio Millennio Ineunte*: "It is not therefore a matter of inventing a 'new program.' The program already exists: it is the plan found in the Gospel and in the living Tradition, it is the same as ever. Ultimately, it has its center in Christ himself, who is to be known, loved and imitated, so that in him we may live the life of the Trinity, and with him transform history until its fulfillment in the heavenly Jerusalem. This is a program which does not change with shifts of times and cultures, even though it takes account of time and culture for the sake of true dialogue and effective communication. This program for all times is our program for the Third Millennium."

as end. And so religion is not a theological virtue, whose object is the ultimate end, but a moral virtue, whose being is directed toward those things that are for the end.[12]

The acquired virtue of religion also has ceremonial precepts that govern the prayers and sacrifices offered by the descendants of Adam and Noah up to Abraham.[13] The virtue of religion is a potential part of justice common to all men. Aquinas understood that, although Aristotle had a notion of creation, he did not grasp how God transcends the whole created universe.

Creation is only a contingent necessity, as is clear in Genesis. Only God as infinite intelligence and love is absolutely necessary. Moreover, the great Greek and Latin philosophers did not grasp that the fact that few humans live by what is highest in them—namely, their reason—is not due to matter, but to their turning away from the God-given light of their reason.

John Paul II realized the depths of Mother Teresa's vocation to teach as evoking the dynamic character of all human beings created in the image of God. Her vocation to teaching was deepened in her service to the poor. As Aquinas states:

> The ultimate ground of our knowing is indeed God, the eternal Light; but the reason why we know is within us. It is the light of our own intellects; and by it we can know because "the very intellectual light which is within us is nothing other than a certain created participation of the eternal light."[14]

The light of our intelligence derives its efficacy from the *Prima Lux* that is God, so that all the certitude we possess comes from the intellectual light within us, and questioning and knowing is a

---

12. *ST* II-II, q. 81, a. 5.
13. *ST* I-II, q. 103, a. 1c. Note that Aquinas does not use, as he did in the Commentary on the Sentences, the expression "sacraments of the natural law."
14. *ST* I, q. 84, a. 5 c.

divine-human cooperation in teaching. Teaching is "sacred" as a theonomic activity. For, "inasmuch as the act of understanding grasps its own transcendence-in-immanence, its quality of intellectual light as a participation of the divine and uncreated Light, it expresses itself in judgment, in a positing of the truth, in the affirmation or negation of reality."[15] Mother Teresa entered deeply into St. Augustine's realization that God is more intimate to us than even we are to ourselves. The hours spent in Eucharistic adoration led Mother beyond her senses into the illumined darkness of her intelligence as a created participation of the Triune God's infinite intelligence, wisdom, and love.

From St. John Paul II's and Benedict XVI's teachings, Mother Teresa deepened her understanding and practice of Jesus's revelation to her in "I thirst." She realized the dynamism of the *imago Dei* manifested in how, from the rational image common to all men, God revealed the covenant with Israel, and how that would prepare for the new covenant in Jesus Christ as truly God and truly man. The theological virtues grace mankind with a knowledge and love of the Triune God. Rational creatures also image the Trinity insofar as their knowing involves a procession of an inner word (concepts, propositions) that in turn brings about a procession of love in the will.[16]

But in this life we know and love God, as Mother Teresa wrote, "imperfectly" as we seek to slake the thirst of Jesus on the cross through our faith, hope, and charity. Only in the Kingdom of Heaven will we see the Triune God in the beatific vision, knowing and loving him as perfectly as our finitude can.

---

15. Bernard Lonergan, *Verbum: Word and Idea in Aquinas*, vol. 2, *The Collected Works of Bernard Lonergan* (Toronto: University of Toronto Press, 1997), 94.

16. *ST* I, q. 93, a. 6c: "Similiter, cum increata Trinitas distinguatur secundum processionem verbi a dicente, et amoris ab utroque, ut supra habitum est (28,3); in creatura rationali, in qua invenitur processio verbi secundum intellectum, et processio amoris secundum voluntatem, potest dici imago Trinitatis increatae per quandam repraesentationem speciei." Also, cf. D. Jurvenal Merriell, *To the Image of the Trinity: A Study in the Development of Aquinas' Teaching* (Toronto: PIMS, 1990).

In her love of the poorest of the poor, Mother Teresa embodied the concrete universality of God's creative and redemptive love. She knew that there is no abstract universality in God. God's love of the human race concretely embraces each and every human being who ever has, is, or will live. Mother realized that Jesus Christ came to redeem creation. The theological virtues heal and elevate the God-given light of reason.[17]

St. Teresa's life of prayer, both personal and sacramental, expanded her conscious self-presence, the light of her mind and heart, to embrace the real presence of Christ in the Eucharist. The hours she spent in prayer enabled her to bring the light of Christ into the darkness of the world. As she wrote in one of her letters collected by Brian Kolodiejchuk in *Come Be My Light*:

> Jesus wanted to help us by sharing our life, our loneliness, our agony and death. All that He has taken upon Himself, and has carried it in the darkest night. Only by being one with us He has redeemed us. We are allowed to do the same: All the desolation of the poor people, not only their material poverty, but their spiritual destitution must be redeemed, and we must have our share in it.—Pray thus when you find it hard—"I wish to live in this world which is so far from God, which has turned so much from the light of Jesus, to help them—to take upon me something of their suffering."—Yes, my dear children—let us share the sufferings—of our poor—for only by being one with them—we can redeem them, that is, bringing God into their lives and bringing them to God.

Mother Teresa knew that genuine love follows from truth. As St. Augustine wrote, we do not love the unknown, but we love to know the unknown. St. Teresa's darkness was the mystical dark night of the soul, as she longed to know the unknown. This is *toto coelo* op-

17. Brian Kolodiejchuk, MC, ed., *A Call to Mercy: Hearts to Love, Hands to Serve* (New York: Image, 2016).

posite to the nihilism of Nietzsche, who went literally mad trying to love the unknown. Following Kant and Descartes, moderns distort reason into an instrument of the will to power. So moderns do not attune their minds and hearts to the God-given order of the universe, the natural law ordering all things from God and returning to God. The will to power results in a relativist nihilism promoting the sins of contraception, abortion, euthanasia, genocides, with the horrors of modern world wars.

In conclusion, we can appreciate how crucial the witness of St. Mother Teresa and her Missionaries of Charity is as we begin the twenty-first century. Only insofar as we join with them in deepening a concrete universal love for Jesus in every human being as created and redeemed images of God can we participate in the return of all things to the Kingdom of Heaven, the new Jerusalem, where for all eternity, with every tear wiped away, we can enjoy the beatific communion with the Father, Son, and Holy Spirit.

7

MORAL VIRTUE, UNION WITH CHRIST, AND TWO TERESAS

~

John Froula

The Big Teresa: that is what Mother Teresa called St. Teresa of Jesus to distinguish her from the little one, St. Thérèse, Mother Teresa's own namesake.[1] The Big Teresa was big indeed: undaunted reformer of the Carmelite order, foundress of numerous monasteries, and a center of the religious revival in sixteenth-century Spain. St. Teresa of Jesus was a historical figure worldwide.[2] She was a brave lover of Christ. She was a spiritual master possessed of mystical intuition, a

1. See Brian Kolodiejchuk, MC, ed., *Mother Teresa: Come Be My Light* (New York: Doubleday, 2007), 15. See also David Scott, *A Revolution of Love: The Meaning of Mother Teresa* (Chicago: Loyola Press, 2005), 47. Scott writes, "She died almost one hundred years to the day after her patron Thérèse, the little flower of Lisieux. And their lives form spiritual brackets around the twentieth century. Thérèse, too, experienced a 'night of nothingness' ... Following Thérèse in to this night of nothingness, Mother Teresa too sought the Holy Face of the Crucified in the crushed and dying, walked the path of spiritual childhood in the small, ordinary realities of her day, and lived her life one little act of love at a time" (158).

2. See William Thomas Walsh, *Saint Teresa of Avila* (Milwaukee: Bruce, 1948).

brilliant mind, and a candid pen who well deserves her place alongside the great doctors of the Church.

Notwithstanding, St. Teresa often in her writing claims not to know what she is talking about. This should not be taken as Socratic irony or a rhetorical self-effacement so as not to appear overly assertive, or even as an implicit comparison between herself and some of her advisors and confessors, many of whom were learned academics and are still read today. No, literary posturing seems entirely foreign to St. Teresa of Jesus. I believe she never wrote an insincere word in her life. Her transparency to the real is so limpid that when St. Edith Stein read her spiritual autobiography—despite St. Teresa's personality being branded on every page—Stein put it down and said, "this is the truth."[3] She did not say that she made some good points or was clever. Rather, "this is the truth." St. Teresa's claim not to know what she is talking about comes from the experience of one who has the godly instincts of the intellectual gifts of the Holy Spirit, someone who knows in a divine way more so than in a human way, and recognizes that her human words are not adequate to the divine realities with which she has contact.[4] As St. Teresa wrote, "For I certainly do not know what I am writing about—God knows."[5]

In writing from her heart of hearts, where God dwelt and prompted her, St. Teresa's literary works often do lack obvious method, as she

3. "In the summer of 1921, she spent several weeks in Bergzabern (in the Palatinate) on the country estate of Hedwig Conrad-Martius, another pupil of Husserl's. Hedwig had converted to Protestantism with her husband. One evening Edith picked up an autobiography of St. Teresa of Avila and read this book all night. 'When I had finished the book, I said to myself: This is the truth.' Later, looking back on her life, she wrote: 'My longing for truth was a single prayer.'" Tessa Benedict of the Cross Edith Stein, website of the Holy See, accessed January 27, 2017, http://www.vatican.va/news_services/liturgy/saints/ns_lit_doc_19981011_edith_stein_en.html.

4. See St. Thomas Aquinas, *Summa theologiae* (*ST*) I-II, q. 68, a. 1.

5. St. Teresa of Avila, *The Way of Perfection*, 16.3, trans. Kieran Kavanaugh and Otilio Rodriguez, in *The Collected Works of St. Teresa of Avila*, vol. 2, (Washington, DC: ICS, 1980), 94.

is quick to remind her readers. One of the key teachings she gives her spiritual daughters, wending its way through her *Way of Perfection*, is that there are three pillars necessary for a life of unitive prayer: fraternal charity, detachment, and humility.[6] At the risk of spoiling St. Teresa's freshness, I apply some of the traditional doctrine of the virtues, as classically expressed by St. Thomas Aquinas, to this teaching in order to show how fraternal charity, detachment, and humility represent a comprehensive perfection of the graced moral life. As such, these three virtues would remove all obstacles to a real, sanctifying, transformative joining to Christ and contemplative prayer.

There is a larger issue at play in bringing together the teachings of St. Teresa of Jesus and St. Thomas Aquinas. A complementarity between them is more than accidental. The object of the systematic theologian's study is the same as the object of the mystic's contemplation. A basic correspondence between a premier theologian and a premier mystic is to be expected, even if one speaks more from study and a learning tradition and the other speaks more from experience and native insight. The true mystic is not swimming in subjectivism any more than the true theologian is lost in pure abstraction. Both are concerned with the realest things.

Also, those familiar with Mother Teresa could not help but notice how these three virtues—fraternal charity, detachment, and humility—figure prominently in her life and work. Examining these virtues could serve as a kind of bridge between St. Teresa of Jesus and Mother Teresa with respect to the way each encountered Christ, whether strictly in prayer or in service to the poorest of the poor. Perhaps by looking at the moral life as condition to contemplative union there is a fuller way to understand how a real, sanctifying, transformative union with Christ on the analogy of contemplative prayer could be operative in doing the corporal works of mercy as Mother Teresa did them.

6. See St. Teresa of Avila, *Way of Perfection*, chaps. 4–18.

So, then, how is it that fraternal charity, detachment, and humility represent the complete perfection of the graced moral life? Moral theologians traditionally see three properly moral virtues as the three highest categories under which all the other moral virtues fit, virtues that habitually perfect the way we are inclined to do things, either by our will, or by the emotions we experience with difficult things, the irascible appetites, or by the emotions we experience with pleasant things, the concupisciple appetites. The three overarching moral virtues are justice, which perfects our will with respect to our neighbor such that we give him his due; fortitude, which perfects us with respect to moral activity, where fear and anger move us; and temperance, which perfects our appetite for good things.[7]

Moreover, there is a certain order of these virtues. Temperance and fortitude are somewhat instrumental with respect to justice. Temperance and fortitude remove interior impediments to the ready practice of justice. Having fortitude helps us to be just if there is some difficulty in being just; think about the courage it can take to offer an apology. Temperance gives us the inner freedom to dispense good things as justice demands without grasping; think about greedy employers who lack the temperance to pay a just wage simply because they do not have to. Because fortitude and temperance enable justice, there is a sense in which justice is the comprehensive moral virtue.[8] It is in this sense that St. Matthew calls St. Joseph a just man: he is a morally virtuous man, merciful and pious.[9]

Fraternal charity in the writings of St. Teresa of Jesus is the perfection of justice, detachment is the perfection of fortitude, and humility

---

7. See *ST* I-II, q. 61, a. 2.

8. Joseph Pieper gives an account of why justice is the highest of the strictly moral virtues. See *The Four Cardinal Virtues* (Notre Dame, IN: University of Notre Dame Press, 1966), 64–69. See also *ST* II-II, q. 141, a. 8.

9. See Mt 1:19. That is the opinion of St. John Chrysostom as reported by St. Thomas Aquinas in his *Commentary on Matthew*, 116.

is the perfection of temperance; these three Teresian virtues represent the perfection of the graced moral life as a whole. The way St. Teresa of Jesus talks about fraternal charity leaves no doubt that it is the single virtue whereby we love God above all things with supernatural love and our neighbor as ourselves for God's sake. But fraternal charity in St. Teresa also bears the marks of the perfection of justice.[10] There is an emphasis on the fraternal side of fraternal charity. Much of the discussion about fraternal charity concerns the equity with which St. Teresa's daughters in religion ought to treat each other. There are long discussions about right behavior with confessors in the section on fraternal charity that seem like a distracted digression, but not when viewed as a consideration of what is due in justice given a certain relationship. Fraternal charity does indeed exceed justice, and we ought to act out of charity in ways that strict justice may not demand. But much like natural friendship, which does not leave justice behind by going beyond it, fraternal charity, as supernatural friendship, is a spiritual love of neighbor that no longer counts so much on natural affection as a unifying bond, but on the common good of beatitude.[11]

Attainment of this ultimate common good requires detachment, which is the perfection of fortitude. At first, the connection between detachment and fortitude may appear tenuous. Detachment seems more to do with temperance, and it would be a mistake to think that there is no detachment involved in temperance. But there is much of the heroic in the way in which St. Teresa of Jesus talks about detachment. She is not talking so much about not being attached to petty pleasure, but a disposition making one ready to give everything. She says when speaking of detachment that "the least that any of us who

10. Joseph Pieper notes that the difference between charity and justice is that charity tends toward union and considering the other as oneself, whereas justice concerns the other as other. See *Four Cardinal Virtues*, 54.

11. Aquinas in *ST* II-II, q. 25, a. 1, explains the bond of fraternal charity in terms of our final end in God.

has truly loved the Lord can offer him is our own life."[12] St. Teresa likens religious life and its detachment to a long martyrdom. In her autobiography, St. Teresa makes a broader statement: "I assert that an imperfect human being needs more fortitude to pursue the way of perfection than suddenly to become a martyr."[13] This at first can have a pessimistic or dour ring to it, but it should not. Classically considered, martyrdom is the ultimate act of the virtue fortitude, the pinnacle of heroism, not something sulky. As the ancients saw the height of fortitude as the readiness to die in battle for the homeland, Christians saw the height of fortitude as the readiness to die in a persecution of the Faith.[14] This strength, consisting of a willingness to fight if necessary but principally consisting of patience and endurance—the patience that obtains all things[15] and determined determination,[16] to use St. Teresa's vocabulary—is needed to consider all worldly goods as relative to the eternal good. The patience of fortitude is impossible if one is attached to the goods one finds oneself losing. No one can have the fortitude of martyrdom or the fortitude to give oneself totally to God without the detachment to give up everything that is not God.

Seeing humility as the perfection of temperance, on the other hand, is the least difficult connection to make on the basis of the classic theology of the virtues. St. Thomas Aquinas includes humility as a potential part or a certain application of the virtue of temperance.[17]

12. St. Teresa of Avila, *Way of Perfection*, 12.1.

13. St. Teresa of Avila, *The Book of Her Life*, 31.18, quoted by Pieper, *Four Cardinal Virtues*, 137.

14. See *ST* II-II, q. 124, a. 3.

15. These verses are known as St. Teresa's Bookmark, found in her breviary: "Let nothing disturb you; / Let nothing frighten you. / All things are passing. / God never changes. / Patience obtains all things. / Nothing is wanting to him who possesses God. / God alone suffices." "Catholic Prayer: Bookmark of St. Teresa of Avila," Catholic Culture.org, accessed May 23, 2017, http://www.catholicculture.org/culture/liturgical-year/prayers/view.cfm?id=874.

16. See St. Teresa of Avila, *Way of Perfection*, 23.1.

17. Virtues have three kinds of parts. Subjective parts are species of a genus or categories within a larger group. Integral parts are essential aspects of the virtue, like the

Because temperance orders our appetite for what feels good, and it feels so good to have exterior validation and to think well of ourselves, temperance is needed for right balance.

Another way we can see humility as the perfection of temperance is that temperance is a beautifying virtue, and humility is most beautifying.[18] St. Thomas explains that temperance, as something honorable, makes one beautiful in terms of the integral parts of beauty, proportion, and splendor.[19] As a naturally beautiful person has orderly parts put together proportionately, contributing to a certain glow or overall expressiveness whereby her personality shines out, so temperance proportionately arranges the appetites in such a way that the order of reason shines out.[20] Temperance is the expression of the right integration of the whole more so than the repression of desire.[21] St. Teresa, for her part, sees the crowning beauty that humility brings

material parts of a body. Potential parts are so called in reference to active potencies, or powers, or abilities to do certain things on the basis of the virtue.

18. The beauty that temperance gives a soul can be further elaborated by the consideration that an integral part of temperance, along with the propensity to feel shame rightly, is *honestas*. *Honestas* is a difficult word to translate. It means something like "honorable" in a full sense, not in a proud sense. *Honestas* is that which is possessed of a spiritual beauty, something that demands intellectual admiration. See *ST* II-II, q. 145, a. 2.

19. A corollary to the attractiveness of temperance is the shamefulness of intemperance. While sins of intemperance may not be the gravest, there is something particularly ugly and embarrassing about them. Whether shame is seen more as a reaction to the body's unruliness, or the making public of something private, or the fear of being misjudged when the part is taken for the whole, there is a kind of disproportion of an expression that does not match a nature.

20. "To the virtue of temperance as the preserving and defending realization of man's inner order, the gift of beauty is particularly coordinated. Not only is temperance beautiful in itself, it also renders men beautiful. Beauty, however, must here be understood in its original meaning: as the glow of the true and the good irradiating from every ordered state of being." Pieper, *Four Cardinal Virtues*, 203.

21. Romanus Cessario sees a kind of a fortiori argument in the Person of Christ that temperance does not mean weak emotions: "The rectification of the sense appetites exists preeminently in the case of Christ, who had full and strong human passions or emotions that remained rightly ordered from within because his virtues of moderation and strengthening were so perfect in their formation." *The Virtues; Or, the Examined Life* (New York: Continuum, 2002), 190. See also *ST* III, q. 15, a. 2.

in terms of its effects rather than integral parts, how it attracts Christ and wins over his love. In St. Teresa's celebrated chess analogy, humility is the queen, the most powerful of all the pieces, who is of most use in checkmating the King who is Christ.[22]

St. Thomas also speaks about how humility is the disposition needed to be free to follow the dictates of reason.[23] St. Teresa has a more purely supernatural way of expressing this. The dictates of reason she is principally concerned with are those of Divine Providence. By humility, we accept what God in his wisdom ordains for our good in the providential order.

Although humility is a key virtue, it does not have the dignity of the theological virtues that link us directly to God as our end, nor does it have the dignity of prudence and justice, which rationally order the means to that end in our reason and will. Humility does have first place, though, among the virtues in removing obstacles to God, the chief obstacle being pride, according to St. Thomas. That is how St. Teresa sees it, too. A recurring theme in *The Way of Perfection* is that contemplative union with God is a gift of God, and our preparation is to not get in the way, which is one way of looking at all three virtues St. Teresa discusses. As humility removes the inordinate self-love as an obstacle to the love of God, fraternal charity removes our inordinate love of neighbor as an obstacle to the love of God, and detachment removes the inordinate love of goods of the world as an obstacle to the love of God.

The three virtues that support prayerful contemplative union with Christ—fraternal charity, detachment, and humility—seem to be the three virtues that support Mother Teresa's spirituality and apostolate of serving the poorest of the poor and seeing Christ in them. Her mission is nearly synonymous with fraternal charity to those who are

22. See St. Teresa of Avila, *Way of Perfection*, 16.1–2.
23. See *ST* II-II, q. 161, a. 5.

most in need of the basic demands of distributive justice.[24] We have a moving expression of her fraternal charity in the sense that her entire life's work would be worth it by having "one child made happy with the love of Jesus."[25]

With respect to detachment, Mother Teresa writes in her 1959 retreat notes, where she is frank about her shortcomings, that she has no attachment to creatures, that she was indifferent to her work, success, failure, and the affection of her companions and those whom she served.[26] This detachment leads to what Josef Pieper calls mystic fortitude,[27] fortitude as a gift of the Holy Spirit, the strength to suffer interiorly the dryness and the sense of the absence of God as chronicled in *Come Be My Light*.[28]

24. "At the time of death, when we meet God face-to-face, we will be judged concerning how much we have loved. Not concerning how much we have accomplished, but rather how much love we have put into what we have done. In order for love to be genuine, it has to be above all a love for my neighbor. Love for my neighbor will lead me to true love for God." Mother Teresa, *Essential Writings*, ed. Jean Maalouf (Maryknoll: Orbis Books, 2001), 81. This is just one example of the many things Mother Teresa has said or written on fraternal charity. Note the echo of St. John of the Cross's maxim that in the evening of life we will be judged on love.

25. Kolodiejchuk, *Come Be My Light*, 61.

26. "3. What use am I making of Creatures? *I have no attachment.* 4. Am I truly indifferent to my work, my companions with whom I work, my health, my success, my failure? *Yes.* Am I indifferent to the love and affection of my companions and of the people for whom I work? *Yes.*" Kolodiejchuk, *Come Be My Light*, 350.

27. Pieper's division of vital, moral, and mystic fortitude corresponds to the acquired virtue, the infused virtue, and the gift of the Holy Spirit. See *Four Cardinal Virtues*, 134–41.

28. "It is difficult to grasp precisely what 'darkness' meant for her at this time, but in the future, the term would come to signify profound interior suffering, lack of sensible consolation, spiritual dryness, an apparent absence of God form her life, and, at the same time, a painful longing for Him." Kolodiejchuk, *Come Be My Light*, 21–22. See also chap. 10 of the same work.

Another powerful expression of her detachment can be seen in one of Mother Teresa's letters: "And when the night becomes very thick—and it seems to me that I will end up in hell—then I simply offer myself to Jesus. If He wants me to go there—I am ready—but only under the condition that it really makes Him happy." Mother Teresa to Jesuit Fr. Franjo Jambrekovic, 1937, in Kolodiejchuk, *Come Be My Light*, 20. To "go there" could mean hell, or it could mean the experience of the absence of God. If it is the former, then "going there" seems a tongue-in-cheek expression, because Jesus is not really

Mother Teresa even expresses the beauty of humility that St. Thomas and St. Teresa of Jesus speak of, albeit in a more active way. Her famous sayings "live life beautifully" and "do something beautiful for God" are applied to a life doing humble things, the small things few will do, that are no longer small because of their beauty. Her beautiful life is an application of St. Thérèse's little way.[29] Mother Teresa's vow "Not to refuse God anything" was the beautiful thing she gave to God, an act of total humble self-effacement. "This is what hides everything in me,"[30] she would say of the vow, gathering up everything she did under the single principle of accepting obedience, hidden in the humility of docility as a lover hides her gifts for her beloved. Mother Teresa invokes another of the senses regarding the pleasing aspect of humility: "humiliations are my sweetest sweets."[31] And who is not personally attracted to the beauty and honorableness of Mother Teresa's humility?

That the necessary moral perfection for contemplative union with Christ in prayer is operative in the mission to serve Christ in the poorest of the poor is just one clue that Mother Teresa's evangelical mission is a real means of unitive transformative contact with Christ. This is not to say that works of mercy replace prayer.[32] Mother Teresa and her daughters are contemplative in the traditional sense. But it is to take seriously Christ's claim that he is identified with those who suffer, the "least of these my brethren," and the persecuted Church. We also want to give maximal attention to the claim in the Letter of St. James that true religion is giving relief the widow and the orphan.

---

made happy by damnation. If it is the latter, then it is real resignation to Providence for the good of those who love God.

29. See Scott, *Revolution of Love*, 50–52.

30. Kolodiejchuk, *Come Be My Light*, 29.

31. Mother Teresa to Jesuit Fr. Franjo Jambrekovic, 1937, in Kolodiejchuk, *Come Be My Light*, 21.

32. Later she would explain to her sisters, "work is not prayer, prayer is not work, but we must pray the work for Him, with Him and to Him." Kolodiejchuk, *Come Be My Light*, 364n19.

One way to look at what it means to find Christ in the poor is that the poor are loved for Christ's sake by the theological virtue of charity on account of our common calling to beatitude.[33] If I help out the daughter of a friend because I love my friend, there is a sense that I am finding my friend in his daughter. Anyone in the state of grace finds Christ in the poor in the sense that they are loved in God and can fulfill the charism of the Missionaries of Charity. Another way of getting at much the same thing is that Christ is the head of all who either possess God fully in beatitude, who possess him as pilgrims by faith or faith enlivened by charity, or even those who possess him potentially.[34] Everyone on earth or in Heaven can be loved as a member of Christ at some level, and so Christ can be loved in everyone we encounter. But what Mother Teresa says seems to go beyond even that. She says, "Our lives are woven with Jesus in the Eucharist. In Holy Communion we have Christ under the appearance of bread; in our work we find Him under the appearance of flesh and blood. It is the same Christ. 'I was hungry, I was naked, I was sick, I was homeless.'"[35] Granting that Mother Teresa saw poverty as including spiritual and not just material poverty, why the specificity in encountering Christ in the poorest of the poor and the abjectly suffering? The following is offered to start a conversation.

By his incarnation, Christ is united to every person, and by his death that union is brought to an operative completion.[36] Christ died for every person and his sin such that when this universally redemptive act is singly applied to a person, it is as though that person

---

33. See *ST* II-II, q. 25, a. 1.
34. See *ST* III, q. 8, a. 3.
35. Mother Teresa as quoted in Scott, *Revolution in Love*, 92.
36. "By his Incarnation, he, the Son of God, in a certain way *united himself with each man*." Vatican Council II, Pastoral Constitution on the Church in the Modern World *Gaudium et Spes*, 22: *AAS* 58 (1966): 1042. Italics as in *Redemptor Hominis*, 8, Encyclical Letter of John Paul II, 1979.

meritoriously died for himself and his own sin.[37] For a Missionary of Charity, it is the love for the suffering person that opens the way for sanctifying contact with Christ, who by his own suffering identifies himself with the poor in the act of redemption.[38] So Christ can move the will in such a way, as a divine gift, such that the Missionary of Charity is no longer simply loving the poor and suffering and dying for Christ's sake, but really loving the suffering Christ directly in a unifying act as he is redemptively identified with the poor.[39] Those in a contemplative vocation are doing nothing wrong by filling their prayer life with active meditation. They still should be open to the passive contemplation that is a gift of God. So, by analogy, a Missionary of Charity, while serving the poor out of charity, should be open to the experience of passively finding Christ in the poor, Christ finding them, and joining them with himself as a sanctifying gift from God.[40]

The mystic and the missionary in their search for Christ each recognize the need for moral perfection. The scholar has something to

37. See *ST* q. III, a. 56, a. 3, ad 4, where St. Thomas speaks of Christ meriting for his members by his passion as though they themselves suffered that meritorious death.

38. "I must go—India is scorching, as is hell—but its souls are beautiful and precious because the Blood of Christ has bedewed them." Mother Teresa to Jesuit Fr. Franjo Jambrekovic, 1937, in Kolodiejchuk, *Come Be My Light*, 21.

39. "Mother Teresa grasped the depth of Jesus' identification with each sufferer and understood the mystical connection between the sufferings of Christ and the sufferings of the poor." Kolodiejchuk, *Come Be My Light*, 43. There are two quotes from Mother Teresa that further support that claim: "Jesus continues to live in his passion. He continues to fall, poor and hungry, just like he fell on the way to Calvary. Are we at his side to volunteer to help him? Do we walk next to him with our sacrifice, with our piece of bread—real bread—to help him get over his weakness?" "When we care for the sick and the needy, we are touching the body of the suffering Christ, and this touch makes us heroic; it helps us overcome the repugnance and the natural reaction that is in all of us. This eye of faith and love, to see Christ in the sick and serve him, sharing their suffering, everything." Mother Teresa, *Essential Writings*, 43.

40. It would be wrong to think that Mother Teresa and the Missionaries of Charity as a group do not have a deep love and concern for the poorest of the poor, or that they tend to see the poor as mere vehicles for union with Christ without their own eternal welfare. Carrying Christ to them, the poorest of the poor, and bringing them salvation and sanctification are what their mission is all about. See Kolodiejchuk, *Come Be My Light*, 43.

say about how that is done within the complex of human nature and practical living. Whether centering around temperance, fortitude, justice, humility, detachment, fraternal charity, or the beauty of completely giving oneself to those in most need as a merciful response to Christ's loving thirst for souls, the heart is purified for the vision of God.

8

MOTHER TERESA'S MYSTICISM AS A SOURCE
FOR THEOLOGICAL RENEWAL

~

Robert M. Garrity, JCL, SThD

St. Teresa of Calcutta (1910–97), though not often thought of as a theologian, nevertheless gives to the Church and to the world a distinctive and significant theology. She provides fresh insight into how the living God is powerfully present today. Twenty years after Mother Teresa's death and ten years after the 2007 publication of her private writings, her theological impact endures through what we can now identify as a *Christo-ecclesio-humano-centric mysticism*.[1] Teresa herself would humbly reject the notion that she provides for the Church anything as grandiose as a theological mysticism focused on Christ, his Church, and his people. Nonetheless, despite Mother's protestations from Heaven, the evidence clearly shows that she contributes mean-

1. Portions of this essay, permitted for publication here by the kindness of Lectio Publishing, LLC, were previously published in my *Mother Teresa's Mysticism: A Christo-Ecclesio-Humano-Centric Mysticism* (Hobe Sound, FL: Lectio, 2017).

ingfully to theological discourse. She does this by taking what is best from the Church's spiritual tradition and expanding that tradition in influential ways for the benefit of humanity today and in the future. A brief prefacing remark is in order here. In what follows, Mother Teresa's mystical journey toward union with God is viewed through the eyes and categories of the Church's Mystical Doctor, St. John of the Cross, who in turn relies on the teleological principles of St. Thomas Aquinas. God ordinarily draws souls to the Divine Union by way of successive *stages* of spiritual growth. The traditional stages of purgation, illumination, and union (*katharsis, photismos,* and *theosis,* to use the Greek from Origen in the third century and Pseudo-Dionysius in the fifth) provide us with a broad interpretive framework, but not a rigid roadmap, for understanding the mysticism of Mother Teresa and other spiritual writers. Mother Teresa lived the second half of her life, from roughly 1947 to 1997 (if not the first half as well), in the highest unitive way, by living a daily and heroic participation in the life of Jesus Christ, expressed in service-oriented faith, hope, and charity. She becomes, by God's gifts of faith and grace, a person who would "share in the divine nature" to an exceptional degree (2 Pt 1:4).

The fact that Mother Teresa also experienced deep spiritual darkness until her death does not imply that she was rigidly "stuck" on any penultimate level of spiritual immaturity. It simply means that, for reasons known to God alone, Mother Teresa was left until her earthly end with the remnants of what St. John of the Cross calls "the dark night of the soul." This is somewhat atypical, as most of the Church's approved mystics (excepting perhaps St. Paul of the Cross) go through the dark night for a while, then emerge with some sense of relief (as for St. Teresa of Avila, after a long "dry spell" in prayer). Yet this was not the case for Mother Teresa, whose suffering in a spiritual darkness remained until her death. St. Thérèse of Lisieux, in contrast to Mother Teresa, did receive shortly before her death some measure of a graced relief from painful temptations against the virtue of faith, even though she suffered terrible physical distress as her illness made it difficult for her to breathe. But Mother Teresa's experience took a slightly different turn, which is investigated here.

Six questions, along with a brief conclusion, are addressed in this essay regarding the significance, for the Church and for the world, of Mother Teresa's mystical theology, with regard to the Church and the world of the twenty-first century and beyond:

1. What is Mother Teresa's "place" or "location" within the Church's spiritual-theological tradition, particularly within the mystical framework of St. John of the Cross, the Church's most trusted Doctor in mystical matters?
2. In what sense (if any) is Mother Teresa a genuine "mystic," within the complete doctrine on mysticism, which the Church provides?
3. In what ways does Mother Teresa's theory and praxis contribute to the theological renewal of the Church?
4. What will be Mother Teresa's enduring impact to theological theory and pastoral practice?
5. Did Mother Teresa make any mistakes in her theology or in her pastoral practice?
6. How is Mother Teresa's theological and pastoral impact to be evaluated today?

WHAT IS MOTHER TERESA'S "PLACE" WITHIN THE SCIENCE OF SPIRITUAL THEOLOGY?

Mother Teresa routinely *receives* and *shares* an experiential knowledge of God's mysterious presence in the world, especially in the poor. This happens partly through Mother's reception, and handing on, of private revelations (which are important yet infinitely less central to

Christian life than public revelation in Scripture and tradition). That is, God gives important insights to Mother, and she hands them on to others. This is a basic part of her spiritual journey, as she receives and hands on to others her own experiential knowledge of Christ in the darkness and in the poor, in the manner of St. Paul: "For I received from the Lord what I also handed on to you"; that is, Paul "hands on" the central content of the Christian faith regarding the Eucharist and the Resurrection of Jesus Christ (cf. 1 Cor 11:23ff. and 15:3ff.).

In India between 1946 and 1950, Teresa first *receives* through non-binding private revelation an experiential knowledge of the mystery of God in Jesus Christ and in his poorest people; later, Teresa *shares* with others her experience. "Come be My light ... Carry Me with you into [the] ... dark unhappy homes [of the poor]," Teresa hears Jesus call to her, followed by a call from Our Lady, "Bring them to Jesus."[2] Secondarily, Teresa then *shares* with others, through generous service, her experiential knowledge of Christ in the poor. One could say that Mother Teresa's spirituality is reminiscent of the motto of the Dominicans: *Contemplare et contemplata aliis trader*, or "To contemplate and to hand onto others the fruits of one's contemplation." Mother Teresa contemplates Christ's presence in the poor and in the sacraments, and then shares with others the fruits of her contemplation.

This pattern of *receiving* and then *sharing* the love of Jesus Christ marks the entire spiritual theology of Mother Teresa. Hers is truly a Christo-ecclesio-humano-centric mysticism, that is, a heightened awareness of the mystery of God in Christ and in his Church and in his people, especially in the poor. In other words, Mother *discovers* the presence of God in several "places" both old and new, especially in Christ, who speaks to her and who is present in his Church's sacraments and who lives within his poorest people. And then Teresa glad-

---

2. Mother Teresa to Archbishop Perier, December 3, 1947, in Brian Kolodiejchuk, MC, ed., *Mother Teresa: Come Be My Light* (New York: Doubleday, 2007), 99–101.

ly *hands on* to others the fruits of her discovery. This sharing occurs through Mother's own self-giving love and through her empowering others to expand the practice of self-sacrificing charity on a daily basis.

Of Mother Teresa it must be said that she exhibits both a distinctive *theological theory* and a zealous *pastoral practice*. That is, Mother affirms God's presence in the poor through both thought and action. This integration of theory and practice places Mother in a position within and yet transcending a distinguished and long tradition of heroic servants of God and of human dignity. It is true that there have been quite a few noble souls in the past two millennia who have affirmed the presence of Ultimate Reality and of Jesus Christ in the poor and suffering. Included here in the Church's tradition are such iconic figures as SS. Elizabeth of Hungary and Vincent de Paul, to name just two of the great saints who saw and served Christ in the poor, not to mention St. Basil, who in the fourth century established for the poor one of the first hospitals in Western Civilization. St. Vincent de Paul, for example, like Mother Teresa herself, saw Christ in the poor street people of seventeenth-century Paris:

> Even though the poor are often rough and unrefined, we must not judge them from external appearances … On the contrary, if you consider the poor in the light of faith, then you will observe that they are taking the place of the Son of God who chose to be poor … We also ought to … imitate Christ's actions, that is, we must take care of the poor, console them, help them, support their cause … [Christ] went so far as to say that he would consider every deed which either helps or harms the poor as done for or against himself … So when you leave prayer to serve some poor person, remember that this very service is performed for God.[3]

3. St. Vincent de Paul, Epistle no. 2546, September 27, in *Liturgy of the Hours*, vol. 4, *Correspondence, entretiens, documents* (Paris: 1922–25), 7. See also James A. Wiseman, OSB, *Spirituality and Mysticism: A Global View* (Maryknoll, NY: Orbis Books, 2006), especially the section on "Asian Spirituality," 165–74.

In Mother Teresa's spiritual theology and humanitarian action, we find a new depth of meaning, fresh vigor, and unsurpassed impact toward the good, flowing in and from a long tradition in which Christ is affirmed as linked with the poor: "For I was hungry and you gave me food" (Mt 25:35). Yet Mother Teresa's words and deeds take our awareness a step further regarding the vision of Christ in his poor. This is because Mother's theology and praxis extend divine mercy and human kindness beyond all bounds of religion or race or culture or ethnicity or societal condition, as we can see by studying her life and writings.

And so Mother Teresa's "place" within the spiritual tradition is among the true giants who have selflessly served God and neighbor. Yet we must also be as precise as possible when considering in another sense Mother's "place" in the spiritual life, that is, her own personal level of progress toward union with God in this life. Therefore we now look at Mother Teresa's personal "location" or "position" in her individual spiritual development. We do this through the eyes of St. John of the Cross, the Church's Mystical Doctor and the most trusted theologian in the science of spiritual theology.

Suffice it to say that Mother Teresa obviously attains by God's grace an advanced state of abiding in a daily union with God in this life through the human virtues and through the theological virtues of faith, hope, and especially charity. Yet we cannot simplistically state that Mother attains *absolutely perfect* union with God in this life (since absolutely perfect union with God is reserved for heaven, even though Mother and the other great saints attain a *relatively perfect*, or relatively complete, union with God in this life through heroic faith, hope, and charity). Nor can we say that Mother in her later years was entirely exempt from the remnants of the spiritual darkness that St. John of the Cross attributes to the soul's being in "the dark night of the soul." The "dark night" is "an inflowing of God into the soul" and is the penultimate, but not the final, stage of a soul's spiritual transformation, causing pain because the soul is still so dull and the Light of God is so infinitely bright. Again, for reasons known only to God, God leaves some of the remnants of the "dark night" in Mother's later days on earth, even though she lives already in a consistent union with God.

This fact of Mother's continuing to suffer the negative effects of the dark night until her death belies the Mystical Doctor's general insight that an advanced soul will experience before death some degree of the "serene freedom" of union with God. For most good souls, there is some relief from the dark night, rather than an unremitting continuation of the "painful transformation" that marks the penultimate stage of spiritual development known as the dark night. Mother's experience of painful darkness lasted until her death, although Mother did abide for decades in the "serene freedom" of union with God, an experience that was lived out in Mother's unique way, in the midst of interior spiritual emptiness.[4]

Mother arrives at a point where she can say, "I have come to love the darkness" (indicating a high degree of her own unique and humble appropriation of the serene freedom of the unitive stage of personal transformation). Yet, still, her own description of the virtually unremitting loneliness and coldness in her heart runs somewhat counter-

4. See St. John of the Cross, *The Dark Night of the Soul* II, 5, 1, along with St. John's major works: *The Spiritual Canticle, The Ascent of Mount Carmel, The Dark Night of the Soul,* and *The Living Flame of Love.* Texts from Luciano Ruano, ed., *Vida y Obras de San Juan de la Cruz,* 10th ed. (Madrid: Biblioteca de Authores Christianos, 1978); translations from E. Allison Peers, *The Complete Works of Saint John of the Cross,* 3 vols. (Westminster, MD: Newman Press, 1945). The sequential order used here reflects the fact that St. John probably wrote *Spiritual Canticle* first, along with the fact that *Dark Night of the Soul* is actually the second part of *Ascent of Mount Carmel* but is often referred to as the third of St. John's four major works. See also my *Mother Teresa's Mysticism,* especially the section on the stages of spiritual growth, "Insights from St. John of the Cross," 35–48; see also my "Bernard of Clairvaux and John of the Cross: Divergent Views of Human Affectivity in Christian Spirituality," STD diss., Catholic University of America, 1990, especially the section on the stages of spiritual growth according to St. John of the Cross, 64–110.

intuitively to the description of the serene freedom of divine union as given by St. John of the Cross in his final work, *The Living Flame of Love*. Here St. John describes the deep peace and serenity of the advanced soul, as the Holy Spirit "breathes" within it, causing her to feel "disencumbered ... [and] peaceful," in the serene freedom of being "God by participation."[5] Mother Teresa never articulated at any length this kind of experience of lasting serene freedom, as far as we can tell, beyond her affirming that she came "to love the darkness"— that is, to accept darkness—and even to prefer it, as her pathway to a complete union with Christ.

Mother Teresa's union with God is of a unique kind, for her union with God remains an experience of darkness and loneliness until her death, which is atypical for most saints. Most saints who have gone through some measure of "the dark night of the soul" (excepting possibly St. Paul of the Cross) have at least some brief experience late in life of God "turning the lights back on" for them, so to speak. For example, St. Thérèse of Lisieux, the Little Flower, had some experience with the lifting of the spiritual darkness of temptations against faith shortly before she died, although her physical suffering remained. The Little Flower heard the "voice" of darkness and of temptation against faith saying that "death ... will give you ... the night of nothingness," yet, eventually, just a few weeks before death while stuck mostly in spiritual darkness, the Little Flower experienced "that at times a very small ray of the sun comes to illumine my darkness, and then the trial ceases for *an instant*."[6] But not so for Mother Teresa, who seems to have had virtually no relief in this life, beyond simply "com[ing] to

5. Mother Teresa to Father Neuner, April 11, 1961, in Kolodiejchuk, *Come Be My Light*, 214; see also St. John of the Cross, *Living Flame of Love* III, 34; prologue 3–4; I, 3; III, 8. The "flaming forth" of Divine Charity in service to the poorest was a consistent characteristic of Mother Teresa's life, indicating her advanced status in the spiritual life, as described by St. John of the Cross, although St. John places much less emphasis on love of neighbor and much more on love of God.

6. St. Thérèse of Lisieux, *Story of a Soul*, chap. 10, "The Trial of Faith," June 1897.

love the darkness" from the pain of unremitting spiritual suffering in interior darkness.

We are left with a paradox and a mystery, which should not surprise us, since we are exploring here precisely the *mysticism* of Mother Teresa. *Mystical* theology is centered on "the *mystery* hidden from ages past in God," namely, "the mystery of Christ" (see Eph 3:3–9, emphasis added). Mother Teresa would give to the Church and to all an intensified awareness of the mysterious presence of Christ in today's world, in the poorest of the poor. We must not be surprised that Mother Teresa's mystical vision of Christ in the poor will seem a bit mysterious or even confusing, since she both fits into the categories of mystical growth given in the writings of St. John of the Cross and yet bursts those categories to some degree.

We must ask the following question: For much of the second half of her life, from roughly 1947 to 1997, does Mother Teresa live precisely on the *cusp or borderline or intersection* between what St. John of the Cross describes as "the dark night of the soul" and "the transforming union with God"? The answer is, mysteriously enough, yes and no. Yes, Mother experiences many of the distressful aspects of the dark night, such as feeling abandoned by God, even as she lives in a daily union with God through heroic faith, hope, and charity. But no, it would be overly simplistic to state that Mother is later in life rigidly "stuck" between the dark night and "union with God." For this would make it sound as though Mother was not fully advanced in the spiritual life, whereas of course she was fully matured in her participation in God's life in her daily round, even though the remnants of the dark night persisted in her until she died. It is more accurate to state that Mother Teresa's later spiritual journey is compatible with St. John's analysis of the dark night leading into "the transformative union" with God. This is because Mother lives a consistent union with God while still maintaining the experiential remnants of the dark night, for reasons known to God alone.

Mother Teresa in the remnants of the dark night of her personal interior life is, subjectively speaking, according to the doctrine of St. John of the Cross, in the "place" where the soul "experiences great sweetness of peace and loving friendship with God" while simultaneously also feeling "useless" and that "God is against it": "There is no God in me … God does not want me … [Yet] I have come to love the darkness." And so, Mother's own words definitely place her, for much of her later life, in the remnants of the experiential place that the Mystical Doctor names as the dark night, that is, situated within the passive night of the spirit, a place of final spiritual purification. Yet, simultaneously, Mother also feels the effects of being in what St. John describes as the serene freedom of living in union with God: "disencumbered … peaceful … one living flame [with the Holy Spirit Who] sends out flames [of love, as the soul is now] … God by participation (*Dios por participacion*)." She loves Christ in the poor, as a clear sign that the Holy Spirit is "send[ing] out flames" of divine charity from within her.[7] Thus the most we can say here is that the distressing remnants of the dark night remain with Mother, even as the much deeper interior peace of God dwells in her as she receives the gift of the transformational union with God.

Is it possible to conclude that Mother Teresa in some sense "bursts" the theological categories of St. John of the Cross, and that this is why she is so difficult to "place" in terms of personal spiritual development? Perhaps. But it seems more likely that St. John of the

7. See *Dark Night of the Soul* II, 7, 4, and II, 5, 5. See also *Living Flame of Love* III, 34; prologue 3–4; I, 3; and III, 8. See also Mother Teresa to Fr. Neuner, April 11, 1961, and (probably) April 1961, in Kolodiejchuk, *Come Be My Light*, 210 and 214. It is primarily in the second part of *Dark Night of the Soul* and in the first part of *Living Flame of Love* that St. John describes the transition from "the dark night" to "the transforming union with God." St. John's description of the spiritual life at these advanced stages is eerily accurate when applied to Mother Teresa, who grows through the dark night and into union with God. In what follows, St. John of the Cross subdivides the classical "three ways" of the spiritual life (purgation, illumination, and union) into six smaller stages or substages (beginning in the love of God, active night of the senses, passive night of the senses, active night of the spirit, passive night of the spirit, and union with God).

Cross gets it generally right, and that his categories are accurate, and that Mother Teresa actually "fits" quite well into the Sanjuanist categories, properly understood and interpreted. Let me clarify.

St. John of the Cross uses the traditional framework of the "three ways" of the spiritual life to describe the soul's personal spiritual growth toward union with God: purgation, illumination, and union (*katharsis, photismos,* and *theosis*). Yet St. John distinguishes not just three but a total of six stages in the course of "ordinary" spiritual development (if such a thing exists) toward union with God, as follows:

- •**Stage one:** The beginning of the soul's turning toward authentic love for God (as described in St. John's first major work, *The Spiritual Canticle*), corresponding to the beginnings of purgation or cleansing from sins and imperfections.
- •**Stage two:** The active night of the senses, as described in the first part of *The Ascent of Mount Carmel*, corresponding to a process of perseverance in purgation, leading to illumination in Christ.
- •**Stage three:** The active night of the spirit, as described in the second part of *The Ascent*, corresponding to the ongoing process of deeper purgation, moving the soul toward greater enlightenment by Christ.
- •**Stage four:** The passive night of the senses, as described in the first part of *The Dark Night of the Soul*, corresponding to God's continuing to cleanse and to enlighten the soul by doing for the soul what the soul cannot do for herself.
- •**Stage five:** The passive night of the spirit, described in the second part of *The Dark Night* as a darkness that is actually "an inflowing of God into the soul," corresponding to God's leading the soul through intense darkness and suffering toward the serene union that will follow.[8]

8. *Dark Night of the Soul* II, 5, 1, on the dark night, which is "an inflowing of God into the soul."

•**Stage six:** The transforming union with God, as described in *The Living Flame of Love*, corresponding to an experience of serene freedom in which the soul feels God the Holy Spirit "breathing" within herself and causing and experience of being "disencumbered ... [and] peaceful," while "flames of love" burst outward toward God and/or neighbor.[9]

The process of "situating" Mother Teresa within the theological framework of St. John of the Cross suddenly becomes relatively straightforward and easy. Easy, that is, when we acknowledge that Mother Teresa finds herself simultaneously in "union with God" and yet unremittingly subject to the remnants of the difficulties and pains of the "dark night." Mother clearly witnesses the painful experience of being purified by darkness and suffering and pain (the dark night), and also the reality of being deeply conformed to God's will (the transforming union). Thus we can say, in the spiritual-theological terms of the Sanjuanist framework, that Mother Teresa lives for some fifty years in "union with God," all the while having to endure the painful remnants of the "dark night of the soul." But this is not all bad; in fact, it is supremely good, because as St. John says in a critically important statement:

> This dark night is an inflowing of God into the soul, which purges it from its ignorances and imperfections, habitual, natural and spiritual, and which is called by contemplatives infused contemplation, or mystical theology.[10]

In short, Mother Teresa initially receives from God several close communications in private revelation; then God gradually removes from

---

9. See St. John of the Cross, *Living Flame of Love*, prologue; III, 34; I, 3; and III, 8, on the experience of the Holy Spirit "breathing" within the advanced soul and "flaming forth" in charity toward God and neighbor.

10. *Dark Night of the Soul* II, 5, 1.

Mother virtually all of the delightful affective and emotional content of her faith; then Mother's spiritual life is marked by dry prayer, loneliness, and emptiness. This sounds somewhat like clinical depression, but it is not, as several studies show.[11] Rather, God during the second half of Mother Teresa's life is actually accomplishing through the dark night "an inflowing of God into the soul."[12] In effect, the supreme brightness of God's uncreated light is blinding Teresa spiritually, while accomplishing in her what might be called a purificatory and reparatory and preparatory perfection. Teresa is being prepared for a mission to change the world for the better, by seeing and serving Christ in the poor and enabling others to do the same.

IN WHAT WAY (IF ANY) IS MOTHER TERESA A "MYSTIC"?

As is well known, from 1946 to 1950, Mother Teresa in India received from God an interior awareness of Jesus Christ calling her

11. Studies disproving the possibility of Mother Teresa having suffered from clinical depression include Phyllis Zagano and C. Kevin Gillespie, "Embracing Darkness: A Theological and Psychological Case Study of Mother Teresa," *Spiritus: A Journal of Christian Spirituality* 10, no. 1 (Spring 2010): esp. 58; Louise Sundararajan and Chulmin Kim, "Spiritual Suffering from Medieval German Mysticism to Mother Teresa," *Humanist Psychologist* 42 (2014): esp. 172; S. Taylor Williams, "Illness Narrative, Depression, and Sainthood: An Analysis of the Writings of Mother Teresa," *Journal of Religion and Health* 53 (2014): esp. at 294; Susan Rakoczy, "What Does Mysticism Have to Do with Social Justice?," *Scriptura* 12 (2013): esp. at 11. Mother Teresa, since the possible murder of her father in her youth, may have struggled with some degree of what the American Psychological Association (APA) identified in 2013 as a disorder called a "Religious or Spiritual Problem," pertaining to those who have difficulty in matters of faith. See APA, *Diagnostic and Statistical Manual of Mental Disorders, V* (Washington, DC: APA, 2013). Blessed John Henry Newman drew the clear distinction between *difficulties* in faith and *doubt*: "A thousand difficulties do not make a single doubt." Mother Teresa had difficulties in faith, but no real doubt about the existence of God, whose existence, the Church acknowledges, "can be known with certainty from his works, by the natural light of human reason." See the *Catechism of the Catholic Church* (CCC) §47, referring to Vatican I, can. 2, 1.

12. *Dark Night of the Soul* II, 5, 1.

to serve and to love Christ in the poorest of the poor. Initially, this heightened awareness of Christ's presence in Mother's life comes to her primarily through internally experienced allocutions (spiritual moments of voice input) and through visions (spiritual moments of sight imagery). These "visions and voices," as Mother describes them, comprise a part of her mysticism, but only a relatively small part. For there is much more to Mother Teresa's mysticism than merely a few extraordinary spiritual experiences early in her life. The much more significant mystical awareness would unfold later, as Mother from roughly 1947 until her death in 1997 received by grace a realization that God is to be encountered in spiritual darkness and in interior suffering and in the poorest people, who are actually "Christ in the distressing disguise of the poor."[13]

Mother Teresa is a mystic, yes, but not in the sense in which most people understand mysticism. Mysticism, contrary to the common estimation, is not merely strange or bizarre or extraordinary spiritual experiences such as levitation or bilocation or clairvoyance, though these may rarely be part of the mystical experience. Rather, mysticism is a particular form of *knowledge* or *gnosis*. This is not the heretical kind of knowledge of the false *gnostics*, but rather the genuine *experiential knowledge* of the mystery of God in Jesus Christ, as St. Thomas Aquinas indicates. As Louis Bouyer points out, originally in Christian tradition "the word 'mystical' came to be applied to any *knowledge* of the divine realities [like Scripture and sacraments]," beyond merely "experienc[ing] more or less directly the feeling that this is indeed so."[14]

---

13. Mother Teresa to Father Van Exem, October 19, 1947, in Kolodiejchuk, *Come Be My Light*, 86. Over the years, Mother Teresa undoubtedly used many times the description of "Christ in the distressing disguise of the poor," but the phrase is quoted as having been written by Mother in a poem, undated, perhaps from the early years of the Missionaries of Charity; see Kathryn Spink, ed., *Mother Teresa: Life in the Spirit: Reflections, Meditations, and Prayers* (San Francisco: HarperCollins, 1983), 1; idem, *Mother Teresa: A Complete Authorized Biography* (San Francisco: HarperCollins, 1997).

14. Louis Bouyer, *The Spirituality of the New Testament and the Fathers*, vol. 1, *History*

The word "mysticism" comes from the New Testament Greek words *mysterion* and *mysticos*, referring to the mystery of God in Christ that was once secretly hidden but is now made public. St. Paul announces his desire to bring to the entire world "the mystery [that] was made known to me by revelation, ... the mystery of Christ, ... to bring to light [for all] what is the plan of the mystery hidden from ages past in God" (see Eph 3:3–9). Mother Teresa definitely has experiential *knowledge* of the mystery of God in Christ and in the poor. It is this *knowledge*—which in her flows from faith, Scripture, sacraments, and extraordinary spiritual experiences joining her to Christ's poor—*and love of Christ's presence, especially in the poor,* that make her a mystic. As the Church teaches in the *Catechism of the Catholic Church* §2014, it is an ever closer oneness with Christ in his sacramental "mysteries" that makes one's union with Christ "mystical" and enables one to participate in the "mystery of the Holy Trinity." Mother Teresa had that kind of "mystical union" with Christ, through sacramental graces lived out in knowledge and love and service.

There is a useful and threefold definition of who qualifies as a genuine mystic in Catholic tradition. And, of course, there can be some degree of mystical awareness in non-Christian traditions, though the Church affirms that the fullness of authentic mystical experience is closely linked with baptismal and Trinitarian faith, the renunciation of sin, and discipleship in the truth of Christ. The useful definition of a mystic is a person who (1) has experiential knowledge of the mystery

---

of Christian Spirituality, ed. Louis Bouyer et al. (New York: Seabury, 1960, 1963), 408, emphasis added. See also idem, *Mysterion: Du mystere a la mystique* (Paris: 1986), 348, quoted in Louis Dupre and James Wiseman, OSB, eds., *Light from Light: An Anthology of Christian Mysticism,* 2nd ed. (New York: Paulist Press, 2001), 415. See also Louis Dupre, "General Introduction," in *Light from Light,* 3 and 414–15; see also James Wiseman, "Mysticism," in *The New Dictionary of Catholic Spirituality* (Collegeville, MN: Liturgical Press, 1993), 681–92; also idem, *Spirituality and Mysticism: A Global View* (Maryknoll, NY: Orbis Books, 2006), 7–10. See on the special character of mystical knowledge as ordinarily being obscure Olivier Clement, *The Roots of Christian Mysticism: Texts from the Patristic Era with Commentary* (New York: New City Press, 1982, 1993), 27–30.

of God in Christ, (2) writes about the experience or communicates it to others, and (3) is approved by the Church.

Let us attempt to clarify what exactly is the "experiential knowledge" of God in Christ that makes one a genuine mystic. St. Thomas guides us when he quotes Pseudo-Dionysius in referring to a man named Hierotheos who "knew spiritual things by feeling [or suffering] them."[15] This kind of knowing, which includes intellectual knowledge and affective awareness, is what St. Thomas calls *experiential knowledge (cognitio ... affective seu experimentalis)*.[16] In other words, there is frequently within the mystic's encounter with God or with the absolute a heightened affective or emotional content. This affective content makes the mystic's knowledge more than merely intellectual knowledge; it is a felt knowledge as well. But authentic mystical knowledge is more than mere experience; it is compatible with intellectual rationality as well.[17] This experiential knowledge can be described as wisdom, sapiential knowledge, or knowledge of the journey. Aquinas goes on to state: "Knowledge of the truth [often

15. St. Thomas Aquinas, *Summa theologiae (ST)* IIa-IIae, q. 97, a. 2, ad 2; Ia, q. 64, a. 1. See also Marcelo del Nino Jesus, *El Tomismo de San Juan de la Cruz* (Burgos: Tipografia de "El Monte Carmelo," 1930); Reginald Garrigou-Lagrange, *The Three Ages of the Spiritual Life*, vol. 2 (St. Louis: B. Herder, 1948); William J. Wainwright, *Mysticism: A Study of Its Nature, Cognitive Value and Moral Implications* (Madison: University of Wisconsin Press, 1981), esp. 232.

16. Knowledge as "cognitio ... affective seu experimentalis"; see Jean-Pierre Torrell, *St. Thomas Aquinas*, vol. 2, *Spiritual Master*, trans. Robert Royal (Washington, DC: Catholic University of America Press, 2003, orig. 1996), 96. On a mystic as an ordinary Christian with intensified faith, see Karl Rahner, "Mystical Experience and Mystical Theology," *Theological Investigations* 17 (1981): 90–99, and "Everyday Mysticism" and "The Theology of Mysticism," in *The Practice of Faith: A Handbook of Contemporary Spirituality*, ed. Karl Lehmann and Albert Raffelt (New York: Crossroad, 1986, orig. 1982), 69–77. On affectivity in mysticism, see Charles A. Bernard, *Theologie Affective* (Paris: Les Editions du Cerf, 1984), and Jean Baruzi, *Saint Jean de la Croix et le Probleme de l'Experience Mystique*, 2 vols. (Paris: Librarie Felix Alcan, 1924); see also James A. Wiseman, OSB, "Mysticism," in *The New Dictionary of Catholic Spirituality* (Collegeville, MN: Liturgical Press, 1993), 681–92.

17. William James, *The Varieties of Religious Experiences* (New York: Random House, 1902), 370; see also Wainwright, *Mysticism*, 232.

includes a part that is] affective and produces love of God, and this is a gift of the Holy Spirit."[18]

And so a mystic, in the ancient and authentic sense of the term, is not merely someone who has extraordinary spiritual experience. Rather, a mystic is someone who by grace has experiential knowledge (a heightened awareness) of the mystery of God in Jesus Christ. In the case of Mother Teresa, her experiential knowledge lies especially in her knowledge of the presence of Jesus Christ in the poorest of the poor.

Mother Teresa's experiential knowledge of the presence of Christ in the poor becomes a profound and life-changing insight for Mother herself and for anyone who takes this insight seriously. Mother's knowledge of God in the poor shows that there is much more to Mother Teresa's mysticism than merely the extraordinary spiritual experiences from her early life around 1946 to 1950, when she has locutions and visions. Again, these extraordinary spiritual experiences are a significant part of her mysticism but not the entire story. For her mysticism is properly understood as her experiential knowledge of the presence of God in Christ and especially in Christ's poor. Yet simultaneous with Mother's growing awareness of the *presence* of Christ in the poor (her *kataphatic* awareness of God's presence in all things and in all people), is in Mother's personal interior life a growing awareness of the affective *absence* of Christ in her emotional life (her *apophatic* awareness of feeling God's absence from her own heart). In this latter sense, Mother becomes over the years a witness to God's presence even when God seems distant or absent. She gives to us a mystic's unique first-person account of learning to accept spiritual darkness. She writes in 1961:

18. St. Thomas Aquinas, ST Ia, q. 64, a. 1.

[I have] since [19]49 or 50 this terrible sense of loss—this untold darkness—this loneliness … There is no God in me … God does not want me … [Yet] I have come to love the darkness.[19]

One saint who helps us, again, in assessing what makes Mother Teresa a genuine mystic is St. Thérèse of Lisieux, the Little Flower. Thérèse never has any extraordinary spiritual experiences (in fact, she prayed not to have them). But late in life she does have temptations against faith and even an awareness of an evil presence that wants her to think that there will be nothingness and annihilation for her when she dies. Nevertheless, Thérèse perseveres against the darkness and shortly before dying receives "at times a very small ray of the sun that illumines my darkness, and then the trial ceases for *an instant*." Thérèse dies, relieved that God, to some degree, has dismissed the darkness for her. Thérèse of Lisieux is widely considered a mystic (but not so by Hans Urs von Balthasar) despite her lack of extraordinary spiritual experiences. So, again, extraordinary spiritual experiences are not necessary for one to be a mystic-saint. In this, the Little Flower is rather typical of most saints, who by grace conquer their interior darkness and die in some measure in the experience of the Light of Christ.

Not so with Mother Teresa. She lives for some fifty years in virtually unremitting spiritual darkness, and her years from 1950 until her death in 1997 are marked by an experience of God's affective absence (theodicy), rather than of God's presence (theophany). Why is there for Mother this unrelenting darkness, when for most saints (excepting perhaps St. Paul of the Cross) God eventually to some degree "turns the lights back on" near the time of death or even sooner, as when the Little Flower late in life was briefly relieved of temptations against faith, even as her physical sufferings continued? We can only surmise

19. Mother Teresa to Father Neuner, April 11, 1961, in Kolodiejchuk, *Come Be My Light*, 210 and 214.

that, in Mother Teresa's unique case, God is accomplishing in her a purificatory and reparatory and preparatory renewal. God is preparing Mother Teresa to be a distinctive leader in affirming Christ's presence in the poorest and in leading others to do the same through generous service on a daily basis.

It is safe to say that Mother Teresa makes a global impact on the awareness of millions of people regarding the dignity of the poor. This is true for many persons from diverse backgrounds, including Christian, Jewish, Muslim, Hindu, Buddhist, agnostic, secular humanist, and atheist. Mother Teresa enlists people from virtually every background imaginable in her cause of loving Christ in the poor, which includes loving the poor as naturally dignified human persons. Mother is to be understood as belonging to a long line of great saints and humanitarians like SS. Elizabeth of Hungary and Vincent de Paul and Gandhi, who saw and served Christ and/or ultimate reality in the poor. Yet Mother expands the spiritual tradition by reaching out to all in the name of Christ, without reference to religious or cultural backgrounds. It is Mother Teresa's experiential knowledge of Christ in the poor that enables her to have such a far-reaching and lasting impact for good.

MOTHER TERESA'S MYSTICISM AS A SOURCE FOR THEOLOGICAL RENEWAL

Mother Teresa's mysticism is identified here as a Christo-ecclesio-humano-centric mysticism, that is, a God-given knowledge of the presence of God in Christ and in the Church and in human persons, especially the poor. This mysticism is a source for theological renewal in the twenty-first century and beyond. This is because Mother's commitment to the truth of the dignity of the human person has a positive and informing impact on several branches of theology, beyond merely spiritual theology. Of course, Teresa is not a trained professional in systematic or dogmatic or moral or biblical or historical theology. Yet she is well read in the Catholic spiritual classics from Augustine to Aquinas to Alphonsus and beyond. Most of her theological knowledge comes to her as a gift from God, much in the way that, say, a St. Catherine of Siena or a St. Thérèse of Lisieux receives from God the gift of profound theological knowledge despite a lack of extensive formal theological training. Mother provides a significant contribution to contemporary theological discourse in numerous ways. We name just here a few, with a brief comment about each.

•*Christology (and soteriology and Mariology).* Mother Teresa relies on the traditional Chalcedonian theology of Christ's divine personhood saving us through the two natures in Christ, divine and human, as he was born of the Blessed Virgin Mary, who is a secondary mediator of salvation. Nothing new here. Yet Mother Teresa expands the traditional catechetically memorized Christology into what we might call *an experiential Christology.* Mother's is a Christology that flows not just from intellectual thought, as important as that is, but primarily from her deep, prayerful personal relationship with our Lord and our Lady, whom she hears and sees in private revelations concerning God's poor people: "Bring them to Jesus," says Mary; "I have asked you … to take care of them, to bring them to me," says Jesus.[20] Mother Teresa's experiential Christology refreshes contemporary theology with a clear reminder of the salvific importance of "bringing" souls to Jesus and Mary through prayer and service, witness and evangelization. From Mother's intense prayer life comes her real awareness of the presence of Christ in the poor:

20. Mother Teresa to Archbishop Perier, December 3, 1947, in Kolodiejchuk, *Come Be My Light*, 99.

"For I was hungry and you gave me food" (Mt 25:35). From Mother's experiential Christology comes her real awareness that Christ has an infinite "thirst" for souls (Jn 19:28).

•*Pneumatology.* If Mother Teresa's Christology is to be identified as *experiential*, then her pneumatology, her theology of the Holy Spirit, is to be described as *implicit*. This is because Mother *explicitly* says relatively little about God the Holy Spirit, who "helps us in our weakness ... [and] intercedes for the holy ones," as St. Paul says (Rom 8:26–27). The Holy Spirit is, for Mother, the uncreated and mysterious Third Person in the Triune God, the Love who salvifically draws souls to Christ and to the Father: the Holy Spirit who leads us "to all truth" (Jn 16:13). Nothing new here. A rough estimate of the number of explicit references to the Holy Spirit in Mother's writings is that her references to Christ outnumber her references to the Holy Spirit by approximately one hundred to one. Mother avoids the theological error of Christo-monism, for sure, yet we would like to hear more from Mother on the help of the Holy Spirit in the Church's mission and ministry. What Mother does say is excellent, especially on how she thinks and prays to do the work of the Lord: "Jesus Christ imparts to me his Spirit ... [to] work with him, by him and like him ... [And so I pray,] Give me light.—Send me thine own Spirit—which will teach me Thy own Will ... [Each of us must] Come to God as a child ... and say 'Come Holy Spirit, guide me, protect me, clear out my mind so I can pray.'"[21] But we would like to have from Mother a further sharing of her knowledge of the action of the Holy Spirit. This is precisely because Mother's theology of the Holy Spirit is so theologically and spiritually rich, and we want more.

21. Spink, *Mother Teresa*, 31; see also Mother Teresa to Father Van Exem, September 1946, in Kolodiejchuk, *Come Be My Light*, 98.

•*Anthropology.* The Christian anthropology—the philosophy and theology of the dignity of the human person—with which Mother Teresa communicates with the Church and with the world is based on the profound goodness of the human person created in the "image" of God (Gn 1:27). Nothing new here. Each human person exists in Christ and is sustained in being in Christ, for "in [Christ] were created all things … and in him all things hold together" (Col 1:16–17). From a simple awareness of the dignity of each person, Mother draws out from the traditional Christian anthropology several far-reaching and fresh implications, including insights on religious liberty. Mother feels intensely the need to defend human dignity in the face of the evils of oppression and poverty: "souls are dying for want of care—for want of love … God is calling me—unworthy and sinful that I am … to fight the devil and deprive him of the thousand little souls which he is destroying every day."[22] Mother had a profound awareness of the dignity of each human person, body and soul.

•*Ecclesiology.* Mother Teresa proceeds from the traditional self-understanding of the Church as the People of God, the Mystical Body of Christ, and the Temple of the Holy Spirit. The Church is a kind of "perfect society" in which, available for everyone, are all the means of salvation for the salvation of souls, which is the Church's proper mission. Nothing new here. The Church is the distinctive presence of Jesus Christ in the world, the communion of persons created by the unified community of the Trinity especially through Word and sacrament, and particularly through the Lord's presence in the Blessed Sacrament, as he remains with us "always, until the end of the age" (Mt 28:20). But Mother expands the Church's self-understanding by insisting that the Church must

---

22. Mother Teresa to Archbishop Perier, January 13, 1947, in Kolodiejchuk, *Come Be My Light*, 51.

always be a Church for the poor, a Church with a preferential
option for the poor, a Church whose members are always willing
to serve with mercy the poorest who are Christ in a "distressing
disguise." Mother explains: "God is not separate from the Church
as He is everywhere and in everything ... We are serving Christ.
In our house He is head of our family and makes all the decisions
... Who can outdo God is His generosity—if we poor human
beings give Him everything and surrender our whole being to His
service?—No—He is sure to stand by us, and with us, for everything in us will be His."[23] The Church, united with Christ, must
always be ready and willing to serve Christ in his poor.

•*Spirituality.* Mother Teresa's spirituality is not only *old* (emphasizing daily baptismal faith and renunciation and participation
in the life of Christ) but also *new* (focused on serving Christ in
each person we meet on a daily basis). Giving a smile or a cup of
cold water or a small act of service enables us to live such that
each person who meets us is meeting Christ. The utter simplicity
of Mother Teresa's spirituality is what makes it so profound and
accessible to virtually everyone. When asked how she cares for
so many poor people, Mother's famous answer was, in Bengali:
"Ek, ek, ek," one at a time, one by one by one.[24]

THE ENDURING IMPACT OF MOTHER TERESA'S
THOUGHT ON INTERRELIGIOUS DIALOGUE

Perhaps the most significant and enduring impact of Mother Teresa's theology and practice lies in the area of *interreligious dialogue,*

---

23. Mother Teresa as quoted in Lucinda Vardey, *Mother Teresa: A Simple Path* (New
York: Ballantine Books, 1995), 60; see also Mother Teresa to Father Van Exem, October 19, 1947, in Kolodiejchuk, *Come Be My Light*, 87.

24. "Ek, ek, ek" were Mother Teresa's words in Bengali for describing how she cared
for so many poor people: "One by one by one," or "One at a time."

because the Church and the world receive a powerful example, from Mother, in showing us a decades-long positive interaction with people from all faiths or from no faith. There is a deep theological significance to Mother's insistence on the necessity of religious liberty and interreligious dialogue. Mother's commitment to the fullness of the Catholic Faith as God's securest pathway for human salvation, combined with Mother's exemplary respect for non-Christian religious traditions, shows to the Church and to the world a way forward in dealing with interreligious religious tensions, as in today's Christian-Muslim situation.

The watershed moment for the Church's emphasis on interreligious dialogue occurs on October 28, 1965. This is when the Church promulgates at the Second Vatican Ecumenical Council the *Declaration on the Relationship of the Church to Non-Christian Religions*. Here the Church acknowledges its own God-given, irreplaceable role as the distinctive and surest (ordinary) means of salvation, and at the same time the Church affirms the value of respectful communication and interaction between Christians and persons from other religious traditions. There should always be a "sincere respect" for different religious traditions, which often "reflect a ray of that truth which enlightens all men." The saving effects of Christian baptism by water can also be received through a "Baptism of desire" by non-Christian persons who "seek God with a sincere heart, and, moved by grace, try in their actions to do his will as they know it through the dictates of their conscience."[25] Mother Teresa had a deep respect for all who seek the truth, since those who sincerely do so are implicitly seeking Christ, who is "the truth" (Jn 14:6).

Mother Teresa puts into practice the Church's new encouragement after 1965 toward the desirability and necessity of interreligious dia-

---

25. Second Vatican Ecumenical Council, "Declaration on the Church's Relation to Non-Christian Religions," *Nostra aetate* (NA), October 28, 1965, 2.2. See also *CCC* §2104; *NA* 2.2; see also *CCC* §2104; *Lumen Gentium* 16.

logue. Mother gives to us an outstanding model of how the Church, when at its best, relates to other religious traditions and how we can do the same through genuine respect. Mother lives for decades in charity and respect and understanding among persons from Hindu and Muslim and Sikh backgrounds, while also having positive interactions with persons from Jewish, Buddhist, agnostic, secular humanist, and atheist backgrounds, along with Protestant and Orthodox Christians.

But what exactly is *interreligious dialogue*, as properly understood in the Church? Interreligious dialogue is a positive striving for personal encounter and mutual understanding. The Church favors this kind of dialogue, and Mother Teresa's thought and example anticipates the Church's theology on dialogue in our own time. Today, Pope Francis encourages a mutually enriching encounter between Christians and non-Christians, especially among Jewish and Christian and Muslim persons, all of whom celebrate especially *the mercy of God*. The pope urges a dialogue based on mercy in his introductory message for the Year of Mercy in 2015–16:

> There is an aspect of mercy that goes beyond the confines of the Church. It relates to Judaism and Islam ... the pages of the Old Testament are steeped in mercy ... Among the privileged names that Islam attributes to the Creator are "Merciful and Kind" ... I trust that this Jubilee year celebrating the mercy of God will foster an encounter with these religions ... may it open us to even more fervent dialogue so that we might know and understand one another better; may it eliminate every from of closed-mindedness and disrespect, and drive out every form of violence and discrimination.[26]

Mother Teresa makes a significant contribution to the Church's understanding of authentic religious freedom and interreligious tolera-

---

26. Pope Francis, Bull of Induction for the Jubilee Year of Mercy (2015–16), *Misericordiae Vultus* 23.

tion. Obviously, the Church understands itself as having a God-given mission for the salvation of humanity: "Go, therefore, and make disciples of all nations, baptizing them in the name of the Father, and of the Son, and of the Holy Spirit" (Mt 28:19–20). The Church must never betray its own unique and God-given mission by falling into the serious error of syncretism or false irenicism in interacting with other spiritual traditions. But neither can the Church afford to disregard persons from other religious backgrounds. The way forward, as Mother shows us, is to reaffirm in our minds and hearts the indispensable treasure of the fullness of the Catholic Faith, while at the same time respecting the religious traditions of others who may (hopefully) or may not (sadly) yet find their way to the fullness of faith. Mother felt that "we should help a Hindu become a better Hindu, a Muslim become a better Muslim, a Catholic become a better Catholic." In a now-famous letter from Mother to Indian Prime Minister Morarji Desai in the wake of government threats against the Christian minority in India in 1978—a letter that is theologically "perfect," so to speak, in its affirmations and distinctions—Mother summarizes the Church's best stance regarding interreligious dialogue:

> Religion is … a matter of conscience. I alone must decide for myself and you for yourself, what we choose. For me the religion I live and use to worship God is the Catholic religion. For me this is my very life, … and so naturally I would wish to give [to others] the joy of possessing this treasure, but it is not mine to give, nor can anyone force it on anyone. So also no man, no law, no Government has the right to prevent me or force me, or any one, if I choose to embrace the religion that gives me peace, joy, love.[27]

---

27. Mother Teresa to Indian Prime Minister Morarji Desai, 1978, quoted in Spink, *Mother Teresa*, 156. Regarding each person becoming "a better" version of his or her own religious values, see also Mother Teresa, quoted in Vardey, *Mother Teresa*, 31.

Clearly, the Church places a high value on interreligious dialogue. Ironically, since Mother Teresa's death in 1997, the task of interreligious dialogue has become in a way more difficult yet more urgent and perhaps even more possible, especially with our Muslim brothers and sisters. In the aftermath of terrorist attacks against the United States and others since 2001, and with the rise of radical Islamic jihadist terrorist groups like al-Qaeda, Boko Haram, and ISIS (the Islamic State of Iraq and Syria), even as we pray and work and hope for greater mutual understanding, we Christians and other people of good will in the at least nominally Christian West and elsewhere must have proper security and protection against radical Islamic jihadism. Part of the challenge will be, as one enlightened Muslim author puts it, for authentic Islam to disentangle itself from its disingenuous violent minority.[28] This will demand prayer and, among other tasks, a careful study of the roots of the concept of jihad. For the term originally meant, at least for some in the Sufi Muslim tradition, an individual internal spiritual asceticism—an inner jihad—aimed at personal spiritual growth toward God by opposing one's own sinfulness, but certainly not exclusively an external war on other innocent persons with differing religious beliefs.[29]

The example of Mother Teresa in respectfully and charitably relating with persons from non-Christian backgrounds on a daily basis, including praying and serving the poor with them, gives to the Church an unsurpassed model that helps to show us the way forward in interreligious dialogue in the twenty-first century and beyond.

---

28. Shadi Hamid, *Islamic Exceptionalism: How the Struggle over Islam Is Reshaping the World* (New York: St. Martin's Press, 2016).

29. Michael A. Sells, trans. and ed., *Early Islamic Mysticism: Sufi, Qur'an, Mi'Raj, Poetic and Theological Writings*, Classics of Western Spirituality (New York: Paulist Press, 1996), 97–170; "Islam," in *The Concise Encyclopedia of Living Faiths*, ed. R. C. Zaehner (New York: Hawthorne Books, 1959), esp. regarding Sufism at 185–86 and 202–5.

DID MOTHER TERESA MAKE MISTAKES?

Many people often ask whether Mother Teresa made mistakes. The answer is yes, of course, she made a few mistakes, but not many. It is to be expected that any imperfect human being should make mistakes in starting a great enterprise in service to God and to humanity. But Mother made few mistakes—a few in Christian service—and virtually none in the realm of theology. Mother's clear and Christ-centered mission to the poorest, her irrepressible commitment to the truth, and her intentional generosity to the most vulnerable persons helped to prevent her from making serious errors. But there were a few minor mistakes.

A few critics note, mostly either incorrectly or in a petty way, that over the decades of Mother's life there were some imperfections in her and in the noble attempts by her Missionaries of Charity and their collaborators to practice self-giving charity every day. Of course—no reasonable person could expect otherwise. All these criticisms should be taken seriously, in order to prevent errors in the future among the Missionaries of Charity and their cooperators and those who wish to follow the sound example of Mother Teresa today. But even the worst allegations against Mother Teresa and her collaborators are rather minor. Here are some of the main critiques of Mother Teresa, with a brief response to each.

- There are allegations that some of the medical care given in Calcutta, India, was imperfect. In an imperfect world and in a poverty-stricken part of India, where medical care can sometimes be imperfect, these allegations are not surprising. It turns out upon further examination, however, that the medical care offered by Mother and by her cooperators was excellent by both local and international standards. At one point, there was an unconfirmed rumor that one of Mother's collaborators may have reused a medical syringe; if this rumor is true, then obviously such a mistake should be corrected immediately. Overall, the medical and hospice care provided by Mother Teresa and her associates has proven to be excellent and superior to local standards.[30]

•A critic noted that one or more of the postulants or novices who were considering joining the Missionaries of Charity sisters felt stifled creatively or intellectually.[31] The obvious response here is that no one is obliged to join the Missionaries of Charity, and those who explore joining and who are not yet under final vows are welcome to depart freely and amicably. Mother always wanted joyful sisters, and if a postulant was unhappy in the MC lifestyle, then Mother was consistently happy when a prospective sister found her joy elsewhere.

•Some have claimed that the finances of the Missionaries of Charity were at times insufficiently transparent for public scrutiny.[32] If the critics are suggesting that Mother Teresa and the Missionaries of Charity lived luxuriously from misappropriation of finances, then the critics had better look again. Any allegation of financial mismanagement is preposterous on its face, considering the simplicity and poverty of lifestyle that Mother Teresa and her co-religious have always lived by, worldwide. If Mother Teresa and her missionaries gave away a lot of time, talent, and treasure in serving the poorest people on earth, then this kind of humanitarian charity should be considered not as mismanagement but rather as exemplary action toward the good.

•It has been claimed that Mother Teresa was theologically rigid.

30. William Donahue, *Unmasking Mother Teresa's Critics* (Bedford, NH: Sophia Institute Press, 2016); Thomas C. Reeves, review of *Unmasking Mother Teresa's Critics*, by William Donahue, *Catalyst: Journal of the Catholic League for Religious and Civil Rights* (September 2016): 8–9.

31. See Anne Sebba, *Mother Teresa: Beyond the Image* (New York: Doubleday, 1997).

32. See "Criticism of Mother Teresa," *Wikipedia*, accessed February 20, 2016, https://en.wikipedia.org/wiki/Criticism_of_Mother_Teresa.

A better term would be *solidly rooted* in Christ and in Catholic
tradition. One can only hope that all religious orders would be
as solidly grounded in the perennially valid heritage of Catholic
philosophy and theology.

•It was alleged that Mother "imposed" Christian baptism on
persons from Hindu or Muslim backgrounds as they prepared
for death. Obviously, if such an imposition occurred, it ought
not to occur in the future, considering what we now know about
the Church's teaching on the capacity of a "Baptism of desire"
to bring the saving effects of the "Baptism of water" to persons
from non-Christian backgrounds. On the other hand, if a dying
person gives a positive indication of a desire for Christian baptism, then certainly it should be provided immediately, after a
brief catechesis.

Did Mother Teresa make any mistakes of a strictly *theological* nature? Yes, Mother made a few theological mistakes, perhaps three in
number, none of which is serious. Recalling that Mother was a kind
of *practical* and *mystical* theologian, but never a trained dogmatic or
moral theologian, there are a few areas in which her theological guidance toward others can legitimately be critiqued as being defective,
in addition to the shortcomings in her theology of the Holy Spirit, as
noted above.

1. Mother Teresa on one occasion cautioned the sisters that Jesus
   Christ was "rejected" by his Heavenly Father. Likewise, the
   sisters themselves were warned that they could be "rejected" if
   they failed to stay closely united with Christ in complete conformity to the will of God. This was, theologically, a spiritual
   hyperbole that came across as an unfortunate misstatement
   by Mother. In fact, Jesus was not "rejected" by his Heavenly
   Father; rather, the self-offering of Jesus was fully accepted by
   the Father in raising Jesus from the dead, as St. Paul teaches

us: "Because of this [the humble self-sacrifice of Jesus], God
raised him up and bestowed on him the name above every
name" (Phil 2). Mother Teresa sometimes appropriately used
spiritual hyperbole or exaggeration to make a point, but on this
one occasion, regarding Christ being "rejected" by his Father,
Mother goes a bit too far. The accurate theological concept of
what appears as a "rejection" on the cross is that the Father's
permissive will "allows" Jesus's human nature to experience
the human emotion of abandonment, so as to bring about an
infinitely greater good, namely, the salvation of us weak souls
who need to know that God is with us even when we feel most
abandoned. Nevertheless, we can certainly give Mother a "free
pass" on this, as she may simply have been having a bad day.
St. Augustine guides us toward a correct understanding of
the sense in which Jesus in his human nature on the cross uses
Psalm 22 ("My God, my God, why have you forsaken me?")
to express for the healing of humanity the anguish of feeling
abandoned by the living God, who is with us always in some
mysterious way:

> Here [in Christ on the cross], ... we are symbolized. What
> part of [Christ] hung on the cross if not the part he re-
> ceived from us? How could God the Father ever cast off and
> abandon his only Son, who is indeed one God with him? Yet
> Christ, nailing our weakness to the cross ... cried out with
> the very voice of our humanity: ... "why have you forsaken
> me?" The evening sacrifice is the passion of the Lord, ... the
> holocaust acceptable to God. In his resurrection he made
> this evening sacrifice a morning sacrifice ... [which] rises like
> incense from a holy altar.[33]

33. On Christ being "rejected" by his Father, see Mother Teresa, address to the Sisters of the Missionaries of Charity, April 1, 1981, in Kolodiejchuk, *Come Be My Light*,

2. Teresa in her early years makes a "private vow" to Jesus Christ: "I bound myself under pain of mortal sin not to refuse Him anything."[34] Again, this private vow must be understood as a case of spiritual exaggeration or hyperbole. Teresa's purpose was to motivate herself toward a complete commitment to serve Jesus in the poor; this well-intentioned purpose is noble and edifying. Yet, strictly speaking, one cannot "under pain of mortal sin" bind oneself to reject matters that are not mortally sinful. For example, Mother had a bit of a sweet tooth and enjoyed an occasional piece of candy. Suppose that part of her private vow "under pain of mortal sin" was that she would abstain from candy for the rest of her life; suppose further that in a moment of weakness she ate a piece of candy. Could this constitute a mortal sin? Clearly not, for a piece of candy can never be mortally sinful matter (and one must have grave matter and sufficient reflection and full consent of the will in order to commit a mortal sin). Again, Teresa's *intention* in using spiritual hyperbole in striving to refuse nothing to Jesus is a good and holy gesture. But strictly and theologically speaking, the gesture is not representative of the best of the Church's spiritual theology nor of the traditional teaching on what constitutes mortal sin. Most souls who seek union with Christ need not attempt to bind themselves "under pain of mortal sin" in matters that cannot constitute mortal sin. Spiritual direction should be sought if one is inclined toward ascetical hyperbole.

3. Mother Teresa's ability to attract souls to Christ and to serve his poor was exemplary and unparalleled. Nevertheless, it

---

250–51; as a corrective, see St. Augustine, *In Ps. 140*, 6, in *Liturgy of the Hours* II, Tuesday of the second week of Lent.

34. Mother Teresa to Father Neuner, April 11, 1961, in Kolodiejchuk, *Come Be My Light*, 210.

would be imprudent for most persons today to strive uncriti-
cally to follow Mother's example in, for example, the matter of
seeking an unrelenting "dark night of the soul" for fifty years.
Not everyone is called to this kind of trial or tribulation for fifty years. Most of us can hardly tolerate a "dark night" for fifty
seconds, much less fifty years. Theologically speaking, Teresa's
model of perseverance for decades through the remnants of the
"dark night" is exemplary, but it is not for everyone, nor should
it be sought at great length. The experience of the dark night is,
again, whether lengthy or short in duration, "an inflowing of
God into the soul," which will be given ordinarily, we might say,
to those whom God chooses to receive it.[35]

OVERALL THEOLOGICAL ASSESSMENT
OF MOTHER TERESA'S THOUGHT

Mother Teresa's mysticism—her experiential knowledge of the
mystery of God in Christ and especially in God's poorest people—
has had and will have a significant impact toward theological renewal
in the twenty-first century and beyond. Mother combines theology,
philosophy, spirituality, and service in an unmatched way. It is safe
to say that the freshness and gravity, the vitality and vigor of Mother
Teresa's thought and practice will positively influence many souls for
many years to come.

When evaluating the thought of any theologian, there remains
a paradoxical aspect that defies easy categorization, especially when
that theologian is a saint, and a mystic as well, as in the case of Mother Teresa. For here we are dealing with mystery, with a known unknown. We are pondering the unfathomable ways that the living and

---

35. St. John of the Cross, *Dark Night of the Soul* II, 5, 1.

transcendent God, made known to us through public revelation in Scripture and Tradition, also allows himself to be more fully understood through private revelation, as is seen in the thought of Mother Teresa, for she found God in darkness and in people.

And so, in assessing the theological thought of Mother Teresa, we are left with a paradox or, better, with a set of paradoxical mysteries, well worth investigating yet ultimately beyond our complete human comprehension. But we can, and should, attempt to unpack, to some degree, the mystery of Mother's mystical theology. Mother has extraordinary spiritual experiences, which she claims *did not* impact her life, yet in fact they *did*. Mother has an entirely *kataphatic* exterior awareness of God's presence in today's world (i.e., she finds God in all things and in all people and especially in God's poor), yet simultaneously her interior life is thoroughly *apophatic* in character regarding herself (i.e., she finds God removing from her virtually all the positive emotion of faith and presenting himself to her only beyond any attachment to persons, places, and things). Mother's external spiritual experience is based in the *theophany* of seeing God in others, yet her interior experience is grounded in the *theodicy* of feeling the affective absence of God's love.

The question must be asked: Was Mother Teresa a whiner and a complainer? Was she someone who in her private writings simply gives vent to commonplace human emotions, like the fear and loneliness and meaninglessness that most people experience at least some of the time? No, it would not be fair to identify Mother Teresa as a whiner or a complainer, but she does give to all of us the freedom to feel our negative emotions when God seems far away. In a way, she expresses *our* complaints toward God.

What we have from Mother Teresa's writings is a spiritual and theological treasure trove, a first-person account of "the dark night of the soul," absolutely unique and unequalled in the history of spiri-

tual theology. Even the great St. John of the Cross—aside from a rare
mention about imaginative visions of the Crucifix or about Mt. Carmel or a brief disclosure about the Holy Spirit "breathing" within his
soul—even the Mystical Doctor declined to describe his own personal
experience, if any, of the dark night. But he chose instead to speak of
the dark night in a detached and analytical manner.

It is the dimension of *personal disclosure* and *witness testimony* in
Mother Teresa's mystical theology (particularly regarding the presence of Christ in the "dark night" and in the "distressing disguise of
the poor") that gives to us in Teresa's writings something special, moving, and insightful. Mother Teresa gives us not only *general knowledge
of the journey*—that is, *wisdom*, like that in St. Augustine's honest narrative of the process of his own conversion in the *Confessions*—Lord,
"you touched me, and I burned for your peace."[36] But there is even
more. Mother Teresa gives us also a *specific understanding*, like that in
Blessed Julian's commentary on her *Revelations of Divine Love*, about
how on May 8, 1373, a life-changing insight into God's unconquerable
love came to her: "Jesus ... answered, 'Sin was necessary—but it is all
going to be all right; it is all going to be all right; everything is going
to be all right.'"[37]

Mother Teresa in her private writings maintains a distinctive focus on the experience of the remnants of an unrelenting dark night,
which is "an inflowing of God into the soul," as St. John of the Cross
reminds us.[38] Mother Teresa's personal explication of the subjective
dimensions of the remnants of the dark night—especially her explanation of how it *feels* to experience its remnants—is unsurpassed in

---

36. St. Augustine, *Confessions* 10.27, in Mary T. Clark, trans., *Augustine of Hippo:
Selected Writings*, Classics of Western Spirituality (New York: Paulist Press, 1984), 144.

37. Blessed Julian of Norwich, *Revelations of Divine Love*, trans. Clifton Wolters
(New York: Penguin Books, 1966, 1986), chap. 27, 103.

38. St. John of the Cross, *Dark Night of the Soul* II, 5, 1. For the experience of the
"breathing" and charitable action of the Holy Spirit within the soul of the advanced
spiritual person, see *Living Flame of Love*, prologue; III, 8 and 31; I, 3.

spiritual theology, a kind of existentialist witness account of someone tempted toward atheism who never gives in to the temptation. We also have in Mother Teresa an unparalleled affirmation of the dignity of every human person, in whom dwells the presence of Jesus Christ, especially in the poorest, who share in Christ's poverty.

In summary, what we have in Mother Teresa is a mystical theologian of the highest order. She is a witness to God's presence, especially in the poor, when God seems far away. Mother puts her theological theory into pastoral practice, for God is to be found in the poorest of his people. We are grateful for her witness. Currently there are four women Doctors of the Church: SS. Hildegard of Bingen, Catherine of Siena, Teresa of Avila, and Thérèse of Lisieux. Let us not be surprised if a new female saint joins the ranks of the Doctors of the Church in the not too distant future: St. Teresa of Calcutta.[39]

39. We need not be surprised if both St. Teresa of Calcutta and St. Teresa Benedicta of the Cross (Edith Stein) become Doctors of the Church.

9

THE DARK NIGHT OF MOTHER TERESA,
THE THREE AGES OF THE SPIRITUAL LIFE,
AND THE WITNESS OF THE MYSTICS

~

Taylor Patrick O'Neill

During her life, Mother Teresa was considered something of an enigma. The world had been familiar with large-scale humanitarian work before, but there was something different about this small Albanian nun. Unlike the pop spectacles of George Harrison's Concert for Bangladesh in the 1960s or the 1985 Live Aid Concert in Wembley Stadium, which brought together hordes of beloved celebrities and musicians, this barely five-foot-tall founder of a religious order shunned the spotlight (which eventually found her). Her humility and simple devotion to the sick and the poor were grounded not in a secular humanism but in a profound love for Jesus Christ. Her uncomplicated and childlike faith provided an alluring juxtaposition to so much of the doubt and turmoil that plagued the Western world throughout the latter half of the twentieth century. For believers and unbelievers alike, Mother Teresa was revered as a genuine Christian.

But so much of that popular image of Mother changed in 2007 when her personal letters and diaries were published, revealing an immense pain and spiritual struggle that she hid throughout her years serving the poor in India. "I understand a little the tortures of hell— without God,"[1] she wrote. "Pray for me—for within me everything is icy cold.—It is only that blind faith that carries me through for in reality to me all is darkness."[2]

The mainstream media could make little sense of these words without assuming that Mother Teresa had been a counterfeit Christian. She was not really the almost transcendently holy saint of Calcutta. She was riddled with doubt like the rest of modernity, unbelieving and crippled with nihilistic despair. The Guardian published an opinion piece questioning whether Mother Teresa was really an atheist, stating that in her letters she sounded like "an adolescent [Richard] Dawkins."[3] Christopher Hitchens, a longtime detractor of Mother Teresa, wrote, "She was no more exempt from the realization that religion is a human fabrication than any other person, and that her attempted cure was more and more professions of faith could only have deepened the pit that she had dug for herself."[4] Even Jesuit priest Fr. James Martin said in an op-ed for the New York Times, "in its relentless and even obsessive questioning, her life intersects with that of the modern atheist and agnostic."[5] And yet these revelations about Mother's life did not seem to trouble the Catholic Church, which

1. Mother Teresa to Archbishop Périer, September 12, 1957, in Brian Kolodiejchuk, MC, ed., Mother Teresa: Come Be My Light (New York: Doubleday, 2007), 172;
2. Mother Teresa to Archbishop Périer, December 15, 1955, in Kolodiejchuk, Come Be My Light, 163.
3. Andrew Brown, "Was Mother Teresa an Atheist?," Guardian News and Media, August 24, 2007, https://www.theguardian.com/commentisfree/2007/aug/24/wasmotherteresaanatheist.
4. David Van Biema, "Mother Teresa's Crisis of Faith," Time, August 23, 2007, http://time.com/4126238/mother-teresas-crisis-of-faith/.
5. James Martin, "A Saint's Dark Night," New York Times, August 28, 2007, http://www.nytimes.com/2007/08/29/opinion/29martin.html.

moved ahead with Mother Teresa's canonization process. The same *Guardian* article that questioned whether Mother was an atheist stated in an almost dumbfounded fashion, "Even so, only the most hardened atheists will not be shocked by the ease with which the Catholic church has assimilated the news that its most famous saint thought of herself as a hypocrite when she talked about the love of God." Of course, what was lost on the media was an understanding of the spiritual life and the phenomenon of the dark night of the soul, which the Church has studied in the mystics for centuries.

THE THREE AGES AND THE WITNESS OF THE MYSTICS

There are few minds in the history of the Church who have understood the spiritual life like Dominican theologian Reginald Garrigou-Lagrange, one of the most important Catholic and Thomistic scholars of the twentieth century. Fr. Garrigou held the first ever chair in ascetical and mystical theology in the history of the Church, a position he received with the encouragement of Pope Benedict XV.[6] Garrigou has been lauded for his work on the three stages of the spiritual life, an in-depth study and contemplation of God's interior work on the lives of those who are moved toward holiness. Inspired by the lives of the mystics such as St. John of the Cross, St. John Vianney, St. Teresa of Avila, and others, Garrigou's work sought to synthesize the teachings of St. Thomas Aquinas with the spiritual patterns recognized throughout the lives of the saints of history.

While it is beyond the scope of this essay to take a comprehensive

---

6. Richard Peddicord, OP, *The Sacred Monster of Thomism: An Introduction to the Life and Legacy of Reginald Garrigou-Lagrange, O.P.* (South Bend, IN: St. Augustine's Press, 2005), 16: "In 1917 the Angelicum established—with the encouragement and support of Pope Benedict XV—the first chair of ascetical-mystical theology in the Church's history. Garrigou-Lagrange was from the beginning its intended recipient."

look at the three stages of the spiritual life elucidated by Garrigou, a brief word should be said about each. The beginning of grace is the first stage wherein the Christian is a novice to the spiritual life, struggling continually with his passions. It is often difficult to stay away from grave sin because the soul retains a strong affinity for lower goods. Next follows the illuminative way, a stage for those proficient in the spiritual life. The soul in the illuminative way has made, with the help of God, significant progress in subjecting his passions to reason. As such, the proficient soul is not easily tempted into mortal sin but still struggles on a daily basis with lesser temptations, often those linked with pride over one's spiritual progress and blessings. In order for the root of all selfishness to be stamped out, God must purge the soul of its last and most deep-seated defects. The soul must learn to abandon itself entirely to God, dying to itself such that only God remains to animate the soul.[7]

This transition between the illuminative way of the proficient and the third stage of the spiritual life, the unitive way of the perfected, is the most difficult and arduous moment of the spiritual life, the last and most painful tempering in the fire. This final purification is described as a dark night of the soul owing to the sudden absence of all spiritual joys and consolations. For the soul to die and live anew completely in Christ, it must love Christ entirely for himself and not for any other external or self-centered reasons. Garrigou-Lagrange describes this dark night as a *passive purification of the spirit*.[8]

Why is a passive purification of the spirit needed before entering into perfect union with God, the final stage of the spiritual life? Garrigou reminds us of the Gospel of John wherein our Lord states

---

7. See Reginald Garrigou-Lagrange, OP, *The Three Ages of the Interior Life: Prelude of Eternal Life*, vols. 1and 2, trans. Sister M. Timothea Doyle, OP (St. Louis, MO: B. Herder, 1948), and idem, *The Three Conversions in the Spiritual Life* (Charlotte, NC: TAN Books, 2015).

8. Garrigou, *The Three Ages*, 367–421 (chaps. 35–39).

that the Father will prune and purge the vine so as to make sure that it brings forth abundant fruit.[9] In his commentary on this passage, St. Thomas says:

> Considering the literal sense, we see that a natural vine with branches that have many shoots bears less fruit, because the sap is spread out through all the shoots. Thus the farmer prunes away the extra shoots so that the vine can bear more fruit. It is the same with us. For if we are well-disposed and united to God, yet scatter our love over many things, our virtue becomes weak and we become less able to do good. This is why God, in order that we may bear fruit, will frequently remove such obstacles and prune us by sending troubles and temptations, which make us stronger. Accordingly, he says, he prunes, even though one may be clean, for in this life no one is so clean that he does not need to be cleansed more and more.[10]

Even one who is proficient in the spiritual life is still scattered in their focus and love. Only by pruning away all affection that exists outside of or detracts from a singular love of God can we be made perfect.

We might be tempted to think that such pruning is unnecessary for those who are so advanced in the spiritual life, but St. John of the Cross remarks that there are many imperfections and serious temptations that face the proficients of the illuminative way, including pride and distraction by lesser goods.[11] Although these proficients are con-

---

9. Jn 15:1–7.

10. St. Thomas Aquinas, *Commentary on the Gospel of John*, Lectio 1, §1985: "Ad litteram enim in vite naturali contingit quod palmes multos surculos habens, minus fructificat propter humoris diffusionem ad omnes, et ideo cultores, ut magis fructificet, purgant eum a superfluis surculis. Ita est in homine. Nam homo bene dispositus et Deo coniunctus, si suum affectum ad diversa inclinet, virtus eius minoratur, et magis inefficax fit ad bene operandum. Et inde est quod Deus, ut bene fructificet, frequenter praescindit huiusmodi impedimenta et purgat, immittens tribulationes et tentationes, quibus fortior fiat ad operandum. Et ideo dicit purgabit eum, etiamsi purus existat: quia nullus est adeo purus in hac vita ut non sit magis magisque purgandus."

11. St. John of the Cross, *The Dark Knight of the Soul*, book II, chap. 2.

siderably nearer to their end of unity with God, this does not mean that things become easier. On the contrary, Garrigou states, "Evidently there are greater dangers than those at the beginning."[12] The roots of selfish love are the most deep seated and embedded, and thus they are the hardest to remove.

This is the purging fire that eliminates all final impurities of the soul that stand in the way of its ability to negate itself and live entirely in God. Only in this attitude of self-abandonment can the soul be admitted into the beatific vision after death. The passive purification of the dark night is thus the same process of purification that is found in purgatory. It is essentially the undergoing of purgatory on earth.[13]

These passive purifications are experienced as a darkness because the soul is being brought closer and closer to God. The illumination and brilliance of the divine light are exceedingly high above the previously held metaphorical or sense-based conceptions of God. The luminosity is too bright. It obscures the intellect, forcing it to see according to divine rather than human vision.[14] It also reveals to the soul

12. Garrigou, *The Three Ages*, 2:359.

13. Garrigou, *The Three Ages*, 2:320–21: "These passive purifications of a mystical order are thus in the normal way of sanctity and dispense from purgatory those who undergo them generously; they are a purgatory before death in which the soul merits and makes progress, whereas in the other purgatory the soul no longer merits." See also 377–78: "This salutary crisis is a purgatory before death, in which the soul is purified under the influence, not of a sensible fire, but of the spiritual fire of contemplation and love. 'And thus,' says St. John of the Cross, 'the soul which passes through this state in the present life, and is perfectly purified, either enters not into purgatory, or is detained there but a moment, for one hour here is of greater moment than many there' [*The Dark Night*, book II, chap. 6]. The reason is that on earth man is purified while meriting and growing greatly at times in charity, whereas after death he is purified without meriting. And as purgatory is a penalty and every penalty presupposes a sin that could have been avoided, the normal way of sanctity is to undergo the passive purifications of which we are speaking before death and not after death. In reality, however, rare are they who go immediately from earth to heaven, without passing through purgatory. The true order of Christian life is fully realized only in the saints." See also 388–89.

14. Garrigou, *The Three Ages*, 2:385–86. Garrigou also employs an useful example to help us make sense of this mystery. "In nature, when the sun goes down and night falls, we no longer see the objects surrounding us, but we do see distant objects not visible during the day, such as stars, which are thousands of leagues away. And the sun must

its imperfections. The deep-seated habits of self-love are purged only painfully.[15] The charitable soul's increasing awareness of the great chasm between its deficient creaturely state and the splendor of God is a source of tremendous suffering. These souls now develop a great fear of falling to temptation, lest they recede even further from God.[16] The necessary response to this passive purification is a dying to self, a loving acceptance and total surrender to God.[17] Garrigou remarks that with greater intensity and greater acceptance comes faster completion of the dark night, as the soul abandons itself entirely to God's will.

REPARATIVE SUFFERING BORN OUT OF PASSIVE PURIFICATION

Suffering may be prolonged even beyond the necessary personal purification of the soul. Some souls may continue to suffer—not for themselves, but for others.[18] Garrigou says:

> The lives of some great servants of God especially dedicated to reparation, to immolation for the salvation of souls or to the apostolate by interior suffering, make one think, however, of a prolongation of the night of the spirit even after their entrance into the transforming union. In such cases, this trial would no longer be chiefly purificatory; it would be above all reparative.[19]

---

hide that we may see them, that we may be able to glimpse the depths of the firmament. Analogously, during the night of the spirit we see much farther than during the luminous period preceding it; these inferior lights must be taken away from us in order that we may begin to see the heights of the spiritual firmament" (2:389).

15. Garrigou, The Three Ages, 2:386–87.

16. Garrigou, The Three Ages, 2:387–88.

17. Garrigou, The Three Ages, 2:392: "these souls should accept this trial generously for as long a time as, according to the good pleasure of God, it may last, and they should live in abandonment to the divine will."

18. Garrigou, The Three Ages, 2:392: "If it [the dark night] is more intense, it will generally be shorter (like the purification of purgatory) unless the soul is to suffer specially for sinners, over and above its personal purification."

19. Garrigou, The Three Ages, 2:503.

Although spiritual suffering may begin as a personal purification, it may transition (once that purification is complete) to a reparative suffering for others. Suffering can be utilized by those who are no longer (or who never were) in need of purification. There was no need for purification in the lives of Jesus Christ or his Mother. Nevertheless, we know that both suffered tremendously.

Also, while many of the dark nights experienced by the mystics last for hours, days, or weeks, some saints suffer for long periods of time, perhaps over years and up to their time of death, such as was the case with St. John of the Cross, St. Teresa of Ávila, St. Paul of the Cross, and St. John Vianney.[20] This seems to be especially true for saints who work for great spiritual causes. Garrigou gives as examples of great spiritual causes the foundation of a religious order or the salvation of many other souls.[21] Fr. Garrigou could not have anticipated the great life of St. Teresa and her spiritual causes any better, tasked with starting the Missionaries of Charity and helping the poor souls in Calcutta and throughout the world. Garrigou calls these souls who continue to suffer after their own passive purification has ceased "spiritual life-savers," who, "like St. Paul of the Cross, struggle not only for hours and months, but sometimes for years in order to snatch souls from eternal death."[22]

THE DARK NIGHT OF ST. TERESA OF CALCUTTA

Though it is impossible for us to know the details of the interior life of St. Teresa, it certainly seems as though her passive purification gave way to a night of reparation for souls. After learning to surrender herself entirely to God, to love the darkness, she continues to walk in that darkness to share in Christ's efficacious Passion out of love for mankind.

20. Garrigou, *The Three Ages*, 2:504.
21. Garrigou, *The Three Ages*, 2:504.
22. Garrigou, *The Three Ages*, 2:509.

Mother Teresa's dark night seemed to begin as soon as she undertook her work in Calcutta.[23] Although she did not reveal her state to many, she did mention it from time to time in correspondence with her superior, Archbishop Ferdinand Périer. Archbishop Périer had become Mother Teresa's de facto spiritual director. In 1956, Mother Teresa wrote to the archbishop, "I am not writing to you as to His Grace—but to the father of my soul—for to you & from you I have not kept hidden anything. Tell me what your child should do."[24] Périer seemed to believe that Mother Teresa was suffering the dark night of passive purification of the soul. He writes, "In what you reveal there is nothing which is not known in the mystical life."[25] In another letter sent several months later, Périer says:

> With regard to the feeling of loneliness, of abandonment, of not being wanted, of darkness of the soul, it is a state well known by spiritual writers and directors of conscience. This is willed by God in order to attach us to Him alone, an antidote to our external activities, and also, like any temptation, a way of keeping us humble in the midst of applauses, publicity, praises, appreciation, etc. and success.[26]

Several years later, Mother revealed her spiritual state in a long letter to Fr. John Neuner. He later said of her desolation:

---

23. Mother Teresa to Archbishop Périer, March 18, 1953, in Kolodiejchuk, *Come Be My Light*, 214: "Your Grace, ... Please pray specially for me that I may not spoil His work and that Our Lord may show Himself—for there is such terrible darkness within me, as if everything was dead. It has been like this more or less from the time I started 'the work.'"

24. Mother Teresa to Archbishop Périer, February 8, 1956, in Kolodiejchuk, *Come Be My Light*, 214.

25. Archbishop Périer to Mother Teresa, February 9, 1956, in Kolodiejchuk, *Come Be My Light*, 164.

26. Archbishop Périer to Mother Teresa, July 29, 1956, in Kolodiejchuk, *Come Be My Light*, 167.

My answer to the confession of these pages was simple: there was no indication of any serious failure on her part which could explain the spiritual dryness. It was simply the dark night of which all masters of spiritual life know—though I never found it so deeply, and for so many years as in her.... The sure sign of God's hidden presence in this darkness is the thirst for God, the craving for at last a ray of His light. No one can long for God unless God is present in his/her heart. Thus the only response to this trial is the total surrender to God and the acceptance of the darkness in union with Jesus.[27]

And surrender to God Mother did. In 1961, after Fr. Neuner's astute and perceptive response to her descriptions of her suffering, Mother Teresa seemed to make a breakthrough.

For the first time in this 11 years—I have come to love the dark-ness.—For I believe now that it is a part, a very, very small part of Jesus' darkness & pain on earth. You have taught me to accept it as a "spiritual side of your work" as you wrote.—Today really I felt a deep joy—that Jesus can't go anymore through the agony—but that He wants to go through it in me.—More than ever I surrender my-self to Him.—Yes—more than ever I will be at His disposal.... The help you have given me will carry me for a long time."[28]

For the first time since the darkness began, St. Teresa seems to find some solace and peace in it. She recognizes fully that it is a good, and this invigorates her self-surrender. It is a great consolation to her to know that she is sharing in Christ's agony; she is an instrument of his Passion and its efficacy for the salvation of souls. She has come to *love the darkness.*

Given these words, there can be no doubt that Mother Teresa's night of passive purification had given way to a night of reparation for

27. Testimony of Father Neuner, in Kolodiejchuk, *Come Be My Light*, 214.
28. Mother Teresa to Father Neuner, probably around April 11, 1961, in Kolo-diejchuk, *Come Be My Light*, 214–15.

other souls. It is, of course, unclear when such a shift may have happened. While it is possible that the aforementioned moment in correspondence with Fr. Neuner was the decisive one, it is also possible that this was simply an explicit embrace of a reparative suffering that she had been enduring for some time. Perhaps this new embrace of the darkness signals the final hurdle before the perfection of the unitive way. Or, perhaps, Mother had moved into total union with God many years earlier, perhaps even shortly after the dark night began for her in 1947. Whichever the case may be, like St. Paul of the Cross and many mystics before her, her suffering had been prolonged indefinitely as a sacrifice to her new mission and the souls that her missionary work sustained. After being purified so as to become one with Christ, she spent the rest of her life suffering for others, just as Christ had done.

Fr. Kolodiejchuk seems to imply that Mother's dark night had been reparative from an early point, likely around 1947 or perhaps even slightly earlier. He says:

> Thanks to Father Neuner, Mother Teresa's understanding of her interior condition deepened considerably: she came to realize that her darkness was the spiritual side of her work, a sharing in Christ's redemptive suffering. Regardless of how she had understood it, this trial of faith, hope, and love was not a purification from the defects characteristic of beginners in the spiritual life or even from those defects common to those advanced on the path of union with God. At the time of the inspiration [to start the Society, in 1947], she had frankly stated to Archbishop Périer that she had "not been seeking self for sometime now." Moreover, in the months prior to the inspiration of September 10, she was, in the estimation of her confessor, near the state of ecstasy.[29]

---

29. Kolodiejchuk, *Come Be My Light*, 215–16.

It is impossible for us to know simply by reading St. Teresa's words when she began her night of reparation. My assertion here—namely, that Mother moved from a night of purification to a night of reparation at some point—is an important one. The mystical tradition as described by Garrigou speaks of the night of reparation as being born out of the night of purification. It is not until one enters into the unitive way that one suffers with Christ for others. Garrigou states that "all St. Thomas concedes is that a saint transported by love for Christ's honor and the salvation of his brethren, can desire, should Christ's honor and the salvation of souls require it, *to be deprived of the joy of divine union.*"[30] Thus the special reparative suffering that St. Teresa asked to undergo involves a full emptying of satisfaction of the union to which one has been elevated by God. As such, the dark night of reparative suffering is a freely chosen exclusion from the joys of this union. Such an exclusion of its joys must, of course, presuppose that the unitive source of the joys has been accomplished in the soul.

Anyone in any stage of the life of grace may offer up smaller or larger pains for others, but the reparative darkness of which Garrigou and the mystics have spoken is a special, extensive embrace of Christ's Passion for the sake of others.[31] It implies both (1) a unity with Christ that is not hindered by the defects retained by the proficients of the illuminative way and (2) a freely chosen forfeiture of the spiritual consolations born out of the unitive way. In regard to the former characteristic, Garrigou states:

> When this trial is chiefly reparatory, when it has principally for its end to make *the already purified soul* work for the salvation of its

30. Reginald Garrigou-Lagrange, OP, *The Love of God and the Cross of Jesus*, vol. 1, trans. Sister Jeanne Marie (St. Louis, MO: B. Herder, 1947), 124. Emphasis is mine.

31. Garrigou, *The Three Ages*, 2:509: "Reparative souls are *intimately* associated with our Savior's sorrowful life; in them St. Paul's works are fully realized: 'Heirs indeed of God, and joint heirs with Christ; yet so, if we suffer with Him, that we may be also glorified with Him' [Rom 8:17]."

neighbor, then it preserves the same lofty characteristics just described [in passive purification], but takes on an additional character more reminiscent of the intimate sufferings of Jesus and Mary, who did not need to be purified.[32]

The reparative dark night presupposes that the soul is already purified, that is, in union with God.

In regard to the latter characteristic of the reparative dark night—namely, that it is freely chosen—Garrigou says, "Our Lord invites such souls to choose quite freely; but, as if powerless to resist, they abandon joy and choose suffering with all its darkness, so that light, sanctity, and salvation may be given to others."[33]

We can see this working in the life of St. Teresa, who explicitly desires to suffer for souls. She freely chooses to forgo consolation in order to suffer efficaciously for others. "I want to become a real slave of Our Lady—to drink only from His chalice of pain and to give Mother Church real saints."[34] Moreover, based upon the copious personal evidence that we have regarding her interior life, Mother Teresa did not seem to experience a dark night earlier in her life. What began, then, as a personal purification was willingly extended beyond personal spiritual necessity so that others might profit. This is precisely what Garrigou recognizes in the lives of other mystics, especially St. Alphonsus Liguori[35] and St. Paul of the Cross, both of whom suf-

32. Garrigou, *The Three Ages*, 2:509. Emphasis is mine.
33. Garrigou, *The Three Ages*, 2:501.
34. Mother Teresa to Archbishop Périer, April 15, 1951, in Kolodiejchuk, *Come Be My Light*, 141.
35. Garrigou, *The Three Ages*, 2:504: "Let us note first of all, thought without insistence, a fairly characteristic fact, verified toward the close of the life of St. Alphonsus Liguori. A superficial reading of this period of his life, he was then eighty, might give the impression that he was experiencing the passive night of the senses, which is frequently accompanied by strong temptations against chastity and patience, virtues having their seat in the sensible part of the soul. The holy old man had it this time such violent temptations that his servant wondered if they would not cause him to lose his mind. But consideration of all the work already accomplished by grace in the soul of this great

fered the dark night for long periods of time while also attempting to begin or consolidate their religious order.

St. Paul of the Cross shares especially incredible parallels with St. Teresa. He was transformed into the unitive way at the young age of thirty-one, as evidenced by the publications of his own letters, the notes of his confessor and spiritual director, as well as the apparitions that he received.[36] Also like St. Teresa, he formed a religious order (the Passionists) whose mission was directed toward the salvation of souls. And yet, even though St. Paul had crossed over in the unitive way at a young age, he continued to suffer the spiritual desolations of the dark night of the soul for forty-five years. Garrigou even asserts:

> This suffering consisted not only in the subtraction of sensible consolations, but, as it were, in the eclipse of the virtues of faith, hope, and charity. The saint believed himself abandoned by God, he be-

saint leads to the conclusion that this trial in his last years was not precisely for him the passive purification of the senses (although it had all the appearances of being so), but a series of afflictions that he endured chiefly for his neighbor and for the consolation of his Order for which he had already suffered so much."

36. See Garrigou, *The Three Ages*, 2:505–6: "There is an even more striking example in the life of St. Paul of the Cross, the founder of the Passionists. We may form an exact idea of his interior life by his confessor and director, Father John Mary, and from other documents of the period, quoted in the process of canonization and the preparatory work. Father Cajetan of the Holy Name of Mary, C.P., assembled the most important of these documents in his book, Oraison et ascension mystique de saint Paul de la Croix.... Before the age of thirty-one, St. Paul of the Cross received the grace of the transforming union. This fact can scarcely be doubted if, after carefully considering the loftiness of the purifying graces which preceded it, one takes cognizance of the testimony gathered by Father Cajetan. This signal grace was even accompanied by the symbolism which sometimes manifests its sensibly: by the apparition of our Lord, of His Blessed Mother, and of several saints. St. Paul of the Cross also received a gold ring on which were represented the instruments of the Passion. When we see to what close union with Jesus crucified the servant of God attained before the age of thirty-one, and consider that he was to live to the age of eighty-one and found an order vowed to reparation, we are less astonished at seeing him associated afterward for a period of forty-five years with the sorrowful life of our Lord Jesus Christ. In fact, after receiving the grace of the transforming union, he had, according to the testimony of his confessor, to pass through forty-five years of interior desolations, most painful abandonment, during which, 'from time to time only, the Lord granted him a short respite.'"

lieved that God was irritated with him. His temptations to despair and sadness were overwhelming; and yet in this interminable trial, St. Paul showed great patience, perfect resignation to the divine will, and extreme kindness to all who approached him, as Father Cajetan relates.[37]

St. Paul's experience powerfully mirrors the bleak and despondent state of Mother Teresa's soul. It is hard to read of his belief that he had been abandoned or that he was even hated by God without Mother Teresa's letters coming to mind. As with St. Paul of the Cross, Mother Teresa continued to endure this immense suffering even after entrance into the unitive way, a suffering that began as purgative but was voluntarily embraced for the remainder of her life, taking upon herself the misery of others.

That St. Teresa went through a passive purification before suffering for others need not be a comment on St. Teresa's holiness or devotion to God at any point in her push to establish the Missionaries of Charity. It may be that she moved through the dark night of purification in hours, beginning to suffer for her sisters and the lost souls in Calcutta almost immediately after her dark night began. Whatever passive purification she needed would certainly seem to have been small given her already tremendous devotion and abandonment to God even before taking up her mission in Calcutta. As Fr. Kolodiejchuk reminds us, Mother's spiritual director, Fr. Van Exem, had noted all the way back in 1947 that she was already nearing a state of ecstasy in prayer.[38] There is great evidence that Mother Teresa, even from a young age,[39] was simply one of those souls so especially loved

---

37. Garrigou, *The Three Ages*, 2:507.

38. See Kolodiejchuk, *Come Be My Light*, 82.

39. Mother Teresa to Father Neuner, undated, in Kolodiejchuk, *Come Be My Light*, 210: "From my childhood I have had a most tender love for Jesus in the Blessed Sacrament—but this too has gone.—I feel nothing before Jesus—and yet I would not miss Holy Com. [Communion] for anything."

by God that she was unlikely to have ever required much in the way of purification.

But the words of Fr. Neuner and Mother's newfound love for the darkness discovered in 1961 seem to have been a decisive turning point in her spiritual life, perhaps the moment in which she moved from purifying darkness to reparative darkness. Though it does not appear that the spiritual aridity or silence of God lessened afterward, Mother talks now of saying yes rather than being on the verge of saying no. Several months after hearing from Fr. Neuner, she writes to a friend, Fr. Picachy, "the darkness is so dark and the pain so great, but in spite of it all—my retreat resolution was the same: A hearty 'Yes' to God, A big 'Smile' to all."[40]

Though Mother still struggles with the temptation to say no to God,[41] her correspondences with priests like Fr. Neuner eventually mention her darkness less and less. This is not because it has dissipated but because Mother Teresa, now with a full comprehension and appreciation of its place in her life, is able to entirely accept it and the good that it brings. To Fr. Neuner, she writes:

> I have realized something these days. Since God wants me to ab-
> stain from the joy of the riches of the spiritual life—I am giving my
> whole heart and soul to helping my Sisters to make full use of it....
> As for myself, I just have the joy of having nothing—not even the
> reality of the Presence of God.... With my whole heart I want it to
> be just like this—because He wants it.[42]

40. Mother Teresa to Father Picachy, June 1961, in Kolodiejchuk, *Come Be My Light*, 219.

41. Mother Teresa to Bishop Picachy, December 29, 1964, in Kolodiejchuk, *Come Be My Light*, 245.

42. Mother Teresa to Father Neuner, February 17, 1962, in Kolodiejchuk, *Come Be My Light*, 228.

After Fr. Neuner recognizes that they need not correspond anymore because she has found her way,[43] to her friend, she writes, "Sorrow, suffering … is but a kiss from Jesus—a sign that you have come so close to Jesus that He can kiss you.—I think this is the most beautiful definition of suffering.—So let us be happy when Jesus stoops down to kiss us.—I hope we are close enough that He can do it."[44]

To her sisters, she also stresses the importance of reparative suffering, stating, "Yes, my dear children—let us share the sufferings—of our poor—for only by being one with them—we can redeem them, that is, bringing God into their lives and bringing them to God."[45] This sums up the entire mission of Mother Teresa and her work, which is indeed eternal.

CONCLUSION

The secular politicians and media could certainly recognize the temporal good that Mother was doing in giving medical care to the sick, food to the hungry, and comfort to the dying. But what they failed to recognize was that her work would stand for all eternity, evidenced in the immortal souls that she touched and transformed in her work as an instrument of God. As she once told Archbishop Périer, "If you only knew how much I long to immolate myself completely in that absolute poverty and so bring the light of Christ into the unhappy homes of the slums' poor."[46]

While she wished to relieve the bodily suffering of the poor in Calcutta, what she wanted even more was to capture souls for heaven.

43. Testimony of Father Neuner, in Kolodiejchuk, *Come Be My Light*, 265.

44. Mother Teresa to Eileen Egan, December 14, 1976, in Kolodiejchuk, *Come Be My Light*, 281.

45. Mother Teresa to the MC Sisters, First Friday, July 1961, in Kolodiejchuk, *Come Be My Light*, 220.

46. Mother Teresa to Archbishop Périer, October 1, 1947, in Kolodiejchuk, *Come Be My Light*, 85.

Mother Teresa's intention for her order was simple, "To be an Indian—to live with them—like them—so as to get at the people's heart."[47] Externally clothed in the sari, internally St. Teresa was clothed in the suffering of Indian's poor. Out of love for these souls, Mother Teresa experienced reparative suffering for the rest of her life. "God is calling me.... I am longing to give all for souls."[48] This she did.

It should not surprise us at all that someone who so loved and laid down her life for the destitute souls around her would be given the opportunity to suffer spiritually for these souls. She seemed to understand this reparative spiritual mission when, in 1986, she said, "Suffering by itself has no meaning.... But suffering shared with the suffering of Christ has a tremendous meaning. The suffering offered as a reparation has a tremendous meaning."[49] This spiritual suffering, far greater than the temporal suffering that she certainly underwent while working day and night in the slums of Calcutta, would be likewise of much greater efficacy. Mother Teresa unquestionably loved these souls as Christ did, willing to suffer as immensely as possible for them. It is fitting, then, that Mother did not experience immediate consolations after moving through her own passive purification but instead elected to cleave to the darkness, to love it, in order to continue to bring Christ's light to those who needed it most. And this is where she found her beloved Christ. Mother wrote once:

> In my heart there is no faith—no love—no trust—there is so much pain—the pain of longing, the pain of not being wanted.—I want God with all the powers of my soul—and yet there between us—there is the terrible separation.—I don't pray any longer—I utter

47. Mother Teresa to Archbishop Périer, January 13, 1947, in Kolodiejchuk, *Come Be My Light*, 50.

48. Mother Teresa to Archbishop Périer, January 13, 1947, in Kolodiejchuk, *Come Be My Light*, 50.

49. Leo Maasburg, *Mother Teresa of Calcutta: A Personal Portrait*, abridged ed., trans. Michael J. Miller (San Francisco: Ignatius Press, 2016), 185.

words of community prayers—and try my utmost to get out of every word the sweetness it has to give.—But my prayer of union is not there any longer.—I no longer pray.—My soul is not one with You—and yet when alone in the streets—I talk to You for hours—of my longing for You.[50]

Alone in the streets with those crying out in pain was where St. Teresa *did* experience the presence of Jesus Christ. Mother once said, "If I ever become a saint—I will surely be one of 'darkness.'"[51] The Christian faith is the faith of paradoxes. The painful wounds endured by our Lord are not signs of weakness but strength. They are not grotesque but beautiful. We see in the life of Mother Teresa another, similar paradox. In living a life of darkness, Mother now shines with resplendent grandeur in Heaven, drawn from a feeling of abandonment to immediate intimacy with her Beloved. This profound suffering drew St. Teresa not further from Christ but toward his full embrace. And this is what was missed in 2007. Rather than being a counterfeit Christian, Mother's darkness stands as a model for the entire Church. The Christian must love Christ until there is no more love to give. The Christian must cling to him until one's entire being is Christ's. St. Teresa's reparative suffering, embraced as she transitioned to the unitive way, is a perfect illustration of this abandonment.

Regarding a moment on her deathbed, a Missionary of Charity father remarked, "If someone begged, 'Mother don't leave us. We can't live without you,' she would simply say: 'Don't worry. Mother can do much more for you when I am in heaven.'"[52] It is clear that Mother's mission to save souls did not end in 1997, but has only just begun.

---

50. Mother Teresa's letter to Jesus, enclosed with her letter to Father Picachy, September 3, 1959, in Kolodiejchuk, *Come Be My Light*, 193.

51. Mother Teresa to Father Neuner, March 6, 1962, in Kolodiejchuk, *Come Be My Light*, 230.

52. Testimony of Father Gary, in Kolodiejchuk, *Come Be My Light*, 332.

10

LIGHT AND DARKNESS

Catherine of Siena and Mother Teresa
on Sharing Christ's Suffering

~

Sr. Albert Marie Surmanski, OP

Catherine of Siena and Mother Teresa were both women mystics who had great desire to cooperate with Christ in the salvation of others. There is a parallelism even in some of their language: Mother Teresa talked about "satisfying the thirst of Christ." St. Catherine often spoke of her "hunger for souls." Yet there are some contrasts between the two saints that raise significant theological question. These do not arise from the fact that Catherine and Mother Teresa are from different centuries but rather from different ways in which they understand their spiritual progress and sharing in Christ's suffering.

Mother Teresa endured a prolonged "dark night" until the end of her life after earlier experiencing extraordinary closeness with Christ.[1] She identified her sufferings as a sharing in Christ's experi-

1. Benedict Groeschel, CFR, "Mother Teresa Remembered," *First Things*, September 11, 2007, http://www.firstthings.com/web-exclusives/2007/09/mother-teresa-remembered.

ence on the cross. In contrast, as Catherine of Siena matured spiritually, her suffering came to flow directly out of her *vision* of the world in which she saw God's goodness and the evil of sin outlined with heartbreaking clarity. Catherine of Siena is a Doctor of the Church precisely for her teaching on the path of spiritual growth. She went so far as to say that darkness should not be the experience of those who are in deep union with God.[2]

The different experiences of these two women raise questions about mystical experience and Christology. Does experience in the spiritual life follow a characteristic path? To what extent is this a path of deepening identification with Christ? If so, was Christ's experience one of knowledge or of darkness? In this essay, I discuss how considerations from Catherine of Siena and Aquinas show that although Mother Teresa's experience is a significant variation on the path that Catherine describes, there are points of reconciliation between them.

CATHERINE OF SIENA

Catherine of Siena was a fourteenth-century Dominican Tertiary who possessed a passionate and energetic nature but little formal education. Catherine dedicated her life to Christ around the age of seven after a vision. At the age of sixteen, having refused many offers of marriage, Catherine received the habit of the Third Order Dominican Sisters of Penance. This meant that she became a member of the Dominican family but did not take public vows or live a strict com-

2. Catherine of Siena is considered a Doctor of the Church for her inspired insight into "the supernatural life of the individual and of the Church." Apostolic Letter *Mirabilis in Ecclesia Deus*, October 4, 1970, Drawn by Love: The Mysticism of Catherine of Siena, drawnbylove.com. No official English translation was ever published of this work. This translation was done by the late Fr. W. B. Mahoney, OP, Aquinas Institute of Theology, Dubuque, Iowa. The official Latin text is found in *Acta Apostolicae Sedis* (*AAS*) 1970: 672ff.

munity life.[3] Catherine spent the next three years in intense prayer and penance, rarely leaving her room in her parents' house except for Mass.[4] During this time, Catherine experienced periods of extraordinary closeness to Christ, as well as periods of spiritual dryness and temptation. This was the major period of spiritual growth in Catherine's life.

This period culminated with a mystical betrothal, in which Christ gave her a ring that remained visible to her throughout her whole life. Raymond of Capua, Catherine's spiritual directory and biographer, reports that when Christ gave Catherine the ring, he exhorted her to faith and promised her strength to overcome her enemies.[5] The presence and significance of this ring precluded any further experience of spiritual darkness for Catherine. As a miraculous token of God's loving support, it signified and ensured that she would never be without tangible experience of God.[6] And she was not.

In Catherine's major writing, her *Dialogue*, she describes the spiritual life in three stages. They follow the traditional threefold schema of purification, illuminating growth in virtue, and peaceful union. She speaks of three stairs on the bridge of Christ's cross. The Christian climbs along the body of Christ, first reaching Christ's feet as a servant, then drinking from his side as a friend, and finally reaching his mouth as a "true child of God."[7]

In accordance with what John of the Cross would do centuries

3. For more about this way of life, see Maiju Lehmijoke-Gardner, ed., "Introduction," in *Dominican Penitent Women* (New York: Paulist Press, 2005), 1–36.

4. Raymond of Capua, *The Life of Catherine of Siena* (London: Harvill Press, 1960), 71.

5. Raymond of Capua, *Life of Catherine of Siena*, 100.

6. Thomas McDermott suggests this grace was specifically given to strengthen Catherine for her work, a unique and difficult work for a woman at the time. See *Catherine of Siena: Spiritual Development in Her Life and Teaching* (New York: Paulist Press, 2008), 33.

7. McDermott, *Catherine of Siena*, 54.

later, Catherine places the experience of spiritual darkness within the first and second stages of her bridge imagery. She speaks of the withdrawal of the experience of God's presence.[8] This withdrawal is so intense, so painful, that Catherine compares it to being in hell.[9] In the transition between the first two stages, Catherine notes that the "withdrawal of experience" happens because the soul needs to recognize its own imperfection when it loves consolations (or emotional experiences in prayer) more than God. To those who remain steadfast in this trial, the experience of infused contemplation is given, described by Catherine as God "showing himself" to the soul through various insights into God's action in the world, experiences of his presence, and growth in virtue.[10]

Darkness in the second stage has a similar purpose of deepening virtue in the soul and preparing the Christian for greater service of God. Her language and treatment of suffering at the stage in the spiritual life are similar to her previous description. The soul further recognizes her weakness, growing in humility and self-knowledge, waiting with "lively faith."[11] God withdraws from the soul "in feeling but not in grace." Darkness in this stage is intermittent, a part of a series of experiences in which the soul gradually comes to know and trust God more fully.[12] Coming through these periods gives the Christian an opportunity to "experience divine providence."[13] The spirit of Catherine's trust in God's loving education of the soul is captured when she calls it a "lover's game" in which God gently educates the soul in love.[14]

---

8. In her *Dialogue*, Catherine does speak about "darkness" and its mitigation as "light." Catherine of Siena, *The Dialogue*, trans. Suzanne Noffke (New York: Paulist Press, 1980), 144.

9. Catherine of Siena, *Dialogue*, 144.

10. Catherine of Siena, *Dialogue*, 61.

11. Catherine of Siena, *Dialogue*, 63.

12. Catherine of Siena, *Dialogue*, 64.

13. Catherine of Siena, *Dialogue*, 144.

14. Catherine of Siena, *Dialogue*, 78.

Those who have reached the third stage of the mouth have attained a stable knowledge of God and self. In the voice of God the Father, Catherine says that the soul "has come to know herself, and in herself she has come to know my affectionate charity."[15] "To such as these it is granted never to feel my absence. I told you how I go away from others (in feeling only, not in grace) and then return. . . . I am always at rest in their souls both by grace and by feeling."[16] The souls at this stage can still grow in love and do still suffer. This is the stage of greatest missionary effectiveness for Catherine, that of "hunger" for the salvation of others.

The most characteristic suffering at this stage comes from knowledge of God and of the sin by which others offend God and hurt themselves. Catherine speaks repeatedly of this pain born from loving knowledge. She calls it "an anguished love," a "stinging hunger" "crucifying sorrow at the offense done to me [God] and the harm done to their neighbors."[17] It is the depth of the knowledge of God that is the source of this pain. Catherine writes,

> In their loving union with me [God] they have contemplated and known how ineffably I love my creatures, seeing how they reflect my likeness, and they have fallen in love with my creature's beauty for love of me. Therefore they feel unbearable sorrow when they see them straying from my goodness. The sufferings are so great that they make every other suffering diminish in them.[18]

Insight into God's greatness and the horror of sin causes the greatest possible suffering. Knowing the truth of the full beauty of God and seeing the terribly disfigured beauty of his image in creatures causes the great pain that torments Catherine during the mature part of her life.

15. Catherine of Siena, *Dialogue*, 74.
16. Catherine of Siena, *Dialogue*, 78.
17. Catherine of Siena, *Dialogue*, 78, 145.
18. Catherine of Siena, *Dialogue*, 145.

MOTHER TERESA IN LIGHT OF CATHERINE

Mother Teresa's experience is different from Catherine's in many ways. After experiencing great closeness with Christ earlier in her life, she entered a period of darkness for almost all of the time from her founding of the Missionaries of Charity in 1950 until her death in 1997.[19] She came to understand her darkness as the spiritual side of her work, not simply a stage to pass through.[20] She understood her redemptive suffering with Christ precisely as consisting in her darkness. In this she contrasts significantly with Catherine. As a result, several questions arise when turning to the experience and thought of Mother Teresa after reading Catherine. These involve the place of darkness in the spiritual life and its Christological significance. For Catherine, there is no darkness in the unitive way. The Christian cooperates with Jesus through loving knowledge. Pursuing these questions despite the differences between the two women, there are elements in St. Catherine's teaching that can help to shed light on Mother Teresa's experience.

First is Catherine's insight into the personal way in which God deals with each soul. The dark night, according to the thought of John of the Cross, will have its duration so long as impurities in faith make the infused contemplation of God be experienced as darkness. A person will come out of the dark night when purified. Catherine's emphasis God's freedom in this "lover's game" suggests that God might choose to keep even a purified soul in the darkness. Because God's being is always infinitely greater than any creature, there would be no untruth in an experience of God as darkness at any spiritual stage in this life, no matter how pure her faith and love. God could always

19. Catherine of Siena, *Dialogue*, 149.
20. Brian Kolodiejchuk, MC, ed., *Mother Teresa: Come Be My Light* (New York: Doubleday, 2007), 214.

be present to the soul as surpassing it and ungraspable. This insight is compatible with John of the Cross's theology; it is made plausible by Catherine's language and is verified by Mother Teresa's experience.

Second, although Catherine speaks of knowing and Mother Teresa of darkness, what is of value to both of them is the faithful love that underlies their suffering. Catherine's knowledge bears fruit because of the love that it brings forth in her. One of her most famous quotes is "upon knowledge follows love."[21] In a parallel way, Mother Teresa describes the rootedness of her will in God during the darkness, despite the absence of glowing feelings and mystical insights. She wrote, "I have His darkness—I have His pain … I know I have Jesus—in that unbroken union—for my mind is fixed on Him and in Him alone, in my will."[22] Her mind is fixed on him as a result of supernatural charity burning within her heart.

Third, Catherine notes that even those in the unitive way can grow in love: "There is no one in this life, no matter how perfect, who cannot grow to greater perfection."[23] Although, in Catherine's experience, this growth in love after deep union with God took place through a deeper knowledge of God, it is not incompatible with her thought that God could ask further growth of someone by leading them into darkness. The emphasis on growth in virtue suggests that a return to darkness could be something fruitful although unknown to Catherine.

CHRISTOLOGICAL QUESTIONS

Catherine of Siena understood the suffering of the souls at the third stage to mirror that of Christ on the cross. Catherine says that

---

21. Catherine of Siena, *Dialogue*, 1.
22. Kolodiejchuk, *Come Be My Light*, 223.
23. Catherine of Siena, *Dialogue*, 144, 145.

on the cross Christ experienced the vision of God in his intellect while experiencing pain in his body and emotions.[24] Catherine does not claim that the souls in the third stage have the vision of God. Rather, these men and women are like Christ in their mixture of knowledge and deep sorrow.

Following the teaching of her spiritual director Fr. Neuner, Mother Teresa also came to understand her suffering as "a small part of Jesus' darkness & pain on earth."[25] She wrote to her sisters: "Jesus wanted to help us by sharing our life, our loneliness, our agony and death. All that He has taken upon Himself and has carried it in the darkest night."[26]

Does Mother Teresa's emphasis on darkness require a Christology different from that of Catherine? One answer would be in the affirmative, suggesting that Christ called to Catherine out of light in deference to her Dominican formation, which had led her to believe that Christ had the beatific vision even on the cross. He spoke to Mother Teresa out of darkness in affirmation of more modern Christologies, like that of Luther or von Balthasar, which suggest that Christ's experience of abandonment by the Father was central to the redemption of humanity.

A difficulty with this approach is its implicit separation between ontology and experience. It implies that mystical experience changes in response to changing theology rather than being grounded in an experience of the realities that theology describes.[27] It is true that mystical experience is subjective in that it is experienced by a human subject and is interpreted according to her own background. This legitimate variation, however, must be centered in the realities revealed. If revelation is true, there must be some unvarying essential content.

24. Catherine of Siena, *Dialogue*, 78; this teaching is found in *ST* III, q. 10, a. 2; III, q. 46, a. 7.

25. Kolodiejchuk, *Come Be My Light*, 214.

26. Kolodiejchuk, *Come Be My Light*, 220.

27. Another option would be that Catherine radically misunderstood her experience.

So, let us see how both Catherine's and Mother Teresa's experiences of suffering with Christ can fit within a unified Christology. A first shared insight is that all human suffering can legitimately be understood as a sharing in Christ's suffering. This is true no matter exactly what Christ's experience was on the cross. He died to take away the sins of the world, and to ultimately heal all effects of this sin, whether experienced as darkness or as pained insight into the damage that sin has done to creation.

CATHERINE IN LIGHT OF AQUINAS

A further solution would identify *how* both women participate in the suffering of Christ on the cross. Let us begin with Catherine. Thomas Aquinas's teaching on the knowledge and sufferings of Christ gives insight into Catherine's understanding that a great suffering can come from loving knowledge rather than from darkness. In *Summa theologiae* III, q. 46, a. 6, Aquinas discusses the role of Christ's knowledge in increasing his suffering.

Aquinas taught not only that Christ had the vision of God during his earthly life, but also that he had infused knowledge of all those things pertaining to his mission.[28] Aquinas notes that virtue would not have lessened Christ's suffering, since moral virtue orders the passions so that they are in proper proportion to their object. Because Christ was sorrowing over all the sins ever committed, it was appropriate that his sorrow be surpassingly great. Aquinas says that Christ, to satisfy for sins, "took on a sadness absolutely greatest in quantity, but nevertheless not exceeding the rule of reason."[29] For Christ's sorrow to be proportioned to the rule of reason, he would have to

---

28. *ST* III, q. 11, a. 1.

29. *ST* III, q. 46, a. 6, ad. 2: "assumpsit tristitiam maximam quantitate absoluta, non tamen excedentem regulam rationis."

have knowledge of the sins he was bearing. Sadness would result from Christ's infused knowledge of sin, his union with sinners through his shared human nature and vocation as Redeemer, and his rightly ordered will, in which he would detest all sins as a terrible evil.

Aquinas further says that "Christ sorrowed not only over the loss of his own bodily life, but also for the sins of all others. This sorrow in Christ surpassed the sorrow of any other grief, since it came forth from a greater wisdom and love, both of which increase the sorrow of grief and also because he at once sorrowed for all sins."[30] Thus Christ's suffering was brought about by his knowledge of the sins of humanity, his wisdom, by which he judged them rightly and by his charity, in which his will detested them both out of love of the Father and love of sinners. Because Christ's knowledge and love surpassed that of all others, so did his suffering.

Catherine's experience follows the same pattern. Her love and openness to the Holy Spirit made her acutely sensitive to the evils she encountered daily. Her purified emotions and will experienced great sadness and sorrow at the recognition of the evil of sin and the damage it does to the human person. Catherine's suffering thus parallels Christ's and is a sharing in his.

MOTHER TERESA IN LIGHT OF AQUINAS

Mother Teresa's darkness, when viewed through Aquinas's Christology, shows a complementary sharing in Christ's experience. According to Aquinas, Christ on the cross never lost the direct vision of God. In it, he knew himself to be the beloved Son of the Father, and

---

30. *ST* III, q. 46, a. 6, ad. 4: "Christus non solum doluit pro amissione vitae corporalis propriae, sed etiam pro peccatis omnium aliorum. Qui dolor in Christo excessit omnem dolorem cuiuslibet contriti. Tum quia ex maiori sapientia et caritate processit, ex quibus dolor contritionis augetur."

that his death was a meaningful offering for the sins of the world.[31] It provided the grounding for his obedient love, which pleased the Father and made his sacrifice meritorious.[32]

Nevertheless, Christ's direct knowledge of God did not overflow his higher faculties in such a way as to diminish either his sorrow at the insults offered to him, or his physical pain. Aquinas suggests that Christ's interior suffering surpassed all others partly because he was able to stop all considerations from his higher reason from lessening his pain, something that is not possible for others to choose.[33] This would mean that Christ took no emotional comfort in his knowledge of God—a severance of knowledge and emotion that was not present in Catherine of Siena. Mother Teresa shared Christ's lack of emotional comfort, not because of a similar "block" between clear knowledge and emotion, but because of the darkness of her faith. Mother Teresa shared Christ's *feeling* of desolation on the cross in a way that Catherine could not.

Christ's direct knowledge of God played a role in his consciousness parallel to that of Mother Teresa's unshaken faith—foundational for love and grounding identity. As quoted above, she writes, "I have His darkness—I have His pain ... I know I have Jesus—in that unbroken union—for my mind is fixed on Him and in Him alone, in my will."[34] Even in her darkness, Mother Teresa's faith gave her certainty that Christ was with her. She experienced him upholding her as the cause of her anguished desire for him. Her faith made her able to know that she understood the value of the immolation of her life and her service as a Missionary of Charity. Although different in *mode*, Teresa's faith was like Christ's knowledge in that, although grounding the will in heroic love, it did not enliven the emotions.

31. *ST* III, q. 46, a. 7.
32. *ST* III, q. 49, a. 1.
33. *ST* III, q. 46, a. 6.
34. Kolodiejchuk, *Come Be My Light*, 223.

Further, Aquinas understood the unmitigated emotional pain of Christ as a taking on of the sorrow of all men. He writes that Christ experienced all the types of suffering that it is possible to endure, at least in their general categories. Thus Christ recapitulated, suffered through, and overcame all human suffering.[35] Mother Teresa also understood her darkness as a sharing in the suffering of those whom she served. Her identification with the poor began in her way of living; God ratified and deepened it through giving her their darkness. She writes,

> Jesus wanted to help us by sharing our life, our loneliness, our agony and death. All that He has taken upon Himself, and has carried it in the darkest night. Only by being one with us He has redeemed us. We are allowed to do the same: All the desolation of the poor people, not only their material poverty, but their spiritual destitution must be redeemed, and we must have our share in it.[36]

Mother Teresa's suffering imitated Christ's in being a taking on of the sufferings of those to whom she was sent.

CONCLUSION

The key to understanding the Christology underlying the mystical suffering of Catherine of Siena and that of Mother Teresa involves a distinction between Christ's uniqueness as the God-Man and the way in which Christians share in his redemption. The experience of no follower of Christ reproduces Christ's exactly, while that of every believer is nevertheless a sharing in the love and suffering of a God who takes on all human misery.

The wider question of mystical experience in general directs our

---

35. *ST* III, q. 46, a. 4.
36. Kolodiejchuk, *Come Be My Light*, 220.

attention to the flexibility with which God interacts with each soul. Although there are characteristic stages to spiritual growth, and knowing them can equip and encourage us for the journey, God leads each person on a unique path—one ordered not only to match the characteristics of the individual, but also the age in which the individual lived and to which the saint's life was meant to speak. Catherine's luminous desire perfectly fit the age of faith in which she lived—when God's truths were known to those around her but often ignored in practice. Mother Teresa's darkness perhaps better fits our age of unbelief, in which the darkness of suffering has obscured the face of God for so many.

11

SEEING MOTHER TERESA THROUGH THE
EYES OF TWO POPES

A Challenge to Modern Society and a Call to Conversion

~

Michael Dauphinais

Mother Teresa of Calcutta's charitable work was recognized by many
in the secular world, perhaps most notably when she received a Nobel Peace Prize in 1979. Despite her fame in the secular world, it is
the Catholic Church that has declared her a saint. She is perhaps so
familiar to many in the contemporary secular world that some may
forget how much she challenged many of its basic assumptions and
offered an answer to its deepest longings. I suggest that we might find
it helpful to consider Mother Teresa through the eyes of the two popes
who beatified and canonized her. Pope St. John Paul II first beatified
her in 2003, and Pope Francis later canonized her in 2016. In their
eloquent homilies delivered thirteen years apart, these two pontiffs

Full texts of both homilies are available on the Vatican website, www.vatican.va.

present Mother Teresa to the Church as a contemporary example of mercy and charity as well as an authentic disciple of Jesus Christ. Their beatification and canonization homilies reveal a synoptic view that invites the Church and the world to learn anew from this saint, who sought never to refuse anything to God.

Here are six themes highlighted by both Pope St. John Paul II and Pope Francis.

1. Mother Teresa saw Jesus in the poorest of the poor and served and loved him in serving and loving the poor.

"As you did to one of the least of these my brethren, you did it to me" (Mt 25: 40). This Gospel passage, so crucial in understanding Mother Teresa's service to the poor, was the basis of her faith-filled conviction that in touching the broken bodies of the poor she was touching the body of Christ. It was to Jesus himself, hidden under the distressing disguise of the poorest of the poor, that her service was directed.

Pope John Paul II

God is pleased by every act of mercy, because in the brother or sister that we assist, we recognize the face of God which no one can see (cf. Jn 1:18). Each time we bend down to the needs of our brothers and sisters, we give Jesus something to eat and drink; we clothe, we help, and we visit the Son of God (cf. Mt 25:40).

Pope Francis

Mother Teresa famously said that the work of her sisters was not social work. It was not a commodified service provided to others but an act of love, an act of love for Jesus Christ, true God and true man. Although the work could be seen from the outside on a sociological level, the work was profoundly theological. Our contemporary age, especially in the West, has become effective at viewing things from the outside and trying to manipulate inputs and outputs in order to improve efficiencies. This reductionistic impulse, however, leads us to underappreciate and to undercultivate bonds of affection among families and communities. A mother's care of a child constitutes so much more than an economic exchange; a mother's care manifests maternal love. The mother sees the child and loves the child. So, too, Mother Teresa carried out her work as an act of love for the persons in front of her. Moreover, Mother Teresa assented to the words of Jesus about his presence in the least among us. This theological truth allowed her to embrace her beloved, Jesus Christ, in each act of service to neighbor.

2. As an integral part of her commitment to serve the poorest of the poor, Mother Teresa heroically defended the life of the unborn.

> I remember, for example, her pro-life and anti-abortion interventions, even when she was awarded the Nobel Prize for peace (Oslo, 10 December 1979). She often used to say: "If you hear of some woman who does not want to keep her child and wants to have an abortion, try to persuade her to bring him to me. I will love that child, seeing in him the sign of God's love."
>
> Pope John Paul II

> Mother Teresa, in all aspects of her life, was a generous dispenser of divine mercy, making herself available for everyone through her welcome and defense of human life, those unborn and those abandoned and discarded. She was committed to defending life, ceaselessly proclaiming that "the unborn are the weakest, the smallest, the most vulnerable."
>
> Pope Francis

Teresa's commitment to serving the poorest of the poor included a robust defense of the unborn. The unborn were not accidental to her concern. She wrote of her "call within the call" that became her Missionaries of Charity, through whom the light of Christ would be brought into the holes of the poor and to help them live as families. Her defense of the family included her defense of its weakest members through her unfailing criticism of abortion.

3. Mother Teresa responded to the great poverty of being unwanted and being alone.

> In the darkest hours she clung even more tenaciously to prayer before the Blessed Sacrament. This harsh spiritual trial led her to identify herself more and more closely with those whom she served each day, feeling their pain and, at times, even their rejection. She was fond of repeating that the greatest poverty is to be unwanted, to have no one to take care of you.
>
> Pope John Paul II
>
> Just as the Lord has come to meet me and has stooped down to my level in my hour of need, so too do I go to meet him, bending low before those who have lost faith or who live as though God did not exist, before young people without values or ideals, before families in crisis, before the ill and the imprisoned, before refugees and immigrants, before the weak and defenseless in body and spirit, before abandoned children, before the elderly who are on their own.
>
> Pope Francis

Teresa's service to the poor included the poverty of loneliness and isolation. This poverty of love was not contrasted with the poverty of material possessions and food. Rather, she saw that the peculiar poverty of the poorest of the poor was that they lacked everything, including the human love and affection. Having discovered this spiritual isolation in the poor, she responded with love and kindness. In leaving Loreto, she became poor in order to go to the poor. Through her many years of her darkness, she shared in even the feeling of being unloved and unwanted in order to minister more effectively to the unloved and unwanted.

4. **Mother Teresa's life of service flowed from her charity-filled faith in the fullness of God's revelation: her service was the fruit of prayer; her action the fruit of contemplation.**

> With the witness of her life, Mother Teresa reminds everyone that *the evangelizing mission of the Church passes through charity*, nourished by prayer and listening to God's word.... Contemplation and action, evangelization and human promotion: Mother Teresa proclaimed the Gospel living her life as a total gift to the poor but, at the same time, steeped in prayer.
>
> Pope John Paul II

> We are thus called to translate into concrete acts that which we invoke in prayer and profess in faith.
>
> Pope Francis

Teresa instructed her sisters to be rooted in the adoration of Christ present in the Eucharist. This adoration and contemplation of Jesus guided each day. One misunderstands this contemplative prayer if it is reduced to a utilitarian purpose, as if the sisters needed to recharge their batteries each day for their real work of service to neighbor. Instead, the entire life is an overflow of love for Jesus Christ, substantially present in mass and adoration and mystically present in the people they encounter each day. Prayer is an end in itself as an act of love of God. Only as such is it able to guide Christians in the rest of their tasks. This is but one more way in which the two popes assist us in seeing St. Teresa as, above all, a saint in the Catholic Church, namely, a joyful disciple of Jesus Christ communicating his good news through her words and actions.

5. Mother Teresa is a mother! She not only embodies Christian discipleship, but also true femininity.

> As a real mother to the poor, she bent down to those suffering various forms of poverty.... Recognizing him, she ministered to him with wholehearted devotion, expressing the delicacy of her spousal love. Thus, in total gift of herself to God and neighbor, Mother Teresa found her greatest fulfilment and lived the noblest qualities of her femininity.
>
> Pope John Paul II

> Her mission to the urban and existential peripheries remains for us today an eloquent witness to God's closeness to the poorest of the poor. Today, I pass on this emblematic figure of womanhood and of consecrated life to the whole world of volunteers: may she be your model of holiness! ... her holiness is so near to us, so tender and so fruitful that we continue to spontaneously call her "Mother Teresa."
>
> Pope Francis

The modern world struggles to understand femininity and maternity. So many worry about the unjust inequality between men and women worldwide that they affirm an identity between men and women. This is another reductionistic view that defines persons by the duties they perform and the tasks they carry out. Mother Teresa, in her very title as "mother," expressed her motherhood in all of her life. She was a mother to the poorest of the poor, to her Sisters, to so many Christians and non-Christians around the world who saw in her a powerful maternal love, both comforting and challenging. Men and women are equal in dignity, but they are not identical. We are called to find our deepest fulfillment in discovering our motherhood or fatherhood, in whatever forms those take. Moreover, the modern world, with its heavy emphasis on the beauty of the physical form, fails to understand true femininity. By highlighting Mother Teresa as an expression of noble femininity, the popes remind us that the truest feminine beauty is found at the spiritual level, in a heart that gives itself fully to God and to neighbor. This beauty is open to all.

6. Amid the despair and darkness of the contemporary world, Mother Teresa calls us, believers and nonbelievers alike, to hope.

> How often, like the Psalmist, did Mother Teresa call on her Lord in times of inner desolation: "In you, in you I hope, my God!"
>
> Pope John Paul II

> Wherever someone is reaching out, asking for a helping hand in order to get up, this is where our presence—and the presence of the Church which sustains and offers hope—must be.
>
> Pope Francis

The Second Vatican Council document *Gaudium et spes* begins with not only the "joys and hopes" of the current age, but also the "griefs and anxieties." The document engages extensively with the problems of atheism, of the grand scale of human suffering and death, of the loss of purpose, and of the recognition of human dignity. Even believers may be overwhelmed by the effects of sin. *Gaudium et spes* proclaims the answer in "Christ, the final Adam, [who] by the revelation of the mystery of the Father and His love, fully reveals man to man himself and makes his supreme calling clear" (*GS* 22). In the discovery of God's calling for each human being, we recognize that we may receive the gift of our redemption. Furthermore, God calls us to play a role in his providential ordering of history toward its consummation in heaven. Mother Teresa exemplified the virtue of hope in God and trust in his goodness and our salvation. Her love possessed an incarnate and tangible reality that awakened in so many people the awareness of God and of heaven. Heaven is real. Without a real heaven, opened up through the cross, there can be no solid hope. When we see the witness of Mother Teresa and her sisters, we are called to recognize the love of the Incarnate Word at work in them. To know that such love is the love that has created and redeemed the world is to restore hope amid an anxious and despairing age.

May we learn from the words of these two great shepherds of the Catholic Church as they present to us St. Teresa of Calcutta, an icon of Jesus's thirst for souls.

CONTRIBUTORS

~

MICHAEL DAUPHINAIS is an associate professor and the chair of theology at Ave Maria University. He coauthored *Knowing the Love of Christ: An Introduction to the Theology of Thomas Aquinas* and *Holy People, Holy Land: A Theological Introduction to the Bible*. His most recent work is on the theological significance of Aquinas's biblical commentaries as well as the theology of revelation.

JOHN FROULA is an assistant professor at the Saint Paul Seminary School of Divinity, in St. Paul, Minnesota. He has written about Thomistic Christology and the thought of C. S. Lewis. His most recent publication is an annotated translation of the Christological portion of Hugh of Saint Victor's *De Sacramentis*.

FR. ROBERT M. GARRITY, JCL, STHD, is an assistant professor of theology at Ave Maria University. He has published three articles in canon law in *The Jurist* and in *Studia canonica* as well as four books: *O Happy Fault: Personal Recovery through Spiritual Growth* (1994); *Resurrection Power: Spiritual Solutions for an Anxious Age* (2015)—and a later expanded companion volume with supplemental evidentiary material, *The Resurrection: Deception? Or Truth?* (2017)—and *Mother Teresa's Mysticism: A Christo-Ecclesio-Humano-centric Mysticism* (2017). He currently awaits publication of an article on Mother Teresa's mystical theology as a source for theological renewal and a coauthored article on the possibility of secular authorities being involved in episcopal appointments. He is also currently preparing an article on the positive effects of recent liturgical reforms.

ANDREW HOFER, OP, is an associate professor of patristics and ancient languages at the Pontifical Faculty of the Immaculate Conception at the Dominican House of Studies in Washington, DC, where he also serves as master of students. He is the author of *Christ in the Life and Teaching of Gregory of Nazianzus* in the Oxford Early Christian Studies series and of articles in several journals.

BRIAN KOLODIEJCHUK, MC, is the superior general of the Missionaries of Charity Fathers and served as the Postulator for the Cause of Canonization of St. Teresa of Calcutta. He has edited four books on Mother Teresa: *Jesus Is My All in All* (2008), *Come Be My Light* (2007), *Where There Is Love There Is God* (2012), and *Call to Mercy* (2016).

MATTHEW L. LAMB† was the Cardinal Maida Professor of Theology at Ave Maria University. His authored books are: *Eternity, Time and the Life of Wisdom*; *Thomas Aquinas's Commentary on Ephesians*; *History, Method and Theology*; and *Solidarity with Victims*. His edited books are: *Creativity and Method: Essays in Honor of Bernard Lonergan*; *Catholicism and America: Challenges and Prospects*; *Theology Needs Philosophy: Acting against Reason Is Contrary to the Nature of God*; *Vatican II: Renewal within Tradition*; and *The Reception of Vatican II*. He published over 160 philosophical and theological articles in journals and books.

RALPH MARTIN, STD, is a professor of dogmatic and spiritual theology at Sacred Heart Major Seminary in the Archdiocese of Detroit. He is the author of *The Fulfillment of All Desire: A Guidebook for the Journey to God Based on the Wisdom of the Saints* and *Will Many Be Saved? What Vatican II Actually Teaches and Its Implications for the New Evangelization*. His most recent work is focused on doctrinal issues that pertain to evangelization.

DAVID VINCENT MECONI, SJ, is an associate professor of historical theology as well as the director of the new Catholic Studies Center at Saint Louis University; he is also the editor of *Homiletic and Pastoral Review*. He has authored the *Annotated Confessions of Saint Augustine* (2012), *The One Christ: St. Augustine's Theology of Deification* (2013; pbk 2017); edited along with Eleonore Stump *The Cambridge Companion to Augustine* (2014) as well as *The Cambridge Companion to Augustine's City of God*; and has most recently written *On Self-Harm, Narcissism, Atonement and the Vulnerable Christ* (2018) as part of the Reading Augustine series.

MARK MIRAVALLE is a professor of theology and Mariology at the Franciscan University of Steubenville, the president of the *International Marian Association*, and editor of the Mariological journal *Ecce Mater Tua*.

ROGER W. NUTT is the vice president for academic affairs and dean of faculty at Ave Maria University, where he also serves as an associate professor of theology and editor-in-chief of Sapientia Press of Ave Maria University. His recent publications include *Thomas Aquinas, De unione verbi incarnati* (2015) and *General Principles of Sacramental Theology* (2017).

TAYLOR PATRICK O'NEILL is an assistant professor of religious studies at Mount Mercy University. He has written on St. Thomas

Aquinas and the Thomistic understanding of grace, predestination, and the permission of evil.

SR. ALBERT MARIE SURMANSKI, OP, is a member of the Dominican Sisters of Mary Mother of the Eucharist. She is a visiting assistant professor at the University of St. Thomas, Houston, and also teaches at St. Mary's Seminary in Houston. She is the translator of Albert the Great's *On the Body of the Lord* (2017) and has written for *Logos, Antiphon, New Blackfriars,* and *Homiletic and Pastoral Review.*

H. JAMES TOWEY was a friend and legal counsel to Mother Teresa of Calcutta from 1985 to 1997. Now in his eighth year as president of Ave Maria University, he previously served as an assistant to and director of faith-based initiatives for President George W. Bush. Towey is married and has five children.

INDEX

~

225

Mother Teresa and the Mystics: Toward a Renewal of Spiritual Theology was designed in Brioso Pro and composed by Kachergis Book Design of Pittsboro, North Carolina. It was printed on 60-pound Natures Book Natural and bound by Thomson-Shore of Dexter, Michigan.